JULIE ANN GODSON

On this day in
OXFORDSHIRE

AlleyCat Books

First published in 2019
© Julie Ann Godson

The author has asserted their moral right under
the Copyright, Designs and Patents Act, 1988, to be identified
as the author of this work.

All Rights reserved. No part of this publication may be reproduced,
copied, stored in a retrieval system, or transmitted, in any form or by any means,
without the prior written consent of the copyright holder, nor be otherwise circulated
in any form of binding or cover other than that in which it is published and without
a similar condition being imposed on the subsequent purchaser.

A CIP catalogue record for this title is available from the British Library.

For Mr Scott

Introduction

READERS MAY FEEL entitled to expect the author of a book offering an historical event for every day of the year at least to get her dates right. Unfortunately, dates are not what they used to be.

In September 1752, Great Britain switched from the Julian calendar to the Gregorian. Under the Calendar Act of 1751, eleven days were 'omitted', that is, 2 September 1752 was followed immediately by 14 September 1752. The Act also moved the first day of the new year from 25 March to 1 January. Before the change, the day after 24 March 1642 was 25 March 1643. The Act changed this, so that the day after 31 December 1751 was 1 January 1752.

Historians tend to adopt the new style for the year but, somewhat illogically, ignore the change of day and month. Some attempt an old style/new style cover-all device, but then allow the whole business quietly to lapse at some arbitrary point. I have simply slotted each snapshot of Oxfordshire life into the year on the date originally presented in the source material. It seems to me likely that the precise date was rarely the chief concern of the participants—those predecessors of ours who were busy being hanged, beheaded, robbed, born, buried, murdered, and drowned, not to mention the ones who were inventing things, rioting, drinking too much, fighting, and scandalising the neighbours.

Now that images ping freely round the internet on social media, it has become difficult sometimes to track them back to their first appearance. Please do let me know if you feel you have missed out on a credit.

Julie Ann Godson
2019

1 January

On this day in 1863, a mysterious case of highway robbery took place in Cropredy. Edward Stiff, John Jones, and William Strong were charged with assaulting Henry Burnham on the Queen's highway at Cropredy.

The three men were travelling by train to London from Birmingham, and got out at Cropredy to stretch their legs. But the guard did not wait, and the train moved off again for London without them. They asked the time of the next train, and then went in to the Brasenose Inn and ordered ale with cheese and biscuits.

While they were there, Henry Burnham of Upper Boddington came into the pub. Henry, a 27-year-old deaf man, stayed only for a few minutes. Although Henry was almost dumb, landlady Mary Ann Amos understood his request for a pint of ale.

Speaking through his brother in court, Henry claimed that he left the Brasenose and walked in bright moonlight towards his home at Boddington. He left the lane and crossed the fields to the canal bridge. Shortly after this, a man grabbed him by the throat. Another man went through his evidently capacious pockets and took a half-crown piece, four oranges, two half-ounce

The Brasenose Inn at Cropredy

packs of tobacco, two mince pies, a tobacco box and some leather pieces for making shoes. Having divested poor Henry of these items, the men told him to leave quietly, or he would find himself in the canal. Stiff, Strong and Jones were seen returning to Cropredy station and boarding the 7.54pm train for Paddington.

Supt Whadcoat took Henry to London to find the perpetrators. At a pub in Wapping, Henry identified John Jones as the man who searched his pockets. At a gun factory in Blue House Lane, Henry recognised Edward Stiff as being involved in the hold-up. But in court, the jury suddenly stopped the case and acquitted the prisoners, even though Henry was adamant about the identifications. Nobody was ever convicted of the attack on Henry Burnham.

2 January

On this day in 1923, missing Headington man Frank Eltome made himself known at the police station in Solihull. A First World War veteran blinded in one eye during his service with the Royal Army Medical Corps in Russia, 43-year-old Eltome had disappeared from his home at 140 Kingston Street about a year before. A body found floating in the Thames in the following July had been buried in the village of Northmoor under his name. But actually, Frank Eltome and a companion were tramping the countryside around Birmingham, surviving on casual farm labouring work.

One evening they sank down by the side of the road, exhausted and down on their luck. They hadn't even found shelter for the night. Eltome's companion picked up an abandoned newspaper and began to read a story about a fortune that lay unclaimed because the heir had gone missing. Eltome looked at the photograph next to the story. 'Why, he's lost an eye, just like me,' he exclaimed. Then he noticed the name in the story. 'Frank Eltome… Frank Eltome…' Suddenly he leapt to his feet and ran off down the road, shouting: 'Blimey! I ain't dead! I ain't drowned. That money is mine!'

The police wired to Eltome's wife Eliza, and she travelled to Solihull to collect her husband on the same day. He claimed that, after he left his house for the last time a year before, his mind went blank. It was only when he saw the newspaper story about the inheritance that it all came flooding back.

He said that he and his wife now planned to open a little shop in Headington

Delighted Mrs Eltome (left) collects her husband (right) with the assistance of her local MP (centre)

with his new riches. Later in 1923, Eltome wrote politely to the Army requesting his medals. Meanwhile residents in the village of Northmoor were left to puzzle over the identity of the drowned man they had buried the previous July.

3 January

On this day in 1692, Banbury conman and serial husband William Morrell spent his last moments chuckling quietly to himself over his many and various acts of knavery throughout England. These included accumulating some 18 wives, all whilst the others were still living.

He was said originally to have been a shoemaker from Worcester who, after a tour abroad, settled respectably as a surgeon with a wife and family at Banbury. In about 1674, however, Morrell began to yearn for the life of a gentleman and fell to neglecting his business. He travelled throughout England passing himself off as a member of the gentry in order to make bogus marriages with young ladies of fortune.

Wife number three tracked him down to London and threatened to prosecute, but he charmed her into allowing him back—and then took off again, taking all her valuables with him. At Christmas 1691, he was lodging at Cullen's bakery on the Strand, posing as Captain Humphrey Wickham of Swalcliffe. Morrell fell ill and died, but not without promising his carers, the Cullens, a generous legacy.

The Cullens made lavish funeral preparations but, once the provisions of the 'will' proved unenforceable, the Cullens gave Morrell a four-shilling burial in a corner of the nearest churchyard.

4 January

On this day in 1604, John Bridges, dean of Salisbury, was elected bishop of Oxford. During Bridges' time in Salisbury, an undignified incident had occurred between Bridges and Salisbury cathedral organist John Farrant, who was married to Bridges' niece Margaret.

Margaret had frequently complained to her uncle about Farrant's ill treatment of her. Eventually, in front of the entire cathedral chapter, Bridges pulled Farrant up on his behaviour, and Farrant replied less than politely to such public interference in his domestic affairs. Indeed, the organist went so far as to leave the cathedral during the *Magnificat* and confront the dean in his study, drawing a knife and threatening to cut Bridges' throat.

During the ensuing scuffle the dean's gown was torn. However, any escalation of the violence was averted by a quick-thinking chorister who created a diversion which enabled Bridges to scarper to his bedroom and lock the door. Thwarted of his prey, Farrant returned to the cathedral just in time to take part in the anthem but, when the chapter sent for him a few days later, he had perhaps unsurprisingly vanished. A new organist was promptly sought.

5 January

On this day in 1643, the Parliamentarian delegation delivering a petition to King Charles I at his Civil War headquarters in Oxford passed over Magdalen bridge on their way back to the capital. One of the Roundheads tipped the sentinel guarding the bridge a gold twenty-shilling piece, but it was returned scornfully. The Royalist sentinel refused to accept a gratuity from a Roundhead, pointing out that he had a gracious king for his master, a man who was not behind with paying his wages—a dig at the haphazard nature of the payment of Parliamentarian soldiers at the beginning of the war. Upon hearing of this demonstration of loyalty, the king sent the sentinel *two* gold pieces.

In the winter of 1642–43, while Parliamentarian general Essex's army lay inactive at Windsor, Charles by degrees consolidated his position in the region of Oxford. The city was fortified as a redoubt for the whole area, and Reading, Wallingford, Abingdon, Brill, Banbury and Marlborough constituted a complete defensive ring which was augmented by the creation of smaller posts from time to time. Royalist successes in November and December 1642 gave Charles the confidence to scorn Parliament's offer of negotiations. He preferred to fight on, and exploit his opponents' weakness. The position of affairs for Parliament was perhaps at its worst in January; the ever-present dread of foreign intervention, and the burden of new taxation—which Parliament now felt compelled to impose—disheartened its supporters.

Disorder broke out in London, and, while the more determined of the rebels began to think of calling in the military assistance of the Scots, the majority were for peace on any conditions.

6 January

On this day in 1987, the first ever episode of *Morse* aired on ITV. Made by Zenith Productions for Central Independent Television between 1987 and 2000, the series comprised 33 two-hour episodes. *The Dead of Jericho* starred John Thaw as Morse and Kevin Whately as Detective Sgt Lewis. Oxford police officer Inspector Morse first appeared in author Colin Dexter's 1975 novel *Last Bus to Woodstock*. Dexter made uncredited cameo appearances in all but three of the TV episodes. The theme and incidental music for the series used a motif based on the Morse code for 'M.O.R.S.E.', starting with the opening notes and recurring all the way through. The name of the killer was occasionally spelled out in the music, or alternatively the name of another character as a red herring.

The red 1960 Jaguar Mark 2 used by Morse throughout the series was given away in a competition a year after filming ended. In November 2005, it was sold again for more than £100,000.

7 January

On this day in 1355, Thomas of Woodstock, fifth surviving son of King Edward III of England and Philippa of Hainault, was born at the medieval Woodstock Palace.

As 1st Duke of Gloucester, Thomas led the so-called Lords Appellant, a group of powerful nobles hoping to persuade Thomas's nephew, King Richard II to prosecute his unpopular court favourites. Their success in 1388 significantly weakened the king, but Richard II managed to dispose of the Lords Appellant in 1397, and Thomas was imprisoned in Calais to await trial for treason. The trial never happened. Thomas was murdered, probably by a group of men led by Thomas de Mowbray, 1st Duke of Norfolk, and Sir Nicholas Colfox on the orders of the king. This caused an outcry among the nobility of England which is considered by many to have added to Richard's unpopularity.

Thomas was buried in Westminster Abbey, first in the Chapel of St Edmund and St Thomas in October 1397, and two years later reburied in the Chapel of St Edward the Confessor.

A Victorian version of the Lords Appellant, showing Thomas in the centre

8 January

On this day in 1942, theoretical physicist and cosmologist Professor Stephen William Hawking was born—exactly 300 years after the death of Galileo. His parents lived in north London but, during the second world war, Oxford was considered a safer place to have babies. In 1963, while at the University of Cambridge, Hawking contracted motor neurone disease and was given two years to live. Yet he went on to become a brilliant researcher and professorial fellow at Gonville and Caius College, Cambridge. After the loss of his speech, he was still able to communicate through a speech-generating device, initially through use of a hand-held switch, and eventually by using a single cheek muscle. From 1979 to 2009 he held the post of Lucasian Professor at Cambridge, the chair held by Isaac Newton in 1663. Hawking was the first to set out a theory of cosmology explained by a union of the general theory of relativity and quantum mechanics. He wrote several works of popular science in which he discusses his own theories and cosmology in general. His book *A Brief History of Time* featured in the *Sunday Times* best-seller list for a record-breaking 237 weeks. In 2002, Hawking was ranked number 25 in the BBC's poll of the '100 Greatest Britons'. He died on 14 March 2018 at the age of 76, after living with motor neurone disease for more than 50 years.

9 January

On this day in 1852, respected Banbury watchmaker and jeweller John (Giovanni) Kalabergo, 66, was making his rounds of the local villages in company with his 22-year-old nephew, Gulielmo. On the way home in the evening, Kalabergo was shot in the head at point-blank range on the Williamscot Road, not far from the high road to Daventry. Shortly afterwards, Gulielmo, who had been in England for only two or three months, arrived at the Kalabergo home in Banbury High Street demanding to see an Italian-speaking Catholic priest. Dr William Tandy was sent for, and learned from the nephew that the Kalabergos had been set upon by three men. However, this seemed unlikely since a great deal of cash was found on the body of the uncle. The pistol found near to the scene of the murder was identified as having been purchased by Gulielmo, and he was charged with murder. It emerged

The Kalabergos, uncle and son, as depicted in *Jackson's Oxford Journal*

that, having been summoned to England by his uncle with a view to taking over the jewellery business, sharp-dressing Gulielmo resented being ordered to shave off his mustachios and tone down his dandified ways. The strict nature of the regime imposed upon the nephew by the uncle was offered as Gulielmo's motive for murder. Following his arrest, Gulielmo made two attempts at escaping his fate, first by jumping out of a window in Banbury, and secondly in Oxford gaol by climbing a wall round the exercise yard—both without success. Between 8,000 and 10,000 people turned out to see Gulielmo hang.

10 January

On this day in 1939, 25 Basque refugee children arrived at St Michael's House in Shipton-under-Wychwood. The Spanish Civil War had raged since July 1936 between the left-wing Republican government and General Franco's right-wing rebel coalition supported by the Catholic church. It was a brutal struggle, but the welcome offered to the children in Oxfordshire was not universal. The vicar of Shipton-under-Wychwood, Rev Winsor-Cundell, refused to join the local committee to support the children and was instead replaced by Rev Hayward of Milton-under-Wychwood. In order to encourage a charitable response from Oxfordshire residents, the politically neutral and non-religious nature of the project was emphasised; it was framed as a purely humanitarian effort. Even the description of the children as 'Basque' rather than 'Spanish' was designed to appeal to British perceptions of Basques as hard working and devout, as opposed to Spaniards who were considered lazy, cruel and intolerant. In fact the children at Shipton had a mixture of Basque and Spanish names, and few actually spoke Basque. Local people raised funds to provide outings and trips to the seaside. Other homes were provided at Aston, Faringdon, and Thame.

11 January

On this day in 1905, the Early family's Witney blanket mill suffered a major fire. Fire was a much more frequent hazard before the mid-20th century. Rush lights, candles or oil lamps could easily be knocked over and, once a fire started, it spread rapidly through tightly-packed streets. The introduction of gas lighting and steam power only exacerbated the danger.

As the folk of Witney sat down to their evening meal on 11 January, the sudden scream of the factory's steam-whistle raised the alarm. Although Witney's volunteer fire brigade was soon on the scene, it was already too late to save the main buildings. Instead, the firemen directed jets of water onto the steel fire doors which stood as a barrier between the flames and the engine-house and fulling block. A powerful steam pump was sent from Oxford and members of a volunteer ambulance brigade set off, pedalling furiously on bicycles. Machinery crashed down through the floors and the red glow over Witney could be seen as far away as Reading. Onlookers hindered the firemen in Mill Street but the fire burned itself out, and the vital engine house and power plant were saved.

12 January

On this day in 1891, archaeological aerial photographer Graham W Allen was born in Iffley. His father had made a fortune from the Oxford Steam Plough Company, and moved his family to The Elms, now the Hawkwell House hotel. A large garage in the grounds housed Major Allen's renovated vintage cars.

George and James Allen

He was accompanied by his brother James on the Brighton Run in 1937. But motoring was not Allen's only hobby. He was supposedly the first owner of a private plane in the county, and had a private airfield at Clifton Hampden. His evenings and weekends were spent flying over the countryside, taking photographs of known, and previously unknown, archaeological sites. If the weather was unfavourable for photography, he flew backwards and forwards locating sites to return to once conditions improved. In all, he took about 2,000 photographs, and calculated that to take 600 photographs required around 12,000 miles of flying. His collection is now housed at the Ashmolean Museum.

13 January

On this day on 1943, Winston Churchill took off in a Liberator AL504 from Stanton Harcourt airfield and flew to the Casablanca Conference. During World War II RAF Stanton Harcourt was a satellite aerodrome for RAF Abingdon, to where No 10 Operational Training Unit crews would be sent once initial training was completed at Abingdon.

Held at the Anfa Hotel in Casablanca, French Morocco, the Casablanca Conference was an opportunity to plan the Allied European strategy for the next phase of World War II. In attendance were United States President Franklin D Roosevelt and British prime minister Winston Churchill. Also attending to represent the Free French forces were Generals Charles de Gaulle and Henri Giraud, though they played minor roles and were not part of the military planning. Stalin declined to attend, citing the ongoing Battle of Stalingrad as requiring his presence in the Soviet Union.

14 January

On this day in 1914, Hertford Bridge over New College Lane in Oxford was completed. Commonly called the 'Bridge of Sighs', it actually resembles the Venetian Rialto Bridge more closely. And strictly speaking, apparently it's a 'skyway'—an elevated walkway joining two or more buildings. It links the Old and New Quadrangles of Hertford College to the south and the north respectively, and much of its current architecture was designed by Sir Thomas Jackson. It was completed in 1914 despite opposition from New College. The building on the southern side of the bridge houses the college's administrative offices; the northern building is mostly student accommodation.

A false legend says that many decades ago, a survey of the health of students was taken, and as Hertford College's students were the heaviest, the college closed off the bridge to force them to take the stairs, giving them extra exercise. However, if the bridge is not used, the students actually climb fewer stairs than if they do use the bridge. The Grade II listed bridge is always open to members of the college, who can often be seen crossing it.

Jackson was one of the most distinguished architects of his generation. His work at Oxford included Oxford Military College as well as the Examination Schools, most of Hertford College, much of Brasenose College, ranges at Trinity College and Somerville College, and the Acland Nursing Home in North Oxford. The former City of Oxford High School for Boys in George Street, Oxford, is another building designed by him.

15 January

On this day in 1951, Major General Sir Ernest Dunlop Swinton, a key player in the development and adoption of the World War I tank, died in Wolvercote aged 82.

In July 1914, Swinton received a letter from a friend, the South African engineer Hugh Merriot, asking that he look in to the possibility that armoured tractors might prove useful in warfare. Swinton took the notion a step further with the idea of deploying caterpillar tracks. As early as 1911, David Roberts of Richard Hornsby & Sons had attempted to interest British military officials in a tracked vehicle, but failed. Benjamin In 1914 the Holt Manufacturing

Company bought the patents related to the 'chain track' track-type tractor for £4,000. In November 1914, by this time a war correspondent in France, Swinton suggested to the military authorities the construction of a bullet-proof, tracked vehicle that could destroy enemy machine guns. In 1916 Swinton was promoted to lieutenant colonel and given responsibility for training the first tank units, and by 1918 the War Office had received 2,100 Holt tractors.

16 January

On this day in 1879, the elderly rector of Tackley Rev Lancelot Sharpe was obliged to extract a commercial traveller from under his bed. Earlier in the evening the butler Noble Rose had made his rounds to check that the house was properly secured for the night. Spotting a ladder propped against the wall of the house directly under the master's bedroom window, Rose upbraided the gardener, who had been cleaning the windows. But the gardener claimed he had locked the ladder away in the tool-house some time before.

A search of the house was therefore made but, when no intruder was found, the servants went back downstairs. Rev Sharpe announced that he had better check under the bed, whereupon his wife trilled playfully: 'Come on out, boy!' A gruff voice from under the bed replied: 'It's not a boy, it's a man.' As 47-year-old Alfred Tuckey emerged, the 72-year-old rector sprang on him and grabbed him by the throat. The butler Rose reappeared and over-powered the intruder, but not without incurring a bullet wound in his thigh.

Since the witness accounts suggested that the break-in occurred at about a quarter to nine and therefore constituted 'house-breaking', Tuckey was sentenced to five years' penal servitude only. Had the intrusion taken place *after* nine o'clock in the evening, Tuckey would have been guilty of 'burglary', and the sentence could have been much more serious. It was accepted that the revolver had gone off accidentally during the scuffle.

17 January

On this day in 1713, composer and organist Charles John Stanley died. At the age of 17, Stanley became the youngest person ever to obtain the Bachelor of Music degree at the University of Oxford. At about the age of two, he stumbled

Composer Charles John Stanley
on a marble hearth with a china basin in his hand; the sharpened shards of china pierced his eyes and left him almost blind. Fortunately, Stanley developed a remarkable memory which helped him direct many of Handel's oratorios, and to enjoy music-making and card games with his many friends. If he had to accompany a new oratorio he would ask his sister-in-law to play it through just once—enough to commit it to memory. Like the great Johann Sebastian Bach, Stanley was better known in his lifetime as a performer than a composer. But he achieved an almost Handel-like status by the time he died. The antiquary and diarist Thomas Hearne (1678-1735), writing in his *Remarks and Collections* about Stanley's visit to Oxford in 1725, said that Stanley should be 'look'd upon as the best Organist in Europe, it may be, in the World'.

18 January

On this day in 1881, there began a great blizzard, exacerbated by strong gales, which laid down drifts of snow up to 12 feet deep in some villages. Shops remained shuttered and mail carts were abandoned. Many tradesmen were found dead in the snow in the ensuing days. The rail system was paralysed, with the Dean of Christ Church, his wife and two daughters spending the night on a dark, freezing, snow-bound train at Radley. No doubt Mr and Mrs Cantwell experienced some surprise when the gable-end of their house in Bullingdon Road, Oxford, arrived in their bedroom at 11am. Similarly, a few streets away, bootmaker John A'Bear can't have been expecting the roof of his house in Stanley Road to make its way through the bedrooms and down the stairs into the hall. Fortunately, nobody was hurt in these incidents.

There were fears for 16-year-old George Davis, a post office letter-carrier employed to deliver to Kennington via Hinksey. Following his failure to appear at the office at the usual time on Tuesday night, a man on horse-back was sent out to search for him to no avail. The next morning, George staggered in to the office with his mailbag, explaining that he had taken shelter at a cottage in Kennington overnight. He had recommenced his journey at 6am on Wednesday morning, but missed his footing in Kennington Lane, whereupon he had plummeted in to a ditch, and found himself up to his neck in snow. He had eventually extricated himself and continued on his way to work.

19 January

On this day in 1642, diarist and antiquary Anthony Wood's father Thomas died and had to be buried the same day because he was tremendously fat, and therefore 'could not keep'. The family was living in the little house Mr Wood had built a few years before to the rear of Postmaster's Hall in Merton Street, Oxford. The English Civil War was underway and the king had been expelled from London. The Court moved to Oxford and the Woods' main house was now occupied by Lord John Colepeper, Privy Counsellor and Master of the Rolls to His Majesty King Charles I. Thomas Wood died in the room above the kitchen at about 4am, and between 8pm and 9pm on the same day, he was buried in the north part of Merton College church, near to the graves of his younger brother James and his own son John.

20 January

On this day in 1980, pioneering abstract artist William Patrick Roberts died aged 84. Trained at both St Martin's and the Slade art schools, he spent most of World War II living with his wife Sarah in a flat in Marston. Always on his uppers financially, he managed to get a one-day-a-week teaching job at Oxford Technical College, now Oxford Brookes University. Throughout his life he drew inspiration from his surroundings, and a number of watercolour drawings from this period show rural scenes on the River Cherwell and a nearby gypsy camp. There has been a recent revival of interest in the work of a man who described himself as an 'English Cubist'.

21 January

On this day in 1699, Obadiah Walker, Master of University College from 1676 to 1688 and closet Catholic, died. Oxford and its University supported the Royalist side during the English Civil War, particularly in financial terms. But the city surrendered to the Parliamentary forces on 24 June 1646, and by October a 'visitation' was proposed. This was a political and religious purge during which many masters and fellows of colleges lost their positions, including Obadiah Walker. He passed some years in teaching, studying and travelling. Returning to Oxford at the Restoration in 1660, Walker took a leading part in the work of University College. In June 1676, he became master of the college. He remained a Protestant, in name at least, until the accession of James II. Soon after this he became a Roman Catholic, opening a Catholic chapel at University College. He advised the new king with regard to affairs in Oxford, being partly responsible for the tactless conduct of James in forcing a quarrel with the fellows of Magdalen College.

Walker was responsible for the statue of King James II on the tower in the main quad at University College, one of only two in England. After James left England, Walker lost his mastership and subsisted on the charity of friends, mainly his former pupil Dr John Radcliffe.

22 January

On this day in 1644, Charles I opened the Royalist 'Oxford Parliament' at Christ Church. Having been expelled from London on the eve of the English Civil War, Charles made Oxford the Royalist base.

The king was advised that dissolving the Long Parliament would be unconstitutional, so all the members were summoned to assemble for a parliamentary session in Oxford. Most of the House of Lords, and about one-third of the House of Commons, heeded the king's summons.

Royalist lawyer Sir Sampson Eure, who was born in Upper Heyford, was elected as Speaker of the House of Commons. However, some of the members defected back to Westminster because they did not like the king's dealings with Irish Catholics, and others argued strongly for a negotiated peace with the Long Parliament in Westminster Hall. The Oxford Parliament met a number of times during the English Civil War and was used by Charles as a way of raising funds to fight. Not much is known of its proceedings because all its records were burnt just before Oxford fell to Parliamentary forces in 1646.

23 January

On this day in 1620, Sir John Croke, builder of Studley Priory, died. Speaker of the English House of Commons between October and December 1601, Croke spent the early part of his career as a lawyer. As Recorder of London in 1602, Croke was involved in a divisive witchcraft case in which he performed a series of a tests on the 14-year-old accuser, Mary Glover, and the defendant, elderly Elizabeth Jackson; he came to the conclusion that Glover was bewitched after witnessing her reaction to a disguised Jackson, and her unresponsiveness to heat which left visible burns. The evidence obtained was used in trial, and Jackson was convicted to one year's imprisonment and several sessions in the pillory, but released early.

24 January

On this day in 1883, *The Oxford Magazine* first appeared. Not be confused with commercial listings/shopping magazines *Oxford Magazine* and *In Oxford Magazine*, *The Oxford Magazine* provides an independent forum where members of Congregation can debate academic policy, and often carries articles critical of the University's leadership. The magazine was established in 1883 and published weekly during Oxford University terms. Contributors included J R R Tolkien, whose character Tom Bombadil featured in its pages in around 1933 before later appearing in *The Lord of the Rings*. Other early work published in the magazine included that by C S Lewis, Dorothy Sayers, and W H Auden. The magazine continues to publish poetry, including the work of Oxford Professor of Poetry Simon Armitage.

25 January

On this day in 1640, English scholar Robert Burton was found dead in his chambers at Christ Church. A life-long depressive, he was best known for his classic treatise *The Anatomy of Melancholy*. Burton was a mathematician and dabbled in astrology, and a rumour spread that he hanged himself on this day deliberately to verify his own prediction. He wrote *The Anatomy of Melancholy* largely to try and write himself out of being a lifelong sufferer from depression. The work examines in forensic detail the ubiquitous Jacobean malady, melancholy, supposedly caused by an excess of 'black bile', one of the four humours according to theory fashionable at the time. Melancholy was responsible, according to Burton, for the wild passions and despairs of lovers, the agonies and ecstasies of religious devotees, the frenzies of madmen, and the periods of utter absorption of artists like Shakespeare and Milton.

But he could actually be a fun companion, and had favourite sources of amusement. In 1728 his friend Bishop Kennett reported that listening to the bargemen swearing and cursing would have Burton rocking with laughter.

26 January

On this day in 1554, Queen Mary Tudor granted a royal charter bestowing borough status on Banbury. Following the death of Henry VIII's son Edward VI, Banbury had supported Mary's claim to the throne against the machinations of the Duke of Northumberland in favour of Lady Jane Grey.

Under the new charter the town was entitled to return a single Member

Banbury market

of Parliament, thus reinforcing the cause of the pro-Mary party in the area. The charter also conferred the right to select a bailiff, 12 aldermen, and 12 burgesses to govern the borough by means of a common council. The precise geographical boundaries of the town were carefully noted, and permission given for the council to appoint annually a 'sergeant at mace' and constables to ensure that its orders were carried through. The right to hold a Court of Record was granted, and a justice of the peace was to be chosen annually from among the aldermen by the common council. Permission for a weekly market on Thursdays was included in the charter, plus two annual fairs—one on the Feast of St Peter and one on the Feast of St Luke the Evangelist.

27 January

On this day in 1649, Henry 'Harry' Marten of Longworth signed Charles I's death warrant. More of a republican than a Puritan, Marten had spent his youth—and a great deal of his father's money—racketing around Europe on the Grand Tour, drinking and wenching with his boon companion, the poet Mildmay Fane, Earl of Westmorland. He was closely associated with John Lilburne and the Levellers, and was one of those who suspected the sincerity of Oliver Cromwell, whose murder he is said personally to have contemplated. This gave Marten the distinction of having voiced support for the extirpation of both the monarch and Cromwell.

At a meeting of the Commission for the king's trial, Cromwell asked members for suggestions as to how they should deal with Charles's predicted refusal to acknowledge the court's authority. Marten broke the embarrassed silence: 'Why then let it be this: in the name of the Commons and Parliament assembled, and all the good people of England.' Greatly relieved, all concurred. Marten signed the death warrant of Charles I along with 31 other regicides, enjoying a jolly ink fight with Cromwell during the ceremony.

28 January

On this day in 1613, Sir Thomas Bodley died. He was an English diplomat and scholar who founded the Bodleian Library in Oxford. The library at the University began in the 1300s with a small collection of books given by the bishop of Worcester, and in the following century Henry V's younger brother the Duke of Gloucester added many books and manuscripts.

During the Reformation in the 1500s, the library was stripped bare and abandoned, and this was the state in which Bodley found it in 1598. He determined, he said, 'to take his farewell of state employments and to set up his staff at the library door in Oxford.' His offer to restore the old library was accepted by the University. Bodley began his project in 1600, using the site of the former library above the Divinity School, which was almost in ruins.

As well as deploying a good deal of his own and his wife's inheritances, he cajoled donations from rich colleagues and friends, engraving their names in a magnificent vellum-leaved *Benefactors' Book* which was kept on prominent display. Another innovation of Bodley's was the agreement between the Bodleian Library and the Stationer's Company, by which the Company agreed to send to the library a copy of every book entered in their register. This made the Bodleian the first legal deposit library.

29 January

On this day in 1900, blood-curdling screams were heard issuing from the top floor of the New Inn in St Aldate's, Oxford, first thing in the morning.

Landlord Fred Cumberlidge rushed upstairs to find fellow-publican Alexander Sharp Naylor sitting on top of his wife Edith, having attacked her with a knife and then slit his own throat into the bargain. Naylor died within a few minutes, his wife was severely wounded though still living. Subsequent enquiries revealed that the Naylors were no drunken low-lifes. Son of a Brick Lane cook, Naylor had done well for himself and, in his time, become a publican of some standing, having been involved in various hostelries. As a 42-year-old widower with four children, he had remarried to 19-year-old Edith Hicks of King's Farm, Harpsden near Henley-on-Thames, daughter of a respectable registrar (though said on occasion to deploy her pretty looks for the purposes of flirtation). According to Mrs Naylor's brother Thomas Hicks, another publican, Naylor had recently approached him for a loan of £40, having lost £500 betting. Several pawn tickets were found on the body of Naylor, though Mrs Naylor's diamond ring was on the dressing table.

Finding itself unable to decide between pecuniary embarrassment or marital jealousy as a motive for suicide, the court fixed upon that most helpful of Victorian smoke-screens—'temporary insanity'. This kept the way open for a conventional burial in hallowed ground.

30 January

On this day in 1884, Mr and Mrs Joseph Reade of Shipton Court, Shipton under Wychwood, treated 300 villagers to a sumptuous feast of roast beef, plum pudding and pastries. The great house was cheerfully decorated with banners of welcome and, after the food was polished off, tobacco and beer were placed on the tables, with tea for abstainers. The Shipton Brass Band provided music for singing and dancing until 10pm, at which point the National Anthem was played and three cheers given for the hosts. Such hospitality on the part of the big house towards tenants and locals was traditional at the time, but there was something different about the Reades.

Joseph Reade was actually born humble Joseph Wakefield in Leeds. Forty-one years earlier, as footman to Sir John Chandos Reade of Shipton Court, Joseph had been the only witness to an altercation between his master and the butler Thomas Sinden which resulted in Thomas taking a tumble down the stairs and sustaining a head injury that killed him a few days later. Contrary to the evidence of all the other servants, Joseph testified that he heard and saw nothing that might have caused Sinden to fall. Sir John bypassed all his own relatives when he died, and left the entire Shipton estate to Joseph on condition that he changed his name from Wakefield to Reade. He did.

31 January

On this day in 1604, Sir Thomas Crompton became the first burgess to sit as a MP for the newly-created constituency of Oxford University. The constituency, created by royal charter in 1603, was not a geographical area. Its electorate consisted of the graduates of the University of Oxford with a doctorate or MA degree, and it was entitled to return two members. Electors numbered about 500 in the 1754–1790 period; by 1910, it had risen to 6,500.

Following the reforms of 1918, the franchise encompassed all graduates who paid a fee of £1 to join the register. This included around 400 women who had passed examinations which would have entitled them to a degree if they were male. Sir Thomas Crompton was a judge of the High Court of Admiralty in Southwark from c.1605, chancellor of the diocese of London from 1607, and master in chancery from 1608. The Oxford University constituency was abolished in 1950 by the Representation of the People Act 1948.

1 February

On this day in 1328, the orphaned son of a Wallingford blacksmith was elected abbot of St Alban's. Brought up in the care of William de Kirkeby, the prior of Wallingford, Richard of Wallingford was sent to Oxford University where he emerged as something of a mathematical, scientific and mechanical whizz. The abbot of Wallingford Priory died in 1328, and Richard's inspiring preaching led to him be elected to lead the abbey in his place.

During his trip to Avignon to seek Papal confirmation of his appointment, Richard appears to have contracted leprosy. His indisposition first became evident shortly after the commencement of his abbacy when he experienced a period of temporary blindness. When it became clear that the abbot's affliction was leprosy, some of the younger monks began to plot to have him removed. However, Richard's charm, piety and learning gained him many friends, and a rare display of medieval equal opportunities enabled him to stay in power, reassert his authority over the town and rebuild much of the abbey. Richard's greatest achievement is said to have been the design of an extraordinary temporal and astronomical clock, copies of which are on display in both the abbey and the British Museum.

Richard and his clocks

2 February

On this day in 1650, King Charles II's mistress Eleanor 'Nell' Gwynn was born, some say in Oxford. She certainly spent time in Oxfordshire, following the king and his Court here to escape the plague in London. One day as she drove through the streets of Oxford in her coach, the mob mistook her for her rival Louise de Kérouaille. 'Here comes the Catholic whore!' they yelled. Quick as a flash, Nell stuck her head out of the coach window. 'Good people, you are mistaken!' she responded cheerily. ' I am the *Protestant* whore.'

Another clue to Nell's local connections might perhaps be detected in the titles Charles granted to the couple's son when the boy was six— Baron of Heddington and Earl of Burford. Two stories describe the momentous grant. The first is that when Charles arrived one day, Nell called to the boy: 'Come here you little bastard, and say hello to your father.' When the king protested at the unpleasant appellation, Nell replied: 'Your Majesty has given me no other name by which to call him.' In response, Charles created him Earl of Burford on the spot. Another is that Nell grabbed the boy, dangled him out of a window, and threatened to drop him unless he was granted a peerage, upon which the king cried out: 'God save the Earl of Burford!' In 1676, a warrant was passed for 'a grant to Charles Beauclerc, the king's natural son, and to the

'Pretty, witty' Nell Gwynn accompanied the Court to Oxford

heirs male of his body, of the dignities of Baron of Heddington, co. Oxford, and Earl of Burford in the same county, with remainder to his brother, James Beauclerc, and the heirs male of his body.' Shortly afterwards the king granted to Nell and their son a house on the edge of the Home Park in Windsor. It was promptly renamed Burford House.

3 February

On this day in 1458, Thomas Courtenay, 5th Earl of Devon, died at Abingdon Abbey—poisoned, according to rumour. Thomas had succeeded his father as the premier nobleman in the West Country at the age of only eight. Four years later, he was knighted by King Henry VI and served him faithfully during the French Wars. But when factionalism broke out at Court between the Yorkists and the Lancastrians, Courtenay allied himself to Richard, Duke of York, the rival for Henry's throne. This was because Courtenay's chief West Country rival had aligned himself with the king.

The relationship with York broke down, and Courtenay became an advisor to Queen Margaret. He received a summons to appear with York before the king in London and, having been on both sides, he imagined he could become a great hero by brokering the peace. He travelled in Queen Margaret's entourage and the party broke their journey at Abingdon Abbey.

The monastery was a hot-bed of Yorkist sympathisers including the Abbot himself. Before negotiations even had a chance to begin, the Earl died. Poison was suspected, but never proved.

4 February

On this day in 1680, German botanist, Jacob Bobart, the first-ever superintendent of the Oxford Physick Garden (now the Oxford Botanic Garden) died at Rose Cottage at the age of 81. In 1622, former outlaw Henry Danvers, 1st Earl of Danby, keen to rebuild his reputation, had gifted to the University five acres of land opposite Magdalen College to be utilised for the study of physick and botany. Eminent naturalist and collector John Tradescant the Elder was offered the position first, but he turned it down. Bobart was in position by 1641 and, within a year or two, Danvers was dead and his lands sequestrated during the English Civil War. Happily, Bobart's right-of-office entitling him to sell fruit and vegetables from the gardens enabled him to survive through this sticky patch. His organised mind revealed itself in a penchant for planting yew trees in pairs, plus a painstaking alphabetical catalogue of 1,600 plants under his care. Bobart did not lack eccentricity, however. On feast days he would lace strips of fluttering silver into his beard and, in addition to the customary dog, Bobart was accompanied at all times by a goat.

5 February

On this day in 1861, early in the morning, the porter living in the main gate at Blenheim Palace spotted signs of a fire taking hold in the north-east wing of the outer quadrangle. The house steward and a team of helpers hurried at once to the Titian Room, hoping to save the paintings by cutting them out of their frames. However, when they opened the door flames rushed out at them, and melted lead poured down from the roof making entry impossible. Within a few minutes the roof fell in. Fire engines from the Palace itself and from Woodstock were brought to bear on the conflagration, but the whole wing was destroyed except for the strong-room and the bakehouse, both of which were said to be fireproof. *Art Journal* announced sniffily that the works of art destroyed in the fire were no great loss, being probably by Padovanino rather than Titian, and therefore worth only(!) £60,000. The journal did acknowledge, however, that the loss of a fine Reubens was irreparable as there was no copy in existence. The origin of the fire was never discovered.

6 February

On this day in 1990, Diana, Princess of Wales visited the Oxford office of Relate. Just five weeks previously on New Year's Eve 1989, two Oxfordshire radio hams had separately recorded a sensitive phone call between the princess and close friend James Gilbey, to whom she had turned following the departure of another admirer, James Hewitt, for the Gulf War.

Retired savings bank manager, Cyril Reenan from Abingdon, was the first to come forward with a tape of the conversation, followed by another Abingdon resident, Jane Norgrove. The resulting scandal became known as 'Squidgygate',

Diana in Oxford

reflecting Gilbey's use of the nickname 'Squidgy' for the princess. If that wasn't sufficiently toe-curling, a recording of a late-night phone call between Prince Charles and Camilla Parker-Bowles then emerged which included even more cringe-worthy language, and was evidently made only a fortnight before the Squidgygate call. Diana may already have known about the taping of her call with Gilbey at the time of her visit to Oxford, and she certainly knew what was going on between her husband and Mrs Parker-Bowles. After much skirmishing in the press, Charles and Diana announced their official separation in December 1992.

7 February

On this day in 1891, *Jackson's Oxford Journal* carried a report from the proud townspeople of Charlbury: 'ELECTRIC LIGHTING.—Our town is in front of many others with larger claims to importance in the matter of electric lighting. For the last few weeks on Saturdays our enterprising firm Messrs Baughan and Co, manufacturing electricians, have been giving us the advantage of this addition to present day science by having outside their building, carried on a high bracket, an arc-lamp of 2,000 candle-power, which very brilliantly illuminates the town for a considerable area, and may be seen for miles round. They have recently put down a gramme-dynamo capable of giving light equalling 14 to 16,000 candles, together with necessary steam engine and boiler for driving the same. Inside the building, Messrs Baughan show incandescent lamps varying from 2 to 150 candle-power, which glow with remarkable steadiness and brilliancy, also other arc-lamps. As the object of the firm is the temporary (or permanent if desired) lighting of ball rooms, garden parties, bazaars, &c, more than a permanent installation, the light here at present is only run periodically. Anyone interested in this system of lighting, Messrs Baughan invite to view the plant when at work.'

8 February

On this day in 1999, novelist Irish Murdoch died at Vale House in Sandford-on-Thames. Born in Dublin, Murdoch moved to London where she enjoyed a happy childhood. Just before World War II she went up to Somerville College to read Greats. During the war she worked at the Treasury and experienced the Blitz, then moved to the United Nations Rehabilitation and Relief Association, assisting refugees. After a string of tumultuous romantic adventures, Murdoch met Oxford academic John Bayley in 1953, and the couple spent 46 harmonious years together, first in Steeple Aston, then in North Oxford.

Murdoch taught philosophy at St Anne's College until 1963. From there she went to the Royal College of Art to teach general studies. In 1967 she left to commence her writing career which resulted in 27 novels, plus plays, poems and treatises on philosophy. Her often prize-winning novels are populated by highly intelligent people, with the women frequently sporting apparently masculine names and vice versa. Multiple cross-currents of love and longing lead these characters into sometimes comic situations. In 2008 *The Times* ranked Murdoch twelfth on a list of 'The 50 greatest British writers since 1945'.

9 February

On this day in 1933, a debate at the Oxford Union carried by 275 votes to 152 the motion that 'this House will in no circumstances fight for its King and Country'. The motion was proposed by Kenelm Hubert Digby of St John's College and opposed by K R F Steel-Maitland of Balliol.

Debates on pacifism and disarmament had been held before, and in 1927 an almost identical motion had passed in the Cambridge Union by 213 to 138 votes without the outside world taking much notice. But then a group of indignant life-members led by Randolph Churchill and including Quentin Hogg proposed to expunge the motion from the records. Churchill's presence at the second debate was met by a barrage of hisses and stink bombs. In an expression of their indignation at having the Union's affairs interfered with (rather than from any pacifist leanings) students defeated this second motion by 750 to 138 votes. And this second vote is what gave the episode its notoriety.

After the debate, the proposer of the original motion Digby said: 'I believe that the motion was representative neither of the majority of the undergraduates of Oxford nor of the youth of this country. I am certain if war broke out tomorrow the students of the University would flock to the recruiting office as their fathers and uncles did.' He was right. When World War II broke out in September 1939, 2,632, out of a potential 3,000 students volunteered.

10 February

On this day in 1355, there began the notorious St Scholastica Day riot in Oxford, which escalated into a rampage that lasted two days and left 63 scholars and perhaps 30 townspeople dead.

That Tuesday, two scholars, Walter Spryngeheuse and Roger de Chesterfield, went for a drink at the Swindlestock Tavern (on the site of the Santander Bank

St Scholastica Day, 1355

at Carfax). When they complained to the taverner, John Croidon, about the quality of the wine they were served, angry words were exchanged. The scholars threw their wine in Croidon's face and beat him up. Town bailiffs requested Spryngeheuse and Chesterfield to make amends, but they would not.

Over the next two days mayhem ensued. On Wednesday, the scholars closed the town gates, set fire to the town, robbed the homes of Oxford people, and killed and wounded many. Two thousand country people came into town crying: 'Slay, slay, havok, havok, smite fast, give good knocks.' At dinner, when scholars went out to exercise in the fields, they were attacked by 80 townsmen, who had sheltered in St Giles church. It seems that it was now that the first deaths of the riot occurred. On Thursday, townsmen and country people sacked another 14 halls. Scholars were hurt and killed, and some were scalped in mockery of their clerical tonsure and were thrown bleeding and untended into prison. The dispute was eventually settled in favour of the University and, annually thereafter until 1825, on the feast day of St Scholastica, the mayor and councillors had to parade bareheaded through the streets, attend Mass, and pay the University a fine of one penny for every scholar killed, a total of five shillings and thruppence.

11 February

On this day in 1645, Parliamentary spy Bennett Burroughs reported to his masters on state of the Royalists in and around Banbury. 'Bennett Burroughs came this day from Ano and saith that all the horse that were quartered there & at Kings Sutton went away yesterday over the river towards Blox'm whyther or when they return hee knows not. That there are 2 troopes of horse in Banbury under Sir Wm Compton & Sir Wm Farmer [Fermor] and about 700 foote in the Castle. That the Earle of North'ton lyes at Adderbury where hee hath a regiment of horse and about 50 musqueteers which lye in the Lord Willmotts howse [east of Adderbury Green] and they have pulld upp the bridge [Nell Bridge] betweene Ano & Adderbury.'

Sir William Compton, 'the godly Cavalier' as Cromwell called him, was imprisoned after the Civil War. Upon the Restoration of the monarchy, he became MP for Cambridge. Sir William Fermor also survived, and in 1660 he took his seat on the privy council and stood for parliament for Brackley.

12 February

On this day in 1941, Reserve Constable Albert Alexander, a patient at the Radcliffe Infirmary, became the first person ever to be treated with penicillin intravenously, by Howard Florey's team. The ability of penicillin to slow or counteract bacterial infection had first been noticed by Sir Alexander Fleming in 1928, and now Florey (right) and his team at the University of Oxford were working on the medical applications of penicillin. Florey's wife Ethel brought Constable Alexander's apparently hopeless case to his attention.

Howard Florey

Alexander was in a bad way; a scratch from a rose thorn had become infected. His head was covered with abscesses and one of his eyes had been removed. Within 24 hours of an infusion of the new drug, Alexander's temperature dropped, his appetite returned and the infection began to heal.

However, due to the instability of penicillin and the war-time restrictions placed on Florey's laboratory, only a small quantity of penicillin had been extracted and by the fifth day they had run out. Constable Alexander relapsed, and died on 15 March 1941. The next patient to receive penicillin was Arthur Jones, a lad of 15 who had required a hip operation to insert a pin but whose wound had become septic. He was given penicillin, and within two days his temperature was normal. Four weeks later he was fit enough to have another operation to remove the pin that had caused the infection.

13 February

On this day in 1893, according to *Jackson's Oxford Journal*: 'An invitation ball, under the auspices of the Burford Quadrille Society to close the season, took place, and secured a good attendance, between 60 and 70 accepting the invitation from Burford and the neighbourhood. The Infant School-room was the scene of the action, and its preparation, decoration, and transformation, have been entrusted to the committee who performed their work with much care and skill. The orchestra was nicely placed, being secluded by lace curtains and other artistic designs. The wainscot was draped with white and red festooning, and from the gaseliers and other parts of the room were dependant a number of glass balls of variegated colours, which looked very pretty in the gaslight. The Girls' School-room was utilized as a refreshment department, and the cosy Class Room for a quiet chat, &c. Jackson's Quadrille Band from Witney was engaged for the occasion, and played with their usual brightness and finish. The dancing began about 9pm, and was kept up with energy till 2.30am.'

14 February

On this day in 1966, Hollywood stars Richard Burton and Elizabeth Taylor opened in an Oxford University Dramatic Society student production of Marlowe's *Doctor Faustus* at Oxford Playhouse, directed by Professor Nevill Coghill, Merton Professor of English Literature in the University at the time. Burton had agreed to play the title role to thank Coghill who, two decades earlier, had championed Burton's acting talent when the young Welshman studied English briefly at Exeter College. Remarkably, Taylor's non-speaking role in the play as Helen of Troy marked her stage debut. She described the whole affair as something of 'a giggle'.

For the week that the play ran, the couple took over an entire floor at the Randolph hotel and entertained their undergraduate co-stars every night. The students' brush with fame was to continue when they were flown to Italy to appear in the film version of the play that summer. The film was poorly received by critics, but proceeds from the stage play were used to create the Burton Taylor Studio round the corner from the Playhouse, which is now a popular venue for student, fringe and children's shows.

15 February

On this day in 1928, the *Oxford English Dictionary* was completed after 70 years. A small group of intellectuals from the Philological Society in London (and unconnected to Oxford University) began work on the dictionary in 1857, but it was not until 1879 that the OUP finally agreed to publish the dictionary and to pay the editor, James Murray. It was hoped that the project would be completed in ten years, but it was only in 1884 that it began to be published in unbound sections. The first of these was 'A to Ant'.

The dictionary traces the historical development of the English language, providing examples of the earliest usage of words and thereby illustrating the dramatic change of meaning of many over the centuries. William Shakespeare is the most-quoted writer in the completed dictionary, with *Hamlet* his most-quoted work. George Eliot is the most-quoted female writer.

In 1895, the title the *Oxford English Dictionary* (OED) was first used—up till then it had been *A New English Dictionary on Historical Principles; Founded Mainly on the Materials Collected by The Philological Society*.

16 February

On this day in 1963, the Beatles played at the Carfax Assembly Rooms, on the site of the present HSBC bank at the corner of Cornmarket. Compèred by Rolf Harris, this was the Beatles' only live appearance anywhere in the county of Oxfordshire. Tickets cost six shillings in advance from Russell Acott's music shop in the High Street. The Beatles' second single *Please Please Me* was hurtling up the charts at the time.

Support act that night was local group the Madisons, who tuned up alongside John Lennon and Paul McCartney. Neil Robinson, then a 21-year-old keyboard player, recalls: 'It was a sell-out. The word had just started to spread about the Beatles and there were girls standing up on tables around the room. They were screaming and shouting.'

While in Oxford the Beatles met Jeffrey Archer, then at the Oxford University Department for Continuing Education studying for a diploma of education. The future novelist, Conservative Party politician, and disgraced peer had, in circumstances that remain unclear, become a member of Brasenose College, a connection which he exploited fully. The band accepted Archer's invitation to visit the principal's lodging at Brasenose, where they were photographed with Archer and dons of the college. Critic Sheridan Morley, then a student at Merton, was present and recalled the occasion: 'I went to the toilet, and there

The Beatles in Oxford

beside me was Ringo Starr. He asked if I knew this Jeffrey Archer bloke. I said everyone in Oxford was trying to work out who he was. Ringo said: "He strikes me as a nice enough fella, but he's the kind of bloke who would bottle your piss and sell it."

17 February

On this day in 1809, a serious fire broke out at Christ Church. *Jackson's Oxford Journal* reported on 11 March: 'Yesterday se'nnight, about twelve o'clock, an alarming conflagration took place in the Old Quadrangle of this magnificent College. The flames were first observed to issue from the rooms over Dr White's lodgings, which, spreading to the adjoining apartments, threatened destruction to the whole building. The interior of Dr White's house was entirely consumed. Dr White, his wife, sister, and family, happily escaped uninjured, and were immediately conveyed to the opposite lodgings of Dr Burton. So rapid was the progress of the fire, that it was impossible to save the furniture, personal safety was the only consideration. Many of the young Students, who occupied the rooms which fell a sacrifice to the devouring element, lost a great part of their property... The fury of the flames increased so much that the Hall was apprehended to be in the greatest danger, and it was judged expedient to remove the many valuable portraits from there to Dr Hall's and the Chapter House. At one time the great Gateway appeared to be in imminent danger, but providentially the night being calm, and the exertions of the multitude unremitting, the progress of the flames was arrested before any further ruin ensued than that of Dr White's mansion and seven sets of rooms adjoining, and at about eight o'clock the fire was got under.'

The newspaper assured readers that the fire 'did not originate from carelessness or negligence', but that 'it was probably owing to a beam of wood taking fire in a gentleman's room adjoining Dr White's house'.

18 February

On this day in 1943, an armourer from RAF Upper Heyford took a Sten gun to the Crown hotel in Sheep Street, Bicester, and shot two people dead. He then committed suicide, leaving a note explaining: 'I have been let down by a Bicester woman. Life is not worth living.'

The shooter was South African Jacobus Terblanche, aged about 44. His first victim, and object of his passion, was fishmonger's wife Freda Winman, 28, a daily help in the hotel. Second victim, and Terblanche's rival for Freda's affections was Leading Aircraftman Walter Unsworth, 37, also based at the bomber station at Upper Heyford.

The situation was made yet murkier by the fact that both men were also married—Terblanche probably bigamously. When he arrived in Southampton from Capetown in July 1936, he came equipped with a wife and son. He gave his profession as 'soldier' and his proposed address as 'South Africa House, Trafalgar Square', not an unusual device for an immigrant unsure of their eventual place of settlement. The fate of Mrs Terblanche and her son is unclear, but within weeks Terblanche married 20-year-old Mabel Drew from Bristol; Walter Unsworth at least confined himself to one wife, May.

In summing up after the disaster, the coroner gave this advice: 'All the Winmans will be tainted by association in this case; you must get on with your lives and never mention it again.' Mabel Terblanche remarried in Bristol in 1947, and died 1991. May Unsworth never remarried, and was buried alongside her husband in 2005. The Crown hotel was demolished in the 1980s to make way for the Crown Walk shopping centre.

19 February

On this day in 1887, at about 3 o'clock in the morning, two gypsy children knocked on the door of Lock's Cottage in Blenheim Road, Horspath, and told the occupant that their father had murdered their mother. Farm worker Thomas Smith woke his neighbour, thatcher Henry Surman, and the pair reached the shabby tent on Open Brasenose common—in fact, no more than a tattered blanket stretched over some sticks—at about 4am.

Smith knew exactly where he was going, for he and his wife had heard quarrelling from there the day before, and the children's mother had appeared bruised and terrified of her husband. Oceana and Prince Albert were the children of Charles Smith (sometimes Bagley) and Lucy Austin. Charles, a peg and basket-maker, was in the habit of berating his wife for something that happened 30 years in the past, and indeed the births of Lucy's first three children do pre-date her marriage in 1861. Surman and Smith saw the dead woman and fetched two police officers, who discovered under some straw a hammer with a bloodied handle. Lucy Austin's battered body was removed to the Original Swan public house in Cowley for examination by a surgeon.

Charles attempted to persuade the magistrates that his wife's asthma and consumption must have caused her death, but her many head injuries were telling. Charles Bagley Smith was hanged in Oxford on 9 May. Felicia Skene of New Inn Hall Street, philanthropist and elderly spinster daughter of a Scottish landowner, arranged for Oceana to be sent to a home in York, and for Prince Albert to be brought up to acquire an honest means of earning a living.

20 February

On this day in 1547, Tudor courtier and author Sir Anthony Cope of Hanwell Castle near Banbury was created Knight of the Carpet at the coronation of Edward VI, according to antiquary Anthony Wood. Born in Banbury, probably at the now-lost Hardwick Manor, Cope was educated at the University of Oxford. He then completed his education by mingling with learned men at universities in France, Germany, Italy and elsewhere. This was the period during which he is said to have written a number of books, perhaps including translations from Galen and Hippocrates.

When he was 26, his father died and he inherited the manor of Hanwell as well as other property nearby. He completed the building of Hanwell Hall, which had been begun by his father. The Hall was later described by the antiquary John Leland as 'a very pleasant and gallaunt house'. Back in England, Sir Anthony was appointed vice-chamberlain, and later principal chamberlain, to Henry VIII's last queen, Catherine Parr.

Sir Anthony died in 1551, and was buried in the chancel at the church of St Peter in Hanwell. He left a widow, Jane, to whom he bequeathed £100 and an annuity of 100 marks, a mark being an accounting term rather than a coin, denoting the sum of 13 shillings and fourpence.

21 February

On this day in 1881, the village of Combe near Witney witnessed the deployment of a new invention known as a 'snow plough'. A blinding snow storm had blown throughout Tuesday 18 and Wednesday 19, and the snow had drifted to six or seven feet in the lanes. The only way out of the village was over the fields; cottagers were completely imprisoned inside their homes.

Even so, on the morning of 20 February, working men attempted to get to their place of employment, and several agricultural labourers were obliged to crawl through the snow and over walls to reach the farms. The postman, who had journeyed to Combe from Woodstock daily for over 20 years, was last seen at 5pm on Tuesday, and did not reappear until almost midday on Thursday. Then, on the 21st, salvation at last appeared in the form of a new invention, the snow plough. Designed by the Duke of Marlborough's clerk of works at Combe Mill, the contraption appeared in the village being drawn by three horses. Evidently the new invention was some sort of variation on a field plough, rather than the bulldozing snow ploughs we think of today. In a few hours, good roads nine feet wide were created, and village life began again.

22 February

On this day in 1890, *Jackson's Oxford Journal* reported on the appearance of blacksmith Thomas Richens of Faringdon before the magistrates on a charge of habitually keeping his younger brother Gerald away from school. Thirty-two-year-old Thomas's father had died in 1885, and his mother a year later, leaving Thomas with eight-year-old Gerald to look after, and this was his third appearance on the same charge. Mrs Richens had begged Thomas on her death-bed not to let Gerald be taken into the workhouse, and Thomas had faithfully given his word.

The magistrates had on previous occasions urged Thomas to take the little boy to the workhouse, but Thomas felt he must keep his promise. However, leaving home early in the morning to go to his work meant that Thomas was unable properly to supervise the boy on his way to school. Inevitably, young Gerald frequently played truant and ran wild in the streets. Finally, Thomas had to give up on his promise to his mother, and in the court he agreed to take Gerald to the workhouse that same afternoon.

23 February

On this day in 1808, Viscountess Ashbrook, Baroness Castledurrow in the County of Kilkenny, died. She was born plain Betty Ridge at Noah's Ark Inn on an island in the Thames at Northmoor. Her father Thomas was a Thames fisherman, but the end was in sight for commercial fishing of the river once sea-caught fish could be brought as far as Oxford and remain fresh. Thomas set his sights on becoming an inn-keeper, and this is how William Flower, 2nd Viscount Ashbrook, came to meet and fall madly in love with Betty while he was at Christ Church. Family disapproval meant that the couple had to wait three years until William was 21 to marry. Eventually they married in the little church of St Denys at Northmoor. Their family home was at the now-demolished Shellingford Manor near Faringdon. Betty's elder brother went to Ireland to run the Ashbrook estate and climbed through Kilkenny society to become high sheriff. Younger brother John was sent to the University to be trained as a clergyman, but he absconded to marry a village girl. Betty's granddaughter Charlotte Augusta married the 6th Duke of Marlborough.

24 February

On this day on 1684, James Figg, prize-fighter, was born in Thame. He is widely recognised as the first English bare-knuckle boxing champion, reigning

Pugilist James Figg from 1719 to 1730. He made his headquarters at the Greyhound Inn in Cornmarket, Thame, but to earn a living as a prize-fighter he had to venture far from home.

In 1719 he started his own school in Tottenham Court Road, London, where he taught boxing, fencing, and quarterstaff. Figg was also a great fencer who engaged in sword duels and singlestick matches. After 1730 he largely gave up fighting, and relied on his three protégés to bring in spectators: Bob Whittaker, Jack Broughton, and George Taylor. Taylor took over Figg's business upon Figg's death in 1734, though Broughton went on to become his most famous protégé.

Hogarth may have used Figg as model for some of his well-known works such as *A Rake's Progress*. James Figg was 50 when he died. One of his grandsons also became a Boxing Champion some years later.

> *'The Mighty Combatant, the first in Fame,*
> *The lasting Glory of his Native Thame,*
> *Rash, & unthinking Men! at length be Wise,*
> *Consult your Safety, and Resign the Prize,*
> *Nor tempt Superior Force; but Timely Fly*
> *The Vigour of his Arm, the Quickness of his Eye.'*

25 February

On this day in 2015, the bones of a Civil War woman were unearthed during building work at St Cross College. The young female, buried carefully and wrapped in a pin-fastened shroud, was discovered in what would at the time have been a domestic garden. She was still in rigor mortis when she entered her grave, having died while sleeping or in bed, so it is possible that her death may have been a result of an outbreak of typhus or plague.

Overcrowding and insanitary conditions in the town during this period were caused by the billeting of Royalist officers, soldiers and their families. A typhus epidemic, called *'morbus campestris'*— camp fever—was recorded in 1643, and the plagues of 1644-45 during the Siege of Oxford by Parliamentary forces, meant formal burials may have been difficult. An accompanying Charles I silver shilling, from 1640 or 1641 (above), and a silver half-groat from 1635 or 1636 found in the grave could have been placed over the woman's eyes or mouth. This seems to be more a local and cultural practice rather than a universal custom among Christian burials. The closing of the eyes in Britain is cited as being more likely to guard against rigor mortis setting in while they are still open—the eyelids being one of the first parts to be affected.

26 February

On this day in 1934, the art-deco New Theatre in George Street opened. There has been a theatre on the site for almost 170 years. The first theatre built in 1836 was known commonly as the 'Vic', and later as the 'Theatre Royale' after the company that played there. Forbidden to perform plays during the University terms, the lessee of the theatre resorted to presenting 'concerts' or music hall entertainments, and by 1880 the theatre had become run down.

Funds were raised for a new building, and in February 1886 the Oxford University Dramatic Society opened the second New Theatre with *Twelfth Night*. This second New Theatre was damaged by fire in 1892 and altered in

1908, when the seating capacity was increased to 1,200. In 1908 the Dorrill family took over the theatre and in 1933, Stanley Dorrill announced his plan to build 'the most luxurious and comfortable house of entertainment in England'. He commissioned the present building from architects William and T R Milburn of Sunderland. During the Second World War, half a million troops enjoyed free entertainment at the New Theatre, earning Stanley Dorrill an MBE. The Ambassador Theatre Group bought the theatre in 2009.

27 February

On this day in 1970, the first national Women's Liberation Movement conference was held at Ruskin College. It was organised by two Ruskin students as well as others from Canada, the USA, France and different parts of the UK. The event was originally conceived as a women's history conference, but when almost 600 activists from around the UK expressed a desire to attend, it was adapted to address women's issues more broadly. Four demands were discussed: equal pay; equal educational and job opportunities; free contraception and abortion on demand; free 24-hour nurseries. These were passed in Skegness in 1971, but have been only partially achieved 50 years later.

The WLM held national conferences between 1970 and 1978, and many local, national and regional conferences also took place. These focused on subjects such as feminist history, sexuality, socialist feminism and patriarchy.

28 February

On this day in 1734, Prince William IV of Orange passed the first full day of a stay in Oxford at Christ Church. Having stayed overnight, the Prince was at prayers at 10am. He spent the day in Woodstock, presumably at the new Blenheim Palace, returning to Oxford at half past four for a welcome speech from the Recorder at the Council Chamber. As on the previous evening, an entertainment was staged, the city was illuminated, and the bells rang.

The next morning at ten o'clock the Prince was created a doctor of civil law at the Sheldonian. After a tour of the library, the museum, and several colleges, William dined with the vice-chancellor of the University at St John's College. Between eight and nine o'clock on the following morning, 1 March, the Prince left Oxford via Magdalen bridge. On 25 March 1734 at St James's Palace he married Anne, Princess Royal, eldest daughter of King George II of Great Britain and Caroline of Ansbach. Antiquary Thomas Hearne recorded in his diary: 'Dr Holmes, Vice-Chancellour of the university, thinks of getting great favour at court by inviting the prince hither, and by showing such profound reverence to him. 'Tis observ'd, however, that tho' there was such a conflux of people at Oxford and at the Theater upon this occasion, there were no persons of distinction that came to shew their respects out of the country.'

29 February

On this day in 1932, former mayor of Oxford George Claridge Druce died at Yardley Lodge, 9 Crick Road, Oxford at the age of 81. Following a tricky start as the illegitimate son of Jane Druce and farm bailiff George Richard Claridge of Northamptonshire, Druce was apprenticed to a pharmacist at the age of 16. In June 1879, he set up his own chemist's shop, Druce & Co, at 118 High Street, Oxford, but his main interest was botany.

In 1880, Druce helped to found the Ashmolean Natural History Society of Oxfordshire, originally established as the Ashmolean Society in 1828. In 1886, he published *The Flora of Oxfordshire*, in 1887 *The Flora of Berkshire*, in 1926 *The Flora of Buckinghamshire* and in 1929 *The Flora of West Ross*. He was one of very few people to write a flora for more than one county. In 1889, he was awarded the degree of honorary MA by the University of Oxford and in 1895 he was appointed Fielding Curator in the Department of Botany at the University. Druce served on Oxford City Council from 1892 until his death. Druce never married and appears to have attempted to conceal his illegitimacy by describing his mother as a 'widow' when she came to live with him in 1891.

George Claridge Druce

1 March

On this day in 1517, Richard Foxe, Bishop of Winchester, signed the founding charter of Corpus Christi College. Foxe, a trusted diplomatic and political adviser to King Henry VII, began to build on Merton Street between Merton College and Christ Church from 1513. He bought a nunnery, two halls, two inns and the Bachelor's Garden of Merton College. The college buildings were probably complete by 1520. The famous Pelican Sundial in the main quadrangle was erected c.1580, and gradually developed a lean. This was corrected in 1967 when it was discovered that the dial lacked a solid foundation, and that base was made of stone panels loosely packed with rubble.

One of the earliest Fellows, Reginald Pole, was Archbishop of Canterbury under Queen Mary and narrowly missed becoming Pope. The College's seventh president, John Rainolds, was a key organiser and translator of the 1611 Authorised Version of the Bible, sometimes known as the King James Bible.

2 March

On this day in 1628, the Great Fire of Banbury broke out on a Sunday at a time of day when many were in church or chapel. The seat of the fire was thought to be a malt house 'by negligence of a mayde'.

Within four hours the flames raced from one end of the town to the other, burning all night and most of the following day. It was estimated to have consumed 103 dwelling houses, 20 kiln-houses, and other outhouses, as well as a great deal of malt, grain, and other commodities, to the value of some £20,000. The affected roads were West Bar Street, South Bar Street, Calthorpe Lane, Fish Street (George Street) and Broad Street, all scenes of desolation. Soldiers were quartered in the town to maintain law and order amongst people made homeless by the fire, and an official appeal for help was signed by the mayor, the minister, justices of the peace, aldermen and capital burgesses and attested to by ministers of parishes bordering Banbury. A document survives in the City of Coventry Record Office showing a generous response and naming 65 persons of Banbury 'to be relieved by the gift of Coventry, 23 October 1628'. £26 13s 4d was distributed in amounts ranging from £1 down to one shilling. Evidently the behaviour of the people of Banbury was seen to have contributed to their ill fortune, for when the Bar Gate in West Bar Street was re-erected in 1631, an inscription was placed on it emphasising the need for moral vigilance: 'Except the Lord Keepe the City the Watchman watcheth but in vain.'

3 March

On this day in 1698, Dr William Levinz, Regius Professor of Greek and president of St John's College, dropped dead while addressing the fellows of the college.

He had called a meeting having received the shocking news of the destruction the night before of a plantation of young trees in St John's Grove. On the same night, a large quantity of plate had been stolen from Magdalen College chapel, and it appeared that the thieves must have known the layout and routine of the college well. Having secreted themselves in the chapel during nine o'clock prayers, they raided the chest in the vestry, choosing only easily portable items. The great plate standing on the altar table was left in place.

They escaped through the main doors which were bolted from the inside. The value of the stolen items was reckoned at £30. So tempers were already running high among the University authorities when Dr Levinz called his meeting to consider how to hunt down the culprits. Known for his passionate temper, Levinz worked himself into a considerable lather whilst speaking. Then, mid-rant, he suddenly fell back into his chair, stone dead.

4 March

On this day in 1893, *Jackson's Oxford Journal* reported on the discovery of a child's body in Upper Tadmarton. Two men in the employ of John Salmon at New College farm had been detailed to remove the soil from the 'vault connected with a closet' in a corner of the farmyard—presumably an outside privy. Ezekiel Phipps opened the lid and, after he had removed the first lot of waste into the cart, a tiny body emerged from underneath the seat. As some children were playing nearby, Phipps said nothing to his companion Thomas Hawkins, who waited on the far side of the cart. Phipps lifted the body out with the skip, or basket, he was using and placed it in the cart with the rest of the soil, which Hawkins then took to the field.

Once the job was done, Phipps told Hawkins what he had found, and went to the field to locate the body. PC Lambourn was sent for, and the body was removed to the Lampet Arms public house. Surgeon Richard Routh came from Sibford Ferris to conduct the post mortem. In his view the child, a female, had not reached full-term—perhaps a month or two short. He believed that she had taken some breaths, and that she had died at least a month ago, possibly more. The coroner summed up and the jury returned an open verdict of 'Found dead'. The foreman of the jury emphasised that this threw no reflection upon Mr and Mrs Salmon, for whom they expressed their heartfelt sympathy.

No mention was made in the newspaper report of the Salmons' five sons living in the house, aged from 17 to 32, nor of the presence at the same time of two female servants, Hannah Bone aged 26, and Agnes Phipps, aged 16. Nor yet of the fact that young Agnes was the niece of the very Ezekiel Phipps who found the body and was in the employ of farmer Salmon.

5 March

On this day in 1957, a Blackburn Beverley aircraft crashed in Sutton Wick near Drayton, killing 20 people. They included most of the crew, along with eight RAF police-dog handlers and their dogs on their way to Cyprus, plus two people on the ground. The aircraft left RAF Abingdon in the morning and, as it climbed, one of the engines developed a fuel leak. The crew shut down the engine, and requested an emergency landing at RAF Abingdon. Then another engine failed, and the aircraft began to lose speed and height. The captain tried to land in a field but the aircraft was by now uncontrollable. It struck a number of high-tension cables and a group of elm trees that tore off the port wing. On impact, the aircraft destroyed a caravan and a prefabricated house before somersaulting and crashing upside down.

John Dawson was in the garden of the Red Lion at Drayton and described

Sutton Wick air crash, 1957

what he witnessed: 'The plane came towards me flying low when one wing hit a tree. It dived to the ground immediately, crashed through an ordinary brick house and a pre-fab, slid along the ground for about a hundred yards and burst into flames… It was so hot we could not get near to help those inside, but four of the occupants of the plane were thrown clear.' Two farm workers and two RAF officers showed great bravery in their attempts to rescue the victims. One survivor was badly burned in the accident, and later killed himself.

The subsequent investigation found that a non-return valve in the fuel system had been installed the wrong way round, causing two of the engines to be starved of fuel. The tradesman who had fitted the valve, and his supervisor, were prosecuted and charged, and the technician was court-martialled for negligence and punished with a reprimand.

6 March

On this day in 1840, George Spencer-Churchill, 5th Duke of Marlborough, was born. He was destined to ruin the family fortunes to the extent that his son was obliged to accept a comparatively modest dowry to marry the granddaughter of a local fishergirl (see 23 February). His downfall was his love of beautiful things—antiquities, books, pictures, wine and gardens. He installed his young family at White Knights at Earley near Reading and proceeded to turn it into a palace of pleasure and extravagance. Having grown up watching Capability Brown exercise taste and restraint in landscaping the grounds of Blenheim Palace, the Marquis of Blandford, as he was then styled, decided to abandon such a fuddy-duddy approach and crammed every possible fashionable garden feature into the gardens around White Knights.

Lavish entertaining went on, especially when Blandford's wife Lady Susan was away (seemingly most of the time) with a gated wilderness, a refuge designed for secret assignations. All this expenditure persuaded society that Blandford was much richer than he actually was. Charles Sturt MP decided to take advantage of the fact that the Marquis was sleeping with his wife Lady Mary Anne Sturt, and sued Blandford for £20,000. Unfortunately for Sturt, it emerged at the trial that he too had been keeping a mistress in the form of a Bohemian harp player named Fanny Krumpholtz. Damages were awarded to Sturt—of a derisory £100. In fact, Blandford had been trading on future expectations, running up staggering debts with tradesmen and suppliers. Eventually the debts were called in and, with no cash available, the entire contents and estate at White Knights were auctioned off.

7 March

On this day in 1647, Banbury tiler William Wilde's widow Lydia was murdered. *Oxford Flying Weekly Journal* reported with relish: 'We hear from Banbury that last Sunday morning Widow Wilde of that place was found barbarously murdered in her own kitchen; there were several wounds upon her head, one of which is very large and appears to have been done with a hammer, and her throat was cut almost from ear to ear. An Irish fellow, a shag weaver, is strongly suspected, his shoes being found in his lodgings bloody half way up the heels, and much blood sprinkled on the upper leather. He plundered the house of about £20.'

Mrs Wilde's lodger, one Parr, was tried at Banbury, convicted, and hanged in the Horse Fair—opposite the scene of his crime. He was afterwards gibbeted on the same spot on the south side of the way leading from Easington Farmhouse towards Broad Street, which was afterwards known as 'Parr's Piece'. Apparently,

Parr's body fell from the gibbet and a gang of chimney-sweepers seized the opportunity to parade it through the town. A tradesman named John Baxter, then the chief wit of the place, wrote the following lines, on the occasion of this gibbeting, addressed to the farmer who resided at Easington. (Jack Ketch was the infamously incompetent executioner employed by King Charles II.)

> *'Rejoice and sing, old Farmer Wells;*
> *Proclaim your joy with ring of bells;*
> *For now Old Parr's your neighbour;*
> *And if the tree had been made like a T,*
> *It would have serv'd both him and thee,*
> *And sav'd Jack Ketch some labour!'*

8 March

On this day in 1700, the spire of All Saints Church in the High at the corner of Turl Street collapsed, destroying the 12th-century church almost entirely.

Local residents weren't entirely taken by surprise—the spire had been seen to rock in 1662, causing people in nearby houses to flee. The new church, money for which was contributed by, among others, Queen Anne and John Churchill, Duke of Marlborough, was reputedly designed by gifted amateur architect Dean Henry Aldrich of Christ Church. The western tower and spire, completed in 1718, were based on designs by Nicholas Hawksmoor. The poor quality of the stone made repairs necessary to the tower and spire in 1783, 1803, and 1804. In 1872 they were rebuilt to the old designs. In 1971, All Saints Church was declared redundant and the city church moved to St Michael at the North Gate. All Saints was then deconsecrated and offered to Lincoln College. Since 1975 the building has served as Lincoln College's library.

9 March

On this day in 1959, the notorious Cutteslowe Walls in North Oxford were demolished at last. The two walls were built by private developer Clive

The notorious Cutteslowe Walls come down in 1959

Saxton's Urban Housing Company between 1934 and 1959 to keep council house tenants in the Cutteslowe Estate out of a private development between them and the Banbury Road. The northern wall divided Wolsey Road from Carlton Road, the southern Aldrich Road from Wentworth Road. The walls were nine feet tall and topped with spikes. There was outrage from the start; council tenants raised a petition against the walls, and in 1936 supporters led by Communist politician Abe Lazarus marched with pickaxes to knock them down, but police barred their way.

In June 1938, against legal advice, the city council, took the law into its own hands and demolished the walls with a steam roller. Sued by the company and severely criticised by the judge, the city was forced to re-erect the walls. During the Second World War, a tank whose crew was trying to return from Banbury Road to its base on Elsfield Way took a wrong turn and demolished one of the walls rather than turn back. The War Office paid for the wall to be rebuilt.

After escalating public protests and several unofficial attempts, the council bought the 9 inch-wide strips of land the walls stood on for £1,000. At 7.30am on 9 March, Councillor Edmund Gibbs took a ceremonial swipe at the top of the first wall with a pickaxe.

General Stopford

10 March

On this day in 1971, the British officer who received the Japanese surrender in Burma in 1945 died in Chipping Norton.

General Montagu George North Stopford was born into a family with a distinguished military tradition. He enlisted in the Rifle Brigade and saw service in the First World War, earning the Military Cross. In the Second World War he served under Field Marshal Slim in the Burma Campaign 1943–45 where he commanded 33 Indian Corps in the fierce and protracted fighting against the Japanese at Kohima-Imphal. After a hard-won victory which proved to be a turning point in the war in Burma, Slim, Stopford and their fellow generals Scoones and Christison were knighted in the field by special permission of King George VI.

Stopford and his corps fought on to the crossing of the Irrawaddy and the capture of Mandalay. After Slim's departure, Stopford was given command of all the forces in Burma to complete clearing up operations and on 24 October 1945 he received the surrender of the Japanese Commander in Burma. In 1946 he became Commander-in-Chief of Allied Land Forces, South East Asia. On retirement from the Army, from 1950–1971 he lived at Rock Hill House, Chipping Norton.

11 March

On this day in 1921, Queen Mary, grandmother of the present Queen, became the first woman to be awarded an honorary degree by the University of Oxford. The award is conferred as a way of honouring a distinguished visitor's contributions to a specific field or to society in general.

Accompanied by her dutiful daughter Princess Mary, 24, the queen arrived on the train from Paddington, and dense crowds greeted her at the station. At the Sheldonian Theatre in Broad Street, the queen received the honorary degree of Doctor of Civil Law.

After lunch at Balliol College, she visited Barnett House, a social study centre (see 6 June), where she expressed her admiration for a pair of curtains, made, she was told, by 'inmates of the Cumnor Hill Home for the Feeble Minded'. The royal visitors were presented with bouquets when their carriage stopped briefly outside Oxford High School for Girls.

At Lady Margaret Hall, the *Oxford Journal Illustrated* reported: 'Everywhere prevailed the greatest excitement and when the Queen and Princess Mary arrived, they were greeted with cheers by the women students.' At Somerville College, the queen met a detachment of Girl Guides and a group of small children, one of whom exuberantly tossed his cap into the air, only to watch horrified as it dropped onto the royal arm. According to the *Journal*: 'Her Majesty laughed as heartily as the crowd around and, stooping down with a smile for the little one, murmured: "Naughty child!"'

12 March

On this day in 1264, King Henry III suspended all teaching in the University until Michaelmas while he made the city his military headquarters at the outbreak of the Second Barons' War. A baronial faction led by Simon de Montfort, Earl of Leicester and husband of the king's sister, objected to Henry's expensive and disastrous foreign wars, as well as his methods of government which side-lined the barons themselves.

The country was enduring a famine and tenants looked to their lords for relief, but the lords were at the same time facing continuous demands from the king for money. De Montfort became leader of those who wanted to reassert Magna Carta and force the king to surrender more power to the baronial council.

In 1258, initiating the move toward reform, seven leading barons had forced Henry to agree to the Provisions of Oxford, which effectively gave power to a council of 24 barons to deal with the business of government, and provided for a great council in the form of a parliament every three years to monitor their performance. This startlingly modern idea has since allowed a misplaced aura of liberalism to attach to de Montfort.

13 March

On this day in 1879, Gerard Manley Hopkins wrote the poem *Binsey Poplars*. At the time, Hopkins was working as a parish priest's assistant at St Aloysius's Church in the Woodstock Road, Oxford. In wandering north of the city one day he came to the little village of Binsey. It was familiar territory for him, having studied Greek and Latin at Oxford from 1862 to 1867.

There he found to his horror that the familiar avenue of mighty poplars, 100ft high and with 6ft wide trunks, had been felled, destroying the appeal of one of his favourite stretches of countryside. He wrote to a friend: 'I have been up to Godstow this afternoon. I am sorry to say that the aspens that lined the river are every one felled.' So moved was Hopkins by the scene of devastation at Binsey that he composed his famous poem.

Something of a gloomy character, Hopkins' reputation was largely made in 1918, 30 years after his death, when his friend, the poet Robert Bridges, edited a volume of his poetry. The trees in Binsey were replanted in 1918, and when they were cut down again in 2004, Hopkins's poem was used as part of the successful campaign to have them replanted. In 2013, a manuscript of *Binsey Poplars* was acquired at auction by the Bodleian Library for almost £50,000.

> *'My aspens dear, whose airy cages quelled,*
> *Quelled or quenched in leaves the leaping sun,*
> *All felled, felled, are all felled;*
> *Of a fresh and following folded rank*
> *Not spared, not one*
> *That dandled a sandalled*
> *Shadow that swam or sank*
> *On meadow and river and wind-wandering weed-winding bank.'*

14 March

On this day in 1944, an Armstrong Whitworth Whitley V bomber aircraft crashed onto what was then a military firing range at Great Park Farm, Besselsleigh. Aircraft T4337 was based at No 10 Operational Training Unit RAF at Abingdon, a unit formed in April 1940 to train night-bomber crews. While changing from flare-path to instruments during routine circuits and landings practice, Royal Canadian Air Force pilot Sgt D C Adamson lost control. Almost immediately, the aircraft crashed to the ground and burst into flames. At the time US Army soldiers were billeted at nearby Besselsleigh Park preparatory to the D-Day landings. Two US soldiers and a local man, Ron Amey, rushed to the scene and made apparently heroic efforts to rescue the crew, but without success. All three members of the crew were killed.

Ron Amey went on to succeed his father William Amey as head of the Amey quarrying and construction company, and is remembered with great affection in the area. No 10 OTU disbanded on 10 September 1946.

15 March

On this day in 1927, the first women's rowing event between Oxford and Cambridge was held on the Isis at Oxford. In the years up to 1935, the two boats were not on the river together because the heads of the colleges deemed lining up side-by-side to be unladylike. Each team rowed two legs, one going upstream to test speed, the other going downstream to judge 'steadiness, finish, rhythm and other matters of style'. The teams set off from the Free Ferry at the top of Iffley Reach and rowed around half a mile as far as Keble barge. *The Times* reported that 'large and hostile crowds gathered on the towpath' while the *New York Times* stated that, on the contrary, 'a crowd of fully five thousand persons was on hand as a willing cheering section'.

The judges failed to agree on a winner in the style category. As a result, they based their selection of the winner on speed; the race was won by Oxford in a time of 3 minutes 36 seconds, beating Cambridge by 15 seconds.

The men's University Boat Race was initiated in 1829 by Charles Merivale, a student at St John's College, Cambridge, and his Old Harrovian school friend Charles Wordsworth who was studying at Christ Church, Oxford. The

University of Cambridge challenged the University of Oxford to a race at Henley-on-Thames but lost easily. The second race was in 1836, with the venue moved to a course from Westminster to Putney. Over the next two years, there was disagreement over where the race should be held, with Oxford preferring Henley and Cambridge preferring London. Following the official formation of the Oxford University Boat Club, racing between the two universities resumed in 1839 on the Tideway and the tradition continues to the present day, with the loser challenging the winner to a rematch annually.

16 March

On this day in 1973, a bomb hoax disrupted life in the Oxpens area of Oxford. Children, pets and elderly residents were evacuated from the area around the Toomers (Oils) Ltd fuel depot. A call to the home of an *Oxford Times* reporter said the Angry Brigade, a left-wing anarchist group, had planted a bomb primed to explode at 9pm. More than 200 people left their homes as police sealed off the area and fire crews stationed themselves nearby. Families were evacuated from the surrounding streets as well as the Christ Church buildings and taken to the Oxford City Fire Brigade headquarters. As 9pm came and went, two police officers and two representatives of Toomers went into the depot to check the six storage tanks. They emerged unscathed and the alert was called off. Just 24 hours later, the centre of Abingdon was sealed off for almost five hours after a suspected parcel bomb was found in a telephone box outside the post office. The 1970s was a decade of frequent bomb scares—and real bombs too. But the nuisance value of a hoax still remains tempting for trouble-makers.

17 March

On this day in 1040, Harold Harefoot, king of the English, died in Oxford aged 24. The cause of Harold's death is uncertain. The Anglo-Saxons themselves would consider him elf-shot (attacked by elves), their term for any number of deadly diseases. An Anglo-Saxon charter attributes the illness to divine judgment. Harold had reportedly claimed Sandwich for himself, thereby depriving the monks of Christchurch in Dorset. Harold is described as lying ill and in despair at Oxford. When monks came to him to settle the dispute over

Sandwich, he 'lay and grew black as they spoke'. The context of the event was a dispute between Christchurch and St Augustine's Abbey, which took over the local toll in the name of the king. Harefoot ('fleet of foot') also fell out with his half-brother, the crowned king Harthacnut, who was stuck in Denmark due to a rebellion in Norway, another part of the Scandinavian empire. In 1037 Harold persuaded the nobles officially to proclaim him king.

According to the *Anglo-Saxon Chronicle*, Harold Harefoot ruled for four years and 16 weeks, by which calculation he would have begun ruling two weeks after the death of Cnut. Harold was originally buried in Westminster, but Harthacnut eliminated all doubt over his feelings about his usurping half-brother. He had Harold's body dug up, beheaded, and thrown into a marsh in the Thames estuary. A short while later it was picked up by a fisherman, and delivered to the Danes. They reportedly buried Harold honourably in their cemetery at London. The body was eventually buried in a church in the City of Westminster, which was fittingly named St Clement Danes.

18 March

On this day in 1559, Lord Williams of Thame stipulated in his will that the income from part of his estate should be used to endow a grammar school in Thame. The clause stated that: 'the rectories and parsonages of Brill, Oakley, Boarstall and Easton Beston [Northamptonshire] to mine executors for ever, to the intent that they, or the survivor or survivors of them, shall within the same erect a free school in the town of Thame, and to find and sustain with the profits thereof, a schoolmaster and an usher for ever.'

Lord Williams died in October 1559, and ten years passed before sufficient funds had accumulated to begin building the schoolhouse. The original stone building, now much altered, was roughly T-shaped, with rooms for the master and usher in the west front, and a schoolroom 50ft by 20ft behind. The windows of the schoolroom contained the royal arms, together with those of the founder and of his connections. The attics above accommodated boarders. Teaching began in 1570. At first the main entrance was via Church Row, but a more imposing entrance from the High Street was created later. For the first few years the executors superintended the affairs of the school, but in 1575 they handed the job over to New College. The buildings were sold off in 1876.

19 March

On this day in 1832, 32-year-old John Gibbs of Steeple Aston was executed for arson. A wheat rick, a straw stack and two wagons had been destroyed at the farm of Mr Wing. Earlier in the evening of 12 February Mr Wing's son William had checked the yard and all was in order with the gates closed. He retired to bed at 9pm—farmers have always been early risers. William was first made aware of the incident at about 11pm when he heard the cry of 'Fire!' accompanied by banging on his door. 'I saw the glare of the fire from my window,' he told the court which tried Gibbs at the Lent Assizes in March. 'The greater part of the wheat rick, the staddle on which it stood, the straw stack, the staddle, and two wagons loaded with straw, were consumed by fire.'

The fire took four hours to bring under control, and the damage was reckoned at £200. Gibbs was among the villagers at the scene, and William Wing particularly noticed how lackadaisical were his attempts at assisting at the water pump. Gibbs seemed far more intent on eavesdropping on the conversation between Mr Wing and his neighbour, the magistrate Captain John Lechmere. Next day, Wing and Lechmere went accompanied by the constable to find Gibbs. They demanded of him that he surrender a shoe. He did so without complaint. Wing, Lechmere and the constable then went to the scene of the crime and matched the shoe exactly to some footprints leading directly from the lane to the rick yard, right down to the missing nails in the sole. A flint and steel, for striking a spark, were found discarded nearby. By the time the constable took Gibbs away, the prisoner was in tears.

Five days before his execution, Gibbs was visited by his father and one of his eight brothers. He never gave any reason for committing his crime.

20 March

On this day in 1816, Banbury baker Thomas Colley took on the challenge of walking 1,020 miles in 20 successive days. The quarter-mile course lay in a field alongside the Bloxham Road as it passed through Neithrop. The wager necessitated 39-year-old Colley commencing at 4am every day and walking around 51 miles, which would take him until around 11pm. In addition to his measured distance per day, Colley of course had also to walk the round

Thomas Colley

trip to his home in Bridge Street.

The craze of 'pedestrianism' swept the country at the time, generally involving a wager against a record-breaking feat. Colley actually exceeded his target, adding an extra mile on the final, twentieth, day. Perhaps he was spurred on by the aroma of an ox being roasted to feed the many thousands (so it is said) of spectators who had assembled to witness his triumph.

The next day he was taken around the town in a chaise and four, and a subscription was started for his benefit. Colley died in December 1818, but his wife, Sarah does not seem to have benefitted for long from any funds raised by her husband's efforts; she died a pauper in one of the almshouses in Church Lane in Banbury.

21 March

On this day in 1957, the marriage took place between C S Lewis and divorced American writer and poet, Joy Davidman. Lewis's best-known work, the children's fantasy The *Chronicles of Narnia*, had been published between 1949 and 1954. During this time he had begun corresponding with Davidman. Two years later, in August 1952, Joy came to England.

After several lunch meetings and walks accompanied by Lewis's brother Warren Lewis, a rapid friendship developed between the two. Davidman spent Christmas with the brothers at their home, The Kilns in Risinghurst near Headington. She fell deeply in love with Lewis, but her feelings were not returned; Lewis regarded her only as an agreeable intellectual companion and personal friend. She received a letter from her husband in America saying that he wanted a divorce in order to marry her cousin.

Joy returned home in January 1953 to try and save her marriage but, having failed, she returned to England with her sons in November 1953. Lewis purchased a house for her near his own. In 1956, Davidman's visitor's visa was not renewed by the Home Office, and she and her sons were required to return to America. Lewis agreed to enter into a civil marriage contract with her so that she could continue to live in the UK, telling a friend that the marriage was 'a pure matter of friendship and expediency'. The civil marriage took place at the register office at 42 St Giles' in Oxford on 23 April 1956. The couple continued to live separately after the civil marriage.

In October 1956, Joy was diagnosed with bone cancer. This prompted the couple to seek a Christian marriage too, which eventually took place at her bedside in the Churchill Hospital the following year.

22 March

On this day in 1196, the monks at the Benedictine Abbey of Eynsham entered their church and found there the senseless body of their brother Edmund, lying bare-foot and face down at the foot of the Abbot's throne. They carried him back to his bed where he had been lying sick for some weeks, and wondered how he could have got from his cell to the church unaided. When they returned to the church they discovered blood running from the wounds of a statue of the crucified Christ.

Naturally perplexed, they agreed to be beaten with birch sticks, but inexplicably this didn't seem to help. In the infirmary, brother Edmund lay unconscious all through Good Friday, all the following night and the following day as well, almost until sunset. At last, in the evening on the day before Easter Day, Edmund awoke and reported that he had experienced a vision of Purgatory and Paradise. Whilst out for the count, he had interviewed a variety of contemporary sinners in the other world, from the soul of a local alcoholic goldsmith, through to a prostitute, a lawyer, and an archbishop. He even encountered Henry II, trapped inside red-hot armour as punishment for oppressing his people with unfair taxes.

Edmund made a full recovery and from that time onwards, whenever he heard a sustained peal of bells he felt the most exquisite joy, because it reminded him of the sound that he had heard when he was in Paradise.

23 March

On this day in 1840, Charles Morley, 34, was hanged for murdering 84-year-old Fanny Phillips in her bed at South Stoke near Woodcote. Frail Fanny lived alone and relied on her neighbour Mary Lambden to get her up in the morning and put her to bed in the evening. Mrs Lambden would lock up Fanny's cottage overnight and take the key away with her ready for the morning.

On 8 March 1800, Mrs Lambden arrived at 7am to find the lock smashed and the front door open. She fetched her husband James, who found poor Fanny lying dead with dreadful head wounds. Her wedding ring had been wrenched from her hand with some force. Morley, meanwhile, drew suspicion upon himself by appearing suddenly to have come into money, when the day before he had not been able to afford even a beer. Police officer Henry Stephens went to Morley's home and found a sawyer's file hidden in the chimney. Morley was taken, drunk, to Oxford gaol where he related to his cell-mate how he had murdered Fanny Phillips. But it was not until 26 July that a really thorough search of Morley's cottage was made.

Hidden in the thatch were two bags, one containing 232 sovereigns and 10 half-sovereigns, the other 19 guineas, 10 half-guineas, 2 half-sovereigns, a 7 shilling piece and an old silver coin. By November, Morley had been transferred to a prison hulk at Woolwich. His brother-in-law Henry Burgess visited him there and Morley told him he had hidden Fanny's wedding ring in his razor case. It was found there on 6 February.

At the assizes later that month the jury took ten minutes to reach a guilty verdict, but Morley went to his death protesting his innocence.

24 March

On this day in 1877, for the only time in history, the University Boat Race was declared a 'dead heat'. Experiencing strong head-winds and rough water, the Oxford bow-man Cowles suffered serious damage to his oar, putting him out of action. A spectator recalled: 'Suddenly Oxford staggered and stood still in a mass of foam: the bow-oar, Cowles, had struck the top of a big wave in feathering and broken his blade clean off.' Almost immediately Cambridge took the advantage, but were held off by a determined Oxford crew who 'spurted magnificently and drew up steadily inch by inch, so that it was a near thing as they passed the post'. At that date there were no finishing posts and therefore no clear finishing line. Moreover, 'Honest John Phelps', the professional waterman who had judged the finish for some years, was in a small skiff, which it appears had drifted off the reputed finishing line. Certainly Oxford felt that they had won by several feet and, 'Honest John' in the contemporary records is said have described the result drily as a 'dead-heat to Oxford by five feet'.

The resulting controversy led to two changes. First, posts were placed at Mortlake so that there could be no doubt about the finish line. Secondly, this was the last time that a professional waterman acted as judge, this function from then on being taken by a member of one of the two Universities.

25 March

On this day in 1811, Romantic poet Shelley was expelled from the University. He had anonymously published a pamphlet called *The Necessity of Atheism: the belief that there is no God* which expounded ideas so shocking at the time that, together with his roommate Thomas Jefferson Hogg, who may have been co-author, he was called to appear before the college's fellows including the dean, George Rowley. He refused to repudiate the authorship of the pamphlet and was consequently expelled from Oxford on 25 March 1811, along with Hogg. Shelley's father intervened with the University, and Shelley was given the chance of reinstatement on condition that he recant his published views. He refused, and as a result he fell out with his father.

Shelley drowned in the Mediterranean Sea just before his 30th birthday in July 1822.

Percy Bysshe Shelley

26 March

On this day in 1942, a Handley-Page Hampden AE139 aircraft crashed into the wall of the church of St Peter at Wootton near Abingdon. Three of the four crew died. The RCAF 408 Squadron aircraft took off the day before from its base at RAF Balderton in Nottinghamshire for an operational Nickel sortie, dropping propaganda leaflets over Rennes in France.

Details of the mission are unknown but on its return the aircraft landed at RAF Stoke Orchard near Cheltenham. The next day the aircraft took off to return to base. The accident record card states that the aircraft had a faulty fuel gauge and was running low on fuel. It seems the aircraft was attempting to land at Abingdon. A witness confirmed that, at 4.30pm, the plane was approaching from an easterly direction towards the church. Its engines cut out and it hit the high trees on the east side of the cricket field. Sliding across the ground, it turned turtle and smashed in to the wall. The repair in the wall can still be seen today, just to the right of the church gate. A young girl playing on the swings had a narrow escape when the plane crashed right next to her.

27 March

On this day in 1883, George Harris, porter on the London and North Western Railway, was checking the line under High Bridge on the edge of Port Meadow after the 4.35pm train had passed through. He saw a body in the culvert which drains water from the meadow. It was a young woman, lying face up in about two feet of water, with just her nose breaking the surface. The marks of her boots on the bank revealed that Clara Dadswell, 25, had deliberately stepped over some planks and a ditch in order to get into the water.

Clara and her brother Edward Dadswell had come from Eastbourne about a year before, amid rumours of trouble in the family business there. Their brother Frederick died suddenly aged 24 in the summer of 1882, and this had apparently affected Clara deeply. She constantly complained of weakness in her legs, and her behaviour struck those around her as strange. She would spend all day alone in her room in Kingston Road; she and her brother lodged there with railwayman Henry Rosier and his wife Eliza.

On the morning of Clara's death, she and Mrs Rosier had gone out together and Clara complained of her legs. Mrs Rosier suggested Clara might walk as far as High Bridge where she could rest on the bench. In the afternoon Clara called in at the Anchor Inn on the corner of Hayfield Road and Polstead Road, where she took a brandy and lemonade to soothe the cramp in her legs. She sat for about an hour chatting with the landlord's wife. Clara left the pub just before four, and half an hour later she drowned herself.

28 March

On this day in 1913, the first Morris Oxford—nicknamed the 'Bullnose' because of the distinctive shape of its radiator—came off the production line in Cowley. London motor traders Stewart and Ardern had placed a large order for the car on the strength of drawings on display at the 1912 Motor Show. The two-seater, 8.9 horse-power Morris Oxford, while not the cheapest car on the market at £165, was on its way to becoming a world-beater. William Morris's rise as an entrepreneur is well documented, from running his own cycle business at his parents' home at 16 James Street, East Oxford, and in High Street, through to moving into car manufacturing in Longwall Street and eventually at the former Oxford Military Academy at Cowley. Some 1,300 cars were built in the run-up to the First World War when the Cowley factory switched to the manufacture of munitions. It was not until the 1920s that Morris was able to fulfil his ambition to become Britain's biggest car producer.

William Morris at the wheel of a Morris Oxford

29 March

On this day in 1880 a distressing accident occurred when the two young Comley brothers of Clanfield were out bird-scaring. The elder brother was carrying a loaded shotgun. The gun exploded and the younger boy was blasted in the face, injuring him 'very severely'. The boys were aged around 9 and 5 at the time. This gives us a glimpse of the sort of work young children were expected to undertake in order to supplement the family budget, and how a familiarity with shotguns at an early age was not considered inappropriate.

Apparently the assistance of Dr John Atkinson from Bampton was promptly sought but, according to the report in *Jackson's Oxford Journal*, a few days later the boy's prospects were still uncertain.

30 March

On this day in 1979, Abingdon MP Airey Neave was killed in bomb blast at Westminster. From the early 1970s until his death, Airey Neave and his wife Diana lived at the Old Rectory in Hinton Waldrist.

Neave had an illustrious war-time career. Captured by the Germans in 1940, he escaped in 1941 only to be re-captured and sent to Colditz Castle. His first attempt to escape from Colditz failed because his hastily-contrived German uniform was completely the wrong colour—apparently Neave was hopelessly colour-blind. His second attempt succeeded, and he became the first British officer to make the 'home run' from Colditz. Neave was killed by a car bomb planted by the Irish National Liberation Army as he exited the House of Commons car park. He is buried in the graveyard at Hinton Waldrist.

31 March

On this day in 1901, archaeologist, military officer, diplomat, and writer T E Lawrence made his first appearance in the Oxford census. At the age of 12 he lived with his family at 2 Polstead Road. Lawrence attended the City of Oxford High School for Boys from 1896 until 1907, then read history at Jesus College. In the summer of 1909, he set out alone on a three-month walking tour of crusader castles in Ottoman Syria, during which he travelled 1,000 miles

T E Lawrence while at Oxford

(1,600km) on foot. Having gained some experience in archaeology and a command of Arabic, in January 1914 Lawrence was co-opted by the British military. The Arab Revolt began in June 1916, but after a few early successes it became bogged down. In October 1916, Lawrence was sent on an intelligence-gathering mission. His unique ability to connect with the competing Arab leaders, to understand their psyche and his willingness to learn their various dialects allowed him to accomplish the near-impossible task of uniting the tribes to oppose the Ottomans.

1 April

On this day in 1710, Sir Richard Kennedy was buried at Cogges, having been run through the body in a duel. His adversary was John Dormer of Ascott Park near Stadhampton, a man described by a contemporary, antiquary Thomas Hearne, as a 'young gentleman of a most wicked, profligate, debauch'd Life, a Person of no Conscience nor Religion, and who is not known to have ever done one virtuous or good thing...'

In 1704 Sir Richard had married Catherine the daughter of Sir Francis Blake, lord of the manor of Cogges. John Dormer had married pretty Katherine, one of the daughters and co-heiresses of Sir Thomas Spencer, third baronet of Yarnton. During the building of Blenheim Palace, Kennedy and Dormer met in the park at Woodstock. A disagreement arose, apparently because Sir Richard 'took the Wall or upper side with his Lady', ie, he would not hand her over to Sir John for his gratification. Dormer promptly ran Sir Richard through with his sword and fled the scene. But he gave himself up to justice and was committed to Oxford gaol.

At the subsequent trial, he was found guilty of manslaughter, not murder, and was afterwards pardoned; this may have been partly due to the fact that his distant cousin, Sir Robert Dormer of Lee Grange near Quainton in Buckinghamshire, was one of his judges. Furthermore, according to Hearne, the jury was nothing but a bunch of 'rascals and villains'.

2 April

On this day in 1940, British Grand Prix motorcycle road racer Mike Hailwood was born at Langsmeade House in Great Milton. Regarded by many as one of the greatest racers of all time, 'Mike the Bike' went on to compete in Formula One and other classes of car racing, becoming one of the few men to compete at Grand Prix level in both motorcycle and car racing. By 1967, he had won the Isle of Man TT 12 times. He won what many historians consider to be the most dramatic TT of all time, the 1967 Senior TT against his great rival, Giacomo Agostini.

Hailwood never achieved the same level of success in car racing, but he achieved respectable results in Formula One and World Sports Cars. He was awarded the George Medal for bravery when, in the 1973 South African Grand Prix, he pulled Clay Regazzoni from his burning car after the two collided on the second lap. Hailwood's overalls caught fire, but he returned to help rescue Regazzoni. The George Medal is the second highest gallantry award for a British civilian.

On Saturday 21 March 1981, Hailwood set off in his Rover SDI with his children to collect fish and chips. A truck made an illegal turn and collided with their car. Michelle, 9, was killed instantly. Mike died two days later. He was 40. The truck driver was fined £100.

Mike 'The Bike'

3 April

On this day in 2009, the Oxford Channel shut down; it was the UK's last free-to-air analogue terrestrial television station. Launched on 6 June 1999 by Oxford Broadcasting, within a few months the station had built a considerable following: over 25 per cent of the potential audience of 500,000 watched each week. Debora and Thomas Harding raised the capital to launch the station, and set up a broadcast studio in an old nuclear bunker on Woodstock Road.

From the beginning, the channel focused on local stories, particularly sports, business, arts, music and politics. According to a Reuters Institute report, the channel 'also had a strong training programme, which made formal in 2000 through the Local Television Training company that attracted government money to train unemployed young people from Oxford and taught them the skills of broadcast television. This scheme had a high success rate of placing trainees within the television industry.'

In 2001, with the station financially broke, the board voted to sell the station and its operating company to Milestone Group. Milestone concluded that the lack of digital licences rendered the station non-viable and ceased broadcasting in April 2009.

4 April

On this day in 1899, PC John Charlton of East Hanney died of injuries sustained in an affray outside the Chequers pub in Harwell during the evening before.

He and his friend PC Thomas Hewett were off-duty and having a drink together. It was Easter and several customers had been drinking all day. Hawkers Joseph Slatter and Robert James had become particularly rowdy; instead of leaving, Slatter broke into song despite the protests of the other patrons. Just after 7pm landlord Isaac Day asked Charlton and Hewett to eject the two men. Charlton asked the men to leave quietly, but Slatter went for Hewett, so Day pulled him off and threw him outside.

Once outside, one of the hawkers said: 'Come out and fight, you 'tecs!' PC Charlton replied: 'No one has asked you to fight.' Slatter and James set about the officers anyway, and a nasty brawl ensued. According to a witness,

Joseph Slatter and Robert James outside Wantage magistrates' court

Slatter ran a few steps and took a flying kick at Charlton's stomach, and at the same time punched him in the face. Charlton fell backwards and hit his head 'very forcibly' on the road. Slatter then urged James to knife the constable, whereupon James kicked the fallen man in the head while he was lying on the ground. Then the two miscreants, both ex-servicemen, went for Hewett. The witness and the landlord pulled the men off Hewett, saving him from serious injury. Someone else brought out Hewett's truncheon and handcuffs which had been left behind in the pub. Slatter was cuffed, but James made his escape.

PC Charlton was taken insensible to the Harwell police house occupied by his colleague Hewett. He was laid on the floor of the parlour where he vomited blood, but remained unconscious for 24 hours. He died on the evening of the 4th. The post-mortem concluded that the cause of death was a fractured skull. Robert James was arrested at Stoke Row on the following day. At the summer assizes in June, both Slatter and James were found guilty of manslaughter and sentenced to 20 years' hard labour.

Slatter died in 1926 aged 73 at Fair Mile Hospital at Moulsford near Cholsey, a mental hospital. The fate of Robert James is unknown.

5 April

On this day in 1810, Major-General Sir Henry Creswicke Rawlinson, 1st Baronet, was born in Chadlington. He was a British East India Company army officer, politician and Orientalist, sometimes described as the 'Father of Assyriology'. Having learned the Persian language, in 1827 he was sent to Persia (present-day Iran) with other British officers to drill and reorganise the Shah's troops. Disagreements between the Persian court and the British government ended in the departure of the British officers. Rawlinson served as political agent at Kandahar for three years. He settled in Baghdad, but a riding accident in 1855 obliged him to return to England. He remained active, and was one of the most prominent figures arguing that Britain must check Russian ambitions in South Asia.

6 April

On this day in 1752, Mary Blandy was hanged at Oxford Castle for the murder of her father, the last woman to be hanged in Oxford. Mary Blandy was the only child of Francis Blandy, an attorney and town clerk of Henley-upon-Thames. It was said that Francis had a fortune of £10,000 to leave to his daughter. An avaricious officer in the marines, William Henry Cranstoun, son of Lord Cranstoun, proposed to marry her.

The two were lovers for six years, often meeting along 'Miss Blandy's Walk' at Park Place across the Thames in Remenham. Her father, however, objected, suspecting Cranstoun to be already married. He was right. Cranstoun had married Anne Murray in 1745, and the couple had two children. Cranstoun sent Mary arsenic to administer in small doses to her father, apparently telling her it was a love potion that would soften Blandy's heart towards their plight.

Blandy became ill, and so did some of the servants who had eaten the leftovers. When he realised he was dying by his own daughter's hand, Blandy only pitied Mary and tried to prevent her from incriminating herself. He appears to have believed her story about mistaking the poison for a love potion. After months of agony, he died on 14 August 1751.

Mary's last request was that, for the sake of decency, she should not be hoisted too high. Cranstoun escaped, but died abroad in 1752.

7 April

Friar Bacon's Study

On this day in 1779, 'Friar Bacon's Study' at Folly Bridge was sold for demolition. Oxford's first stone bridge, known as South Bridge, was built over the Thames in the 11th century by William the Conqueror's local henchman Robert d'Oilly. It was part of the great causeway, or grand pont, which carried what is now the Abingdon Road over water meadows from St Aldate's to the bottom of Hinksey Hill. A defensive tower with a portcullis, drawbridge and heavy gates was built at the southern end of the bridge, probably in the 13th century. It was known as New Gate and presented a barrier to anyone approaching from along the causeway to the south gate of the city, which was on St Aldate's, where Christ Church now stands. Timber, iron bars and locks were bought for it in 1310-11 and repairs were made regularly throughout the later Middle Ages. The defensive tower became known as Friar Bacon's Study because Franciscan friar Roger Bacon (1214–1292) apparently used it as an observatory to study astronomy. South Bridge was largely maintained by charity, and bridge-hermits were appointed to collect alms at the chapel of St Nicholas on the causeway leading up to it.

From early in its life the tower on the bridge was a place of residence but it continued to be viewed as a defensive structure; as late as 1565 the city, in leasing the gatehouse for the Berkshire archdeaconry court, reserved the right of entry at all times for the city's defence. But by the 17th century the defensive gate was no longer in use, and shortly after 1611 the gatehouse was heightened by Thomas Waltham alias Welcome, and became known as Welcome's Folly, giving the bridge its present name.

8 April

On this day in 1698, Tsar Peter the Great left London at 8am for an informal sight-seeing trip in Oxford. Taking time out from his study of shipbuilding on the London docks, he arrived in the city incognito at about 10pm. He stayed at the Golden Cross Inn at 5 Cornmarket where he clearly enjoyed a jolly evening, helped along by four bottles of sack wine and a couple of bottles of brandy.

By the time he set out to see the sights the next morning, the innkeeper had become such a good friend of his that the Tsar took him along for company in his carriage. Peter visited the bookshop, Convocation, and the Sheldonian Theatre. Next on the list was the Ashmolean museum. Assistant keeper of the museum, William Williamson, described the visitor as 'a very uncouth fellow' dressed in an enormous, scruffy black wig and a black kaftan with gold buttons, whose dirty hands were 'scratched as though from scabies'. Peter lingered in the museum for all of 15 minutes. Heading across the road to Trinity College chapel, he realised that he had been recognised (after all, a black kaftan with gold buttons was hardly designed to blend in in an English university town) and students and townspeople were flocking to get a look at him. Irritated by the crowd, at midday he simply turned tail and fled back to London.

9 April

On this day in 1962, Windrush Tower was opened, the first tower block at Blackbird Leys. The city's population grew massively in the inter-war period and demand for housing was high—there were 5,000 on the council waiting list in 1946 and Morris Cars was expanding. Workers were needed.

Planning permission was granted in 1953 on 260 acres of land then occupied by a sewage works and farm in Blackbird Leys for an estate of 2,800 dwellings with a projected population of 10,000. By 1958 there were ten families living in or around the Sandy Lane area, and work began shortly afterwards on the estate's two most recognisable features: Windrush Tower and Evenlode Tower. The first pub, the Blackbird, opened in December 1962, then five years later the Bullnose Morris. Some of the shops in the Balfour Road parade began trading from garages at the back even before construction was finished, such

Windrush Tower at Blackbird Leys

was the demand for local services and the unreliability of public transport links.

As with so many initiatives conceived with optimism and good intentions, the pressures of the 1980s led to an outbreak of social unrest on the estate. In the context of wider urban turbulence in the summer of 1991, discontent in Blackbird Leys peaked when a police crackdown on joy-riding led to three days of rioting which has tainted the reputation of the estate to this day. Many residents, on the other hand, whilst acknowledging the shortcomings of the building techniques used and the gap between social aspiration and the outcome, look back on their childhoods on the Blackbird Leys estate in the 90s with affection and loyalty to a tight-knit community.

10 April

On this day in 1941, RAF gunners at Arncott shot down a German bomber returning home from a raid on Birmingham. At about 11pm the Junkers

Ju 88A-5 4203 V4+FV emerged from low cloud above a group of ground defence crews of the RAF Army Co-operation Command. The plane swept the ground with a hail of machine-gun bullets. 'Disregarding this vicious attack,' reported the *Bicester Advertiser*, 'the RAF ground crews held their fire and then took a steady aim. The raider, still firing, circled around them. But the gunners continued firing too—and fired so accurately that the Nazi aircraft crashed a few miles away and its crew were killed.'

The German plane is believed to have cart-wheeled across a field, coming to rest against the hedge line. The bodies of the four crewmen were recovered from the wreckage and buried together in one plot in the churchyard of St Lawrence's Church, Caversfield.

In 1959 the German government began the process of gathering all the individual German war burials in the country together at Cannock Chase, just north of Birmingham. In November 1961 the bodies at Caversfield were moved to Cannock Chase and reburied.

11 April

On this day in 1995, Mansfield College was chartered as a full college in the University of Oxford. The college was founded for Nonconformist students as Spring Hill College in Birmingham in 1838. In the 19th century, although students from all religious denominations were legally entitled to attend universities, only members of the Church of England could take degrees. In 1871, the Universities Tests Act abolished all religious tests for non-theological degrees at Oxford, Cambridge, London, and Durham Universities. For the first time the educational and social opportunities offered by Britain's premier institutions were open to some Nonconformists. Prime Minister William Ewart Gladstone encouraged the creation of a Nonconformist college at Oxford, so Spring Hill College moved to Oxford in 1886 and was renamed Mansfield College.

The Victorian buildings, designed by Basil Champneys on a site bought from Merton College, were formally opened in October 1889. Initially the college accepted men only. The first woman was admitted to read for an external degree in 1913. During World War II, staff from the Government Code & Cypher School were based in the college.

12 April

On this day in 1215, 'bad' King John entered Oxford for the Palm Sunday celebrations. Given that by April 1215 King John was a pledged Crusader (which gave him special protection under church law), and given also that the Palm Sunday celebrations in the Latin church of Jerusalem included a solemn procession or *'adventus'* for the kings of Jerusalem, we might speculate that John's entry into Oxford on Palm Sunday 1215 was hedged with particularly elaborate ceremonial. The unpopular king was facing serious discontent among many of his barons, who were unhappy with his fiscal policies and his treatment of many of England's most powerful nobles.

Palm Sunday itself was very likely spent by the king at St Frideswide's, a reminder that in the 12th and early 13th centuries kings regularly entered the city of Oxford. By the 1260s, the legend was growing that the curse of Frideswide (an Anglo-Saxon princess threatened with abduction by Aethelbald, king of Mercia) forbade all future kings from entering Oxford. It may be that the legend of Frideswide's curse owed at least something to the association between King John's visit in April 1215 and his subsequent humiliation at Runnymede.

13 April

On this day in 1886, a long legal case was at last settled between an undergraduate of Worcester College and the proprietor of Ginnett's travelling circus. The Ginnett family came to England in the early 1800s as captives in the Napoleonic wars. Once peace broke out some of the family stayed in England, and Jean Pierre Ginnett devised his Pony and Budgerigar show which gradually expanded into a full-blown travelling circus. In March 1885, the circus was at Oxford, and on 28th of that month a letter appeared in the *Pall Mall Gazette* complaining of the ill treatment meted out to child apprentices at Ginnett's show.

'As usual there are several boys attached to this circus,' reported the sender, 'and out of natural curiosity a friend of mine asked one of the managers how they were trained to perform so well'. The gullible inquisitor was informed drily that the lads were made to perform their various feats 'surrounded by men holding whips, who each time they failed lashed them severely, till sometimes their backs were a mass of blood.' The letter was written by 20-year-old George Napier-Whittingham, an undergraduate at Worcester College.

The Ginnetts, who had hitherto enjoyed a respectable reputation, claimed that Mr Whittingham's libel had cost them much business. Frederick Ginnett was booed and hissed in Bristol and Bath to such an extent that he was afraid to appear in the traditional procession. He took his troupe to Ireland until the libel was removed. A claim for £2,500 in damages was laid against the *Pall Mall Gazette* for not publishing a full retraction of the groundless allegations when requested. The judge found for the Ginnetts, and awarded them £1,500. Whittingham went on to become a minister in the Church of England.

14 April

On this day in 1386, New College took possession of its buildings on land that had formerly been the City ditch, a haunt of thieves, and a place of burial during the Black Death. Founded in 1379 by William of Wykeham, bishop of Winchester, the full name of the college is 'the College of St Mary of Winchester in Oxford'. The name 'New College', however, soon came into use following its completion in 1386 in order to distinguish it from the older, existing college of St Mary, now known as Oriel College.

New College was founded in conjunction with Hampshire school Winchester College (opened 1394), which was envisaged as a feeder to the Oxford college. Their striking architectural similarities reveal that they were both the work of master mason William Wynford.

When William of Wykeham acquired the land on which to build the college, he agreed to maintain the city wall. Every three years the Lord Mayor and Corporation take a walk along the wall to make sure that the obligation is being fulfilled, a tradition dating back to the college's foundation in 1379. Both Winchester College and New College were originally established for the education of priests, there being a shortage of properly educated clergy after the Black Death. Wykeham forbade wrestling, dancing and all noisy games in the hall, and decreed the use of Latin in conversation. New College was the first college in Oxford deliberately designed around a main quadrangle with an entrance tower and a T-plan chapel.

Wroxton Abbey

15 April

On this day in 1754, Frederick North, 2nd Earl of Guilford, better known by his courtesy title Lord North, was elected unopposed as the Member of Parliament for the constituency of Banbury. Although he had been born in London, North spent most of his time at the family seat of Wroxton Abbey near Banbury. A skilled statesman, and prime minister at the age of 37, North was placed in office by George III to contend with the mounting crisis in the American colonies. He served as prime minister for almost the whole of the American Revolution. His imposition of the tea tax and other repressive measures against the colonists lead to the Declaration of Independence in 1776. Despite his wish to resign when the war turned against Britain, the king kept him in office; afterwards he claimed to have felt more the agent of the king than a responsible adviser.

Eventually, the king was forced to accept North's resignation. North remained an active speaker until he began to go blind in 1786.

16 April

On this day in 1832, Sir Robert James Loyd-Lindsay, Baron Wantage of Lockinge, joint founder of the British Red Cross, was born.

Until the middle of the 19th century, there were no organised army nursing systems for casualties and no safe and protected institutions to accommodate and treat those who were wounded on the battlefield. In June 1859, a French businessman wrote a book to draw attention to the terrible aftermath of the Battle of Solferino, the suffering of the wounded soldiers, and the near-total lack of medical attendance and basic care. In October 1863, the newly-formed International Committee for Relief to the Wounded was held in Geneva to develop possible measures to improve medical services on the battlefield. On 22 August 1864, the conference adopted the first Geneva Convention establish the standards of international law for humanitarian treatment in war.

Upon the outbreak of the Franco-Prussian War in 1870, humanitarian reformer John Furley asked Loyd-Lindsay if he would help set up a British Red Cross society in the United Kingdom. Furley had already been in touch with the International Committee in Geneva, and he knew that Lindsay also supported the goals of the new Red Cross movement. A letter from Loyd-Lindsay was published in *The Times* on 22 July calling for a national society in the United Kingdom, and pledging £1,000 of his own money.

On 4 August, he chaired a public meeting in London which resolved that 'a National Society be formed in this country for aiding sick and wounded soldiers in time of war, and that the said Society be formed upon the Rules laid down by the Geneva Conventions'. The society was renamed the British Red Cross in 1905.

17 April

On this day in 1518, Catherine of Aragon visited the shrine of St Frideswide on the site now occupied by Christ Church Cathedral. Since her marriage to Henry VIII in 1509, Catherine had suffered the loss of three baby boys before she gave birth to a healthy child at last. It was a girl. On 12 April 1518 the king's secretary, Richard Pace, reported to Wolsey that it was secretly said that the queen was with child. Pace prayed heartily to God that the child might be a prince.

The court then travelled to Woodstock, and Catherine took the opportunity to visit Oxford along the way. She lunched with the warden of Merton, who had preached at the funeral of the first of her three dead boys. She also visited the shrine of St Frideswide in the Priory and sought a miracle—a male heir for the Tudors. The pregnancy was kept secret but, in July, when Henry arrived at Woodstock, Catherine greeted him at the door of her chamber, proud to display 'for his welcome home her belly something great'. Henry was so delighted that he gave a great banquet to celebrate, and wrote to Wolsey that he was 'so loath to repair to London, because about this time is partly of her dangerous times, and by cause of that I would remove her as little as I may'.

On the night of 9/10 November the queen gave birth to a daughter. The baby was weak and died before she could be christened. Not only had the Anglo-Saxon princess-saint failed Catherine, but in June 1519, the poor queen had to endure Henry's triumph at the birth of a son with his mistress Bessie Blount, which he felt proved that any fault lay with Catherine and not him.

18 April

On this day in 1884, 40-year-old Edwin Reeves last saw his brother Daniel alive in Chipping Norton. Edwin worked as a groom, probably at the Fox and Hounds Inn next door to the cottage where he lived. But Daniel, who was around ten years older, had no fixed abode and survived by begging.

'He appeared well,' Edwin reported to the jury at the inquest in the Black Horse at Salford on the following Tuesday. 'I gave him some coppers and told him to go to Mr Hartley and enter the Union.' Henry Hartley was the relieving officer for the workhouse. At 4.15pm the next day, the Rev Richard Nash Bricknell, rector of Salford, met Daniel Reeves in the village. Bricknell claimed that Daniel was evidently unwell, but refused the rector's entreaties to go to the workhouse.

On Sunday evening at 7.30 Edwin Reeves was in Mr Wrighton's field with Wrighton's groom Robert Matthews. There was a hovel in the field, and Matthews said he would look inside 'to see if anything had been pulled about. We opened the door and saw something covered up; all we could see was a man's hand. I called very loudly three times, but got no answer. I did not go near him. Matthews said: "Come away for goodness' sake; we will go to the police." We did so. We did not know whether he was alive or dead, but by the noise we made, and receiving no reply, we concluded he was dead. We did not know who the man was.'

Edwin and Robert Matthews fetched PC Dickinson, who revealed: 'He was covered with hay and a sack. By his left hand was a piece of bread, matches, pipe, and tobacco. We brought the body here. On searching him I found fivepence in coppers in his pockets.' A doctor told the jury: 'I knew the deceased. He has been constantly in and out of the Union. Four years ago he lost two toes by frostbite; he has a weak heart. I found him covered with vermin. I should say the cause of death was pneumonia.'

The day after the coroner's inquest, Daniel Reeves finally found a permanent resting place when he was buried at the Church of St Mary in Salford.

19 April

On this day in 1950, Gerald Hugh Tyrwhitt-Wilson, 14th Baron Berners of Faringdon House, died. A renowned eccentric, he dyed his estate doves multiple colours and kept a pet giraffe—but he also wrote highly-regarded music.

Berners worked at a grand piano adorned with a beer mug that played the national anthem when lifted. He could also compose on the move, having installed a clavichord in his Rolls-Royce—the same Rolls-Royce, in fact, that Berners liked riding around in wearing a pig's-head mask to frighten the locals.

His eccentricities appeared early. On hearing you could teach a dog to swim by throwing it into water, the young Gerald promptly threw his mother's dog out of the window to teach it to fly. Thankfully, the dog suffered nothing more serious than understandable surprise. Despite flunking the entrance exam, he joined the diplomatic service, but upon inheriting his family estate in 1918, Berners retired to Faringdon House.

Here he built the Faringdon Folly, widely acknowledged as the last folly erected on an English estate. Salvador Dali was one of many illustrious visitors to Faringdon House, and Penelope Betjeman's Arab stallion was invited into the drawing room for afternoon tea. Berners' dogs padded around wearing fake pearl necklaces, and the entrance to the folly bore a stern warning that 'Members of the public committing suicide from this tower do so at their own risk'.

The doctor who attended Berners during his last years declined to send a bill, saying that his patient's company had been payment enough.

20 April

On this day in 1986, Oxford United won the Football League Cup, known at the time as the Milk Cup. The final scoreline was 3-0 against Queens Park Rangers. It was the team's first major honour.

Founded in 1893 as Headington United, Oxford United adopted its current name in 1960. It joined the Football League in 1962 after winning the Southern Football League, reaching the Second Division in 1968. In 1982, as a Third Division side, Oxford United faced closure because of the club's inability to service the debts owed to Barclays Bank, but were rescued when businessman Robert Maxwell took over the club. Oxford won the Third Division title after the 1983–84 season under the management of Jim Smith, who also guided them to the Second Division title the following year. This meant that Oxford United would be playing First Division football in the 1985–86 season, 23 years after joining the Football League.

The final was played at Wembley Stadium in front of 90,396 spectators. Trevor Hebberd opened the scoring in the first half, and Ray Houghton added a second. Jeremy Charles scored the third following up when John Aldridge had a shot saved by QPR goalkeeper Paul Barron. Because UEFA had voted that the ban imposed on English clubs in European competition following the May 1985 Heysel Stadium disaster would continue for a second season, Oxford United were denied a place in the 1986-87 UEFA Cup.

21 April

On this day in 1956, Soviet leaders Nikita Khrushchev and Nikolai Bulganin visit Oxford as part of a state visit to Britain. 'Crowds 20-deep lined St Aldate's from the Post Office to Carfax traffic lights, with sightseers viewing from the windows of the four-storey buildings opposite the town hall,' reported the *Oxford Mail*. Blackwell's book shop in Broad Street painted its name in Russian to greet the visitors. 'Very few even got a glimpse of the pair as they got smartly out of the car and were enclosed by newsreel and press photographers at the entrance to the town hall,' continued the *Oxford Mail*'s reporter. 'Some climbed the stairs of stationary buses to try to see. The three cars which brought the official Soviet party were escorted by six police motorcyclists.

Blackwell's bookshop repainted their sign to welcome the visitors

The Russian leaders, who were visiting Britain to try to ease tensions between East and West as the Cold War intensified, met political leaders at the town hall. President Khrushchev waved from inside his car before getting out, but he stopped only for a matter of seconds at the foot of the town hall steps when greeted by the mayor.'

A large crowd of undergraduates met the Russian contingent outside the Clarendon Building in Broad Street, with calls for free speech, and invitations to go home. During talks with university representatives, it was agreed that a mahogany desk chair looted during the fall of Sebastopol in 1855 should be returned. It was taken from the study of the Russian commander-in-chief by the servant of Colonel (later General) R J Baumgarten and bequeathed to his grandson, the Master of St Peter's Hall, who offered to hand it back.

22 April

On this day in 1865, readers of *Jackson's Oxford Journal* learned the tragic details of the senseless death of Sophia Vallis on her way to Oxford market.

Sophia, a sawyer's wife from Headington, was accompanied by her sister-in-law Harriet Gammon, and both women had a child with them. As they got to the trees by Magdalen School, a runaway horse and cart came racing over the bridge. Driving the cart was 20-year-old Thomas Valentine of Merton Street. He had been despatched by the horse's owner, Turner, to deliver a message in Littlemore. He invited 17-year-old Richard Buckle to go with him for the ride. The lads collected the horse and trap from the Horse and Jockey in Woodstock Road and drove safely to Littlemore. The mare was very quiet during the trip, but returning over Magdalen bridge she began to kick and then set off at a tremendous gallop. Buckle and Valentine both pulled on the reins, but they could not slow her.

Buckle bailed out opposite Rose Lane, landing on his shoulder. Valentine's seat tilted up and he was pitched out of the cart, landing on his head and left arm. Dazed, he got up and ran after the mare who had by this time arrived in Alderman Thompson's shop, jamming Mary Franklin behind the door inside.

Sophia Vallis was taken to the Radcliffe Infirmary where she managed to saw a few words to her husband. She died the following day. The two children miraculously escaped physical injury. Harriet Gammon was injured, but survived. Mrs Franklin suffered a foot injury that confined her to her bed for several days. The horse sustained only a slight cut.

23 April

On this day in 1327, simmering resentment among the townsfolk of Abingdon against the Abbey boiled over into violence and destruction.

Abingdon was a small, flourishing wool town at the beginning of the 14th century. Its prosperous merchants and clothiers resented the power wielded by the Abbey, particularly its tight control over markets and fairs and the levying of trading dues. On the previous Monday they had gathered together to take the organisation of the market place into their own hands. On Wednesday evening, they held a council of war to decide on the tactics of revolt. On Thursday morning they set fire to the Guildhall, the building where the Abbey collected the townsmen's dues and held its courts. The townspeople then attacked the main gate of the Abbey itself, and when armed defenders sallied forth to repel the onslaught, two townsmen were killed and many taken captive inside the Abbey to await trial by the king's justices.

Worse was to come. Exploiting the unrest to advance their own political aims, the people of Oxford then piled in to the fray. The unusual alliance of Town and Gown and the involvement of leading citizens such as the mayor of Oxford suggest a degree of forward planning, perhaps initiated during the visit of the rebellious Queen Isabella to Oxford six months earlier. During the night of 26 April, the Abbey was looted and burned, and the monks were obliged to flee across the Thames. The aftermath was characterised by endless legal cases—criminal actions and actions for damages. And the abbot obtained a royal licence to crenellate the buildings facing on to the market place: the Abbey gate, St Nicholas's Church and St John's Hospital.

24 April

On this day in 1883, six young men left Bladon for the United States of America—a brave but not unusual step in a time of severe agricultural depression. A succession of bad harvests coincided with the advent of cheap trans-Atlantic travel, and American grain trucks rumbled relentlessly across the prairies courtesy of the new railways. Fast steam ships then conveyed the grain east across the ocean. Cheap imports of vast amounts of American prairie wheat flooded the market and undercut British farmers. Britain's dependence on imported grain during the 1830s was a mere 2 per cent; during the 1860s it rose to 24 per cent; by the 1880s it was 45 per cent, and for corn it was a massive 65 per cent.

During the first half of the 19th century, many British emigrants had been farmers, agricultural labourers or skilled artisans and craftsmen from traditional trades; many emigrated in family groups from rural areas. This pattern began to change in the second half of the 19th century, when emigrants started coming from urban areas, and young, single, male labourers and agricultural workers predominated, like those from Bladon. Thus, during the 19th century, the composition of emigration from Britain transformed greatly, turning from the movement of families into labour migration.

Between 1815 and 1914, approximately ten million people emigrated from Britain—about 20 per cent of all European emigrants. Massachusetts was the destination for the Bladon men, situations as farm labourers having been found for them by Rev W Burnett, curate at Bladon.

Oxford gaol, main entrance

25 April

On this day in 1818, highwayman John Bradley and two accomplices held up Thomas Hankinson on the King's highway near Bicester. All three were charged with violently assaulting and wounding Mr Hankinson and robbing him of six one-pound notes and fifteen shillings in silver. John Bradley was hanged on 2 August that year, along with sheep-stealer Richard Wiggins. After this date, only one further hanging was carried out (for the crime of stealing an animal)—that upon Richard Webbe in 1827 for the theft of a horse. After Webbe, the only crimes for which men were executed were highway robbery, arson and murder.

In all, 100 confirmed executions were carried out at Oxford gaol between 1735 and 1952, with a possible further three in 1742 for which no record of a reprieve has been found. Four women were hanged in the 1735–1766 period, with one more possibly executed in 1742. From 1790, until the ending of public hangings in 1868, the New Drop gallows was erected above the main gate, as was common practice in British prisons.

No executions are recorded for Joseph Elstone and Robert Archer, but Joseph Elstone had another narrow escape in 1827. As one of a gang of six felons, Elstone was charged with violently assaulting and stealing a purse containing seven pounds from Robert Fowler, overseer of Bicester. Even so, Elstone died peacefully in his bed in Bicester aged 80.

26 April

On this day in 1677, the Duke of Rheims visited Oxford while in England to discuss the marriage of the French dauphin and Princess Mary.

The dauphin in question was 16-year-old Louis, eldest son and heir of Louis XIV. Mary was the 15-year-old daughter of King Charles II's brother James, Duke of York. Charles was without a legitimate heir, so the matter of Mary's marriage was one of intense interest. Charles Maurice Tellier, archbishop of Rheims and primate of France under Louis XIV, was described by Oxford antiquary Anthony Wood as 'a tall proper man in a plush coat, sword by his side, and peruque [wig]'.

The duke and his party arrived incognito in the evening, and resorted to the Angel Inn in the High Street. Having been persuaded of the stranger's true identity, Bishop John Fell, Dean of Christ Church, called upon him the following morning and invited him on a tour of the colleges. 'But nothing pleased him,' reports Wood, 'and, as the French commonly do, slighted all things, and spoke uncivilly things to the bishop.'

Poor Dr Fell had to entertain this awkward guest for 11 long days until, at last, the French deputation left Oxford at 11am on 8 May. Almost immediately, a rude poem began to do the rounds:

> *'The blazing comet and the monstrous whale*
> *The breaking shins of Lauderdale*
> *The parliament at the eclipse being called*
> *And Osborne's George fell off before installed*
> *The bishop who from France came newly ore*
> *Did go to Betty Beaulies for a whore.'*

A comet had appeared during April, and a whale beached at Yarmouth during February. The Duke of Lauderdale had stumbled and bloodied his shins, and a solar eclipse adorned the opening of parliament. Lord Treasurer Thomas Osborne, 1st Duke of Leeds, suffered the indignity of losing his decoration from its ribbon at an investiture on 23rd April. Betty Beaulies is described by Anthony Wood as 'an old bawd living in Durham Yard'.

In the event, Princess Mary did not marry the dauphin. Reluctantly, she married her cousin William III of Orange, whom she came to love dearly.

27 April

On this day in 1646, King Charles I fled from Oxford in disguise. Aware that the New Model Army under General Fairfax was just days away and his Civil War capital was about to become besieged for the third time, Charles decided to seek the protection of the Scottish Presbyterian party. But the nearest Scottish army was that besieging the Royalist-held city of Newark-on-Trent in Nottinghamshire. Royal chaplain and sometime military scout Dr Michael Hudson persuaded the king that it was not possible to travel directly from Oxford to the Scottish camp outside Newark, and that it would be better to go by a circuitous route, first towards London, then north-east, before turning north-west towards Newark.

So, at midnight on 27 April, Charles's long hair was cut off—including his fashionable lovelock, and the peak of his familiar pointy beard. He was dressed as a servant to his own faithful courtier John Ashburnham, carrying a cloak bag and wearing a montero cap with flaps that could be drawn down to cover the ears and neck. Completing the party of three was Hudson, bearing a pass for a captain who was ostensibly to go to London to parley with Parliament.

The clock struck three as the little group hurried across Magdalen Bridge. Charles was still hoping to hear from parties in London who would be willing to treat with him, but nothing was heard from that direction, so the king and his companions took a circuitous and dangerous route to Newark. Reaching the Scottish army on 5 May, Charles was immediately arrested and kept under close guard at Kelham House.

28 April

On this day in 1917, Sgt Major Edward Brooks of the Oxfordshire & Buckinghamshire Light Infantry became one of only two soldiers in that regiment to win a Victoria Cross in the First World War. Having captured a German machine gun at Fayet near Saint-Quentin in France, he turned it on the enemy. His citation read: 'This Warrant Officer, while taking part in a raid

The Prince and Edward Brooks

on the enemy's trenches, saw that the front wave was checked by an enemy machine-gun at close quarters. On his own initiative, and regardless of personal danger, he rushed forward from the second wave with the object of capturing the gun, killing one of the gunners with his revolver and bayoneting another. The remainder of the gun's crew then made off, leaving the gun in his possession. C. S./M. Brookes then turned the machine-gun on to the retreating enemy, after which he carried it back into our lines.' Brooks received the VC from the king on 18 July 1917.

For the rest of his life Edward Brooks worked at the Morris car factory, where he pictured during a visit by the Prince of Wales, who would dearly have loved to see genuine action.

29 April

On this day in 1941, an Armstrong Whitworth Whitley P4939 took off at 1.15am in the morning on a circuits and landings exercise—what aircrew call 'circuits and bumps'. The aircraft got into a nose-down position after take-off and then pulled up sharply, stalled and dived into the Sandleigh Road playing fields at Wootton. The playing fields were completely surrounded by houses, just as they are today. The pilot officer, 28-year-old Leonard Sinclair Bradburn from Merseyside, and crew were all killed. The others were Sgt Victor George Pledge aged 20, from Essex (pilot), Sgt Robert Neville 'Bob' Birkhead aged 19 from Nottinghamshire (wireless operator), and Sgt Desmond Fitzgerald Percival aged 25 (wireless operator and air gunner). Sgt Birkhead's brother

George Thomas, another RAF sergeant, also died on active service aged 25.

Fifty-five thousand airmen were killed while serving with Royal Air Force Bomber Command during World War Two. A total of around 180 aircrew lost their lives while stationed at RAF Abingdon, 70 of them in the fields around the Abingdon area. A further 38 aircrew were lost while serving at RAF Stanton Harcourt, and another 112 Abingdon-based Whitley aircrew while on detachment at RAF St Eval in Cornwall.

30 April

On this day in 2014, scientist Professor Julian Lewis died aged 67 at his home in Oxford. He had suffered from prostate cancer for ten years.

Lewis made a huge contribution to the understanding of how embryos develop in the womb. His groundbreaking studies revealed how one of the cells' communication systems, called the 'notch signalling pathway', controls how cells in the embryo come to find themselves in the right place at the right time. When these communication networks go awry in the adult body, it can lead to cancer. A graduate of Balliol, Lewis published his last research paper only a few weeks before his death.

1 May 1847

On this day in 1847, a license was granted for a lottery to allocate shares in the Charterville Allotments near Minster Lovell. Soon after 1842, Chartist leader Feargus O'Connor's National Land Company purchased 244 acres adjoining the Brize Norton Road. O'Connor hoped to take families away from factory-living or unemployment in towns and to set them up to be self-supporting on land in the countryside, thereby also giving them sufficient property to entitle them to vote.

The Minster Lovell estate was built by national subscription, land on both sides of the road and elsewhere being divided into 78 plots of between two and four acres of arable and a small cottage. Settlers came from as far afield as Canterbury, London, and the northern manufacturing towns, though the experiment was at first unsuccessful because the allotments were too small to support a family, and the new tenants were not used to working the land.

By 1851–2 many of the original tenants had left, and the National Land Company itself was bankrupt, and was later dissolved. Local farmers bought or rented the plots, often cultivating them in addition to other land, and Charterville became more prosperous towards the end of the 19th century.

A visitor in 1861 described it as 'a large collection of cottages… all inhabited by labourers and little farmers… mostly exhibiting comfort, cleanliness and good order', and noted with evident approval both the presence of Nonconformist meetings and the absence of an alehouse. Social facilities included a school built by O'Connor. Many of the cottages have now been modernised within an inch of their lives, but one or two remain defiantly un-prettified.

2 May

On this day in 1968, the underground picture gallery at Christ Church was opened. This enabled the collection to be displayed to the public for the first time; previously the paintings had been mainly hung in the library.

Army officer General John Guise bequeathed his collection of over 200 paintings and almost 2,000 drawings to his former college upon his death in 1765. This extraordinary gift enabled Christ Church to introduce art into Oxford education without the necessity to travel to Italy or to gain access to stately homes, which still held the majority of art collections in the country.

The purpose-built gallery was designed by architects Powell and Moya and was opened in 1968 by Her Majesty the Queen. The collection is strongest in Italian art from the 14th to the 18th century. A number of these early religious panels are painted by now-anonymous masters, but they allow the viewer to trace the beginnings of the professional 'artist'.

Later works in the collection include paintings by highly-acclaimed artists like Filippino Lippi, Tintoretto, Veronese, Anthony van Dyck, Frans Hals and Hugo van der Goes. The Old Master drawings include works by Leonardo, Michelangelo, Dürer, Raphael and Rubens.

3 May

On this day in 1645, Royalist colonel Francis Windebank was executed in the grounds of Oxford Castle. On the outbreak of the Civil War, Windebank had been appointed governor of Bletchingdon House. In 1643 at Wolvercote he married Jane Hopton, probably the sister of Royalist general Ralph Hopton.

Cromwell commenced his famous raid into Oxfordshire on 23 April. At dawn on the 24th, Cromwell routed a detachment of Royalist horse at Islip. On the same day, though he had no guns and only a few firearms in the whole force, Cromwell approached Bletchingdon House. And 32-year-old Windebank surrendered immediately. Why?

Some speculate that he had invited his wife and friends into the house for a ball and, having placed these innocents in peril, felt that surrender was the only gallant course. In spite of his impeccable connections—his father was King Charles's secretary of state and he himself was usher of the chamber to Prince Charles—he was removed to Oxford Castle where he was tried by a Royalist court-martial and shot. His daughter, Frances, was born a few months later.

4 May

On this day in 1816, the first Hertford College was finally declared to have been dissolved some 11 years previously in 1805.

The first Hertford College began in the 1280s as Hart Hall, a small tenement built roughly where the college's Old Hall is today, a few paces along New College Lane on the southern side. In medieval Oxford, halls were primarily lodging houses for students and resident tutors. During the 18th century, under educational reformer Rev Dr Richard Newton, Hertford was a relatively spartan college, having received no real endowment. Students were expected to work hard, and many well-to-do families sent their sons there to instil in them some discipline, unlike their privileged contemporaries wining and dining in other colleges. When nobody could be found to succeed the last principal, Bernard Hodgson, Hertford College was dissolved in 1816. In a striking symbol of the college's demise, the decrepit medieval front of the by-then defunct Hertford College collapsed into Catte Street in 1820.

5 May

On this day in 1915, Oxford rugby blue Ronald Poulton was killed by sniper fire in Ploegsteert Wood in Flanders. Second son of evolutionary biologist

Ronald Poulton

Professor Sir Edward Poulton, Poulton is regarded as one of the greatest rugby players of all time. Born at Wykeham House in the Banbury Road, he was educated at Oxford Preparatory School (now the Dragon School), then Rugby School, and finally Balliol College where he read engineering.

On the rugby field he was a charismatic figure with glamorous good looks, noted for his high-stepping style of running and unpredictable swerve. He won three blues playing for Oxford, and the 1909 match against Cambridge is known as 'Poulton's match' for his five tries, still a record in a Varsity match. He played club rugby for Harlequins and Liverpool, and he played 17 times for England, captaining the team in an unbeaten Five Nations series in 1914.

He was commissioned as second lieutenant in a territorial battalion of the Royal Berkshires and volunteered for service abroad on the outbreak of war. He arrived in Flanders in March 1915, and was killed in early May. He was 27. The original wooden cross marking his burial in Flanders was transferred to Holywell Cemetery where Sir Edward and other family members are buried.

6 May

On this day in 1646, the surrender of Banbury Castle was agreed. In 1642 the English Civil War had broken out between the Royalist supporters of Charles I and the supporters of Parliament. Banbury Castle was initially held by William Fiennes for Parliament, and the castle was hastily refortified. After the battle of Edgehill, Charles marched south and forced the surrender of the castle and its stock of 1,500 firearms.

The fortifications were strengthened and in 1644 the castle was besieged again, this time by Parliamentary forces under the command of William Fiennes. The Royalist governor, 18-year-old William Compton, held out between July and October when Compton's brother, James, relieved the siege. In November, Charles I dined in the castle.

In January 1646, Sir Edward Whalley placed the castle under siege again with a force of 3,000 men; the Royalist cause was collapsing, and in May Compton and his force of 300 men surrendered. In 1646 one writer said Banbury had 'scarce the one half (of its buildings) stand to gaze on the ruins of the other'.

Parliament gave the town £300-worth of timber to rebuild. The townspeople were also given stone from the castle, which was demolished in 1648 to prevent its further use; Fiennes was paid £2,000 by Parliament in compensation.

7 May

On this day in 1917, actor David Cecil MacAlister Tomlinson was born in Henley. He played authority figure George Banks in *Mary Poppins*, fraudulent magician Professor Emelius Browne in *Bedknobs and Broomsticks*, and hapless antagonist Peter Thorndyke in *The Love Bug*. He grew up with a stammer. His father secured him a job as a clerk at Shell Mex House. 'But I'd like to be an actor,' he stuttered. 'Be an actor?' expostulated his father. 'Good God, you can't even speak!' During the war, he served as a flight instructor in Canada. In September 1943, Tomlinson married widow Mary Hiddingh. A few weeks later Mary, 34, killed herself and her two sons in a murder-suicide by jumping from 15 floors up at a hotel in New York City. She was said at the time to be despondent because she was unable to join Tomlinson in England. Tomlinson's second wife was actress Audrey Freeman whom he married in 1953, and the couple remained together for 47 years until his death. Tomlinson's flying days continued after the war and he crashed a Tiger Moth plane near his back garden after he lost consciousness while flying. One witness claimed to have seen him looping-the-loop and pretending to dive-bomb his own house.

8 May

On this day in 1963, Balliol College men turfed the Junior Common Room of mortal enemies Trinity College. In the early hours of the morning, six Balliol

Dean David Raven admires the newy-turfed Trinity College JCR in 1963

men slipped quietly over the wall into Trinity, and six others passed the turf through a barred window separating the two colleges. It was carried silently across the Trinity lawn, up a flight of stairs and into the JCR.

The furniture was carefully replaced and even the Dean at Trinity, David Raven, admitted that the intruders had done a good job. This didn't save the offenders however, and they were made to dig up the turf and pay to replace the original carpet. Archibald Whyte, a Trinity student, was quick to lead a revenge attack. He said: 'When the Balliol men came back to collect their sods of turf this morning we threw at least seven of them into the Trinity Rose Pond. It's a good six feet deep and they got very, very wet.'

9 May

On this day in 1734, the weathercock fell off the University Church of St Mary the Virgin while the great bell chimed 9 o'clock in the morning. It had apparently been loose for some time. The cockerel fell onto the church, its tail into the churchyard. The cost of repair to the weathercock and steeple was £53.

A church was established on this site, at the centre of the old walled city, in Anglo-Saxon times; by the 12th century St Mary's was at the heart of the growing medieval University. Students and academics gathered there for special occasions such as the awarding of degrees, as well as for services and lectures. When the University as a whole needed to make decisions, all the academics—so-called members of Congregation—would meet in St Mary's to vote on important matters.

The oldest remaining part of the church is the tower, begun in the 1270s. The decorated spire was added in the early 14th century and is one of Oxford's best-known landmarks.

10 May

On this day in 1870, the library at Christ Church was broken into and 'much wanton mischief' ensued, according to *Jackson's Oxford Journal*.

At about 11pm, one of the windows of the library was removed. Five busts plus a bronze statue were carried into Peckwater Quad and piled round with mats, carpets, two or three valuable old books and a bundle of fagots, and the whole lot set ablaze. The fire was soon spotted and extinguished, but not before several items had been damaged beyond repair. The help of detectives was sought, the property concerned being vested in the Crown.

A motion was passed by the college's Junior Common Room condemning those responsible, but the suggestion that the names of the perpetrators be revealed to the authorities was rejected. The supposed ringleader, one of the most popular members of college, then disappeared during the night. The names of other suspects emerged, and those concerned were gated. Before the month was up, eight undergraduates had been identified as the culprits.

The college authorities decided to deal with the matter in-house rather than resorting to the law. In the presence of the entire college, the offenders were summoned into the Hall and the Dean pronounced expulsion against Edward Marjoribanks, Edmund Pryor, and Robert Russell. Lesser penalties were inflicted on four others, and one was found not to be a Christ Church man at all.

Marjoribanks became a Liberal Party statesman who sat in the House of Commons from 1880 until 1894, when he inherited a peerage and then sat in the House of Lords as 2nd Baron Tweedmouth.

11 May

On this day in 1646, Parliamentarian commander-in-chief Sir Thomas Fairfax sent a demand of surrender in to the governor of Oxford, Sir Thomas Glemham: 'Sir, I do by these summon you to deliver up the City of Oxford into my hands, for the use of the Parliament. I very much desire the preservation of that place (so famous for learning), from ruin, which inevitably is like to fall upon it, except you concur. You may have honourable terms for yourself and all within that garrison if you reasonably accept thereof. I desire the answer this day, and remain your servant, Thomas Fairfax.'

But the governor and the officers of the garrison gave the opinion to the Lords of the Privy Council that the city was defensible. A formal siege of some three months then followed—the third siege of Oxford during the Civil War—but the war was obviously over and negotiation, rather than fighting, took precedence. Being careful not to inflict too much damage on the city, Fairfax even sent in food to the king's second son, James, and was happy to conclude the siege by agreement.

This and other honourable conduct during the hostilities spared Fairfax from the wave of Royalist retributions after the Restoration. He resumed his career as an MP, and provided the horse which Charles II rode at his coronation.

12 May

On this day in 1926, the General Strike stuttered to a halt in Oxford. It had been called by the Trades Union Congress in an unsuccessful attempt to force the government to prevent worsening conditions for coal miners whose pay had dropped from £6 per week to under £4 over seven years.

Middle-class volunteers were quick to answer a government appeal to keep vital services running. When Colonel Luard, in charge of recruitment, arrived at his office in the drill hall at Oxford Town Hall at 9am on 4 May, crowds were waiting to sign on. The *Oxford Times* reported: 'The Drill Hall was a hive of industry, the recruiting of volunteers in order to keep up essential services proceeding at a rapid pace. Scores of willing helpers are giving their assistance in the clerical work involved. All day, there was a stream of people, young and old, offering their services in any capacity.' A total of 3,142 people volunteered,

1,373 from the city, 1,769 from the county and 1,870 undergraduates. In the event, only undergraduates were deployed, with nearly 1,000 of them going off to jobs in other parts of the country.

The strike lasted nine days from 3–12 May, but on the final day Oxford remained in some confusion as to whether the action was over or not. A bulletin posted by the 'Oxford Council of Action' at 2pm on the final day read: 'Dear Brothers, You are instructed to stand firm until you hear from this office. We are waiting for orders from the General Council. Yours fraternally, Frank Penny, Secretary.' When the general committee met that evening, many more telegrams had been received by local officials, and it became clear that the industrial action was over.

13 May

On this day in 1877, New Botley miller William Cummins and landlord of the Jolly Farmers in Paradise Street Henry Quelch were charged by Thames Conservancy with fishing for perch during the fence months (March, April and May), and also with using what the prosecutor called 'one of the most murderous sort of nets possible, a flue net'.

The Jolly Farmers, Paradise Street

In 1866 it was decided to put the navigation of the whole of the Thames under one management because, it was said, the Thames Commissioners were too numerous, the locks and weirs were in a bad condition, and income was insufficient to pay for maintenance. It was believed that under single management with the upper river maintained properly, and with lower tolls overall, the traffic would increase. Under an Act of 6 August 1866, the Thames Conservancy took over management of the river from Cricklade to Yantlet Creek on the Isle of Grain, a distance of 177 miles (285km). In 1868 tolls were placed on three of the four locks then above Oxford—St John's, Buscot and Pinkhill Locks. Rushey Lock was omitted and there were no tolls on the weirs. This reflects the poor state of navigation above Oxford. In 1872 Thames Conservancy promised to reopen navigation between Radcot and Newbridge by repairing Rushey Lock, but in 1874 they recognised that they lacked the funds to meet their promise. There were regular complaints at this time about the poor state of the river, particularly in upper reaches, and the persistence of sewage. Cummins and Quelch convinced the court that they had acted in ignorance of the law, and were let off with a fine of £1 and 18 shillings costs.

14 May

On this day in 1842, photographer Henry Taunt was born in Penson's Gardens, St Ebbe's, the son of a Bletchingdon plumber and glazier. Aged 14, Taunt joined the staff of Edward Bracher, commercial photographer, in High Street in Oxford. At 21, he married 26-year-old dressmaker Miriam Jeffrey. Five years later, in 1868, Taunt set up his own photographic business.

He operated from several premises in Oxford at various times, and also from his houseboat, becoming a familiar figure on the river in his nautical garb and yachting cap. In 1889 he leased what was then known as Canterbury House in the Cowley Road—then an isolated rural property—and extended it to become a photographic and printing base. He renamed the house 'Rivera' to reflect his love of the Thames, and moved in a Miss Fanny Miles, who had formerly kept a shop for him in High Wycombe.

He is regarded as the finest local photographer of Victorian and Edwardian times. Upon his death in 1922, Taunt left his entire estate to Fanny Miles, though his wife Miriam was still alive and lived for another seven years.

15 May

On this day in 1355, King Edward III issued a licence to Nicholas Jurdan, a Bicester hermit, to found 'again' (*de novo fundare*) a hospital connected with the chapel of St John the Baptist, of which he was warden. Jurdan was to endow the hospital with rent from land to the value of 100 shillings a year for the relief of the poor and for the maintenance of a chaplain forever.

Evidently this was not the beginning of the hospital—it was already in existence. Jurdan was its warden, and the chapel of St John was its chapel. But now it was to be endowed. The chaplain was to celebrate divine service daily for the salvation of Edward, his wife Queen Philippa, and of their son Edward, the Black Prince (born at Woodstock, and by now 25).

Hermits might be men of humble origins, without the education or financial means for a career in the priesthood or monastery, who nevertheless felt called to a life of religious devotion and public service. They were generally engaged in what we would now think of as 'public works'—mending roads, maintaining bridges, manning lighthouses and ferries. Such activities were supported not by public levy but by the charity of the faithful. There is no evidence that the plans for a hospital near the chapel of St John were ever carried through, and we do not hear any more of an endowed hospital at Bicester. Sheep Street was formerly known as 'St John's Street', suggesting that the chapel of St John the Baptist stood either in or next to it.

16 May

On this day in 1931, theoretical physicist Albert Einstein lectured at Rhodes House in Oxford. In the years before the war the University offered sanctuary to several Jewish academics fleeing Nazi Germany. Nobel Prize winner Einstein was the first German-Jewish scholar to take up an academic post at Christ Church. He arrived in May 1931 and was soon afterwards offered a studentship (fellowship) at the college, with an emolument of £400 a year.

Einstein's studentship was scheduled to last five years. However, he left after only two. Then, even more concerned about the Nazi threat since Hitler's election as Chancellor of Germany, he departed for Princeton. He asked that his annual £400 be used to assist other Jewish emigrées.

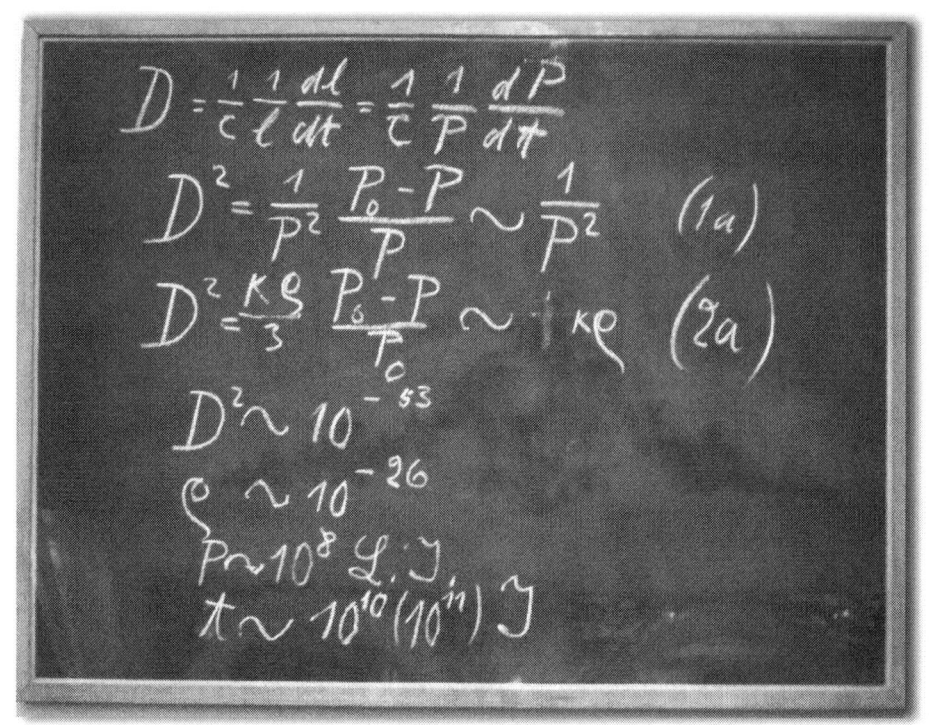

$$D = \frac{1}{c}\frac{1}{l}\frac{dl}{dt} = \frac{1}{c}\frac{1}{P}\frac{dP}{dt}$$

$$D^2 = \frac{1}{P^2}\frac{P_0-P}{P} \sim \frac{1}{P^2} \quad (1a)$$

$$D^2 = \frac{K\rho}{3}\frac{P_0-P}{P_0} \sim \frac{1}{3}K\rho \quad (2a)$$

$$D^2 \sim 10^{-53}$$

$$\rho \sim 10^{-26}$$

$$P \sim 10^8 \, L.J.$$

$$t \sim 10^{10}(10^{11}) \, J$$

The blackboard Einstein used on 16 May 1931

Einstein's appointment at Oxford exposed the ambivalent attitude in England to the business of helping persecuted Germans. When the dean of Christ Church, Henry White, offered Einstein his research studentship, he immediately received a letter from a fellow don branding Einstein's appointment 'unpatriotic', and stating that the college founders had never intended emoluments to go to foreigners. The objector wrote: 'The University cannot carry on its work without a very large Government grant, and yet a college can pay out money to subsidise a German.'

In reply, Dean White emphasised the trans-national nature of scientific and intellectual endeavour: '[Einstein's] attainments and reputation are so high that they transcend national boundaries, and any university in the world ought to be proud of having him.'

17 May

On this day in 1941, Oxford student John Fulljames penned a note to a friend. 'Thank you very much for your invitation and I'm sorry if you have ordered my dinner for nothing, but I'm afraid I won't be able to come to Oriel tonight,' he wrote. 'Unforeseen and pressing engagements will detain me.'

A few hours later, 19-year-old Fulljames loaded a rifle, leaned out of an upstairs window overlooking University College's quadrangle and opened fire on fellow undergraduates walking below. Charles Moffat was shot in the neck and abdomen, killing him immediately. Two more students were badly wounded. All three victims were members of a particularly boisterous clique which Fulljames resented. He then approached the dean, who asked him if he knew which room the shots came from. 'I'm afraid they came from mine,' Fulljames replied. 'Do you know who had the gun?' 'I'm afraid I did. What do you want me to do, sir?'

He had been a quiet young man with an excellent academic record, who had recently become moody and apathetic as the bombs rained down on Britain during the autumn of 1940 and the winter and spring of 1941. He was described by his closest friend as being 'very worried about the war'. Fulljames was by no means the only otherwise law-abiding person to crack. For many people, the appalling mental strain of the war was too much to bear.

Fulljames was spared the death penalty by Stafford Assizes on the grounds of insanity and committed to Broadmoor, but released in 1945. He died in Cardiff in 2013 at the age of 90.

18 May

On this day in 1743, highwayman Mansell Sansbury committed his last crime. *Aris's Birmingham Gazette* tells us that: 'The Birmingham Stagecoach was robb'd about 2 miles from Banbury, and about one hour after the robbery was committed, the noted Sansbury and his accomplice, who have infested these Roads were taken, being drunk, and asleep among the standing corn.'

The Sansburys were hard-working Banbury tradesmen: mercers, bakers, grocers; his father was even described as a 'gentleman'. Mansell himself traded as a grocer. At just 20 years old, Mansell ran off with Margaret Allington, an apothecary's daughter. And exactly nine months after the marriage at St Aldate's in Oxford, a baby was born. Sadly little Samuel Sansbury's time on this earth was brief: Mansell and Margaret's son died at just eight days old. Was this the point at which Mansell Sansbury began to go off the rails?

Highway robbery

It was market day in Banbury when Sansbury lay in wait by the road at Bodicote for the coach returning from London. Following the successful hold-up, Sansbury sensibly settled down in a cornfield to lie low until the heat was off. One of the items purchased in London by the travellers in question on that day turned out to be brandy, so he celebrated his success with enough drink to send himself off to sleep. Sansbury was taken into custody until the Buckingham assizes in July, where he was sentenced to death and hanged the next morning at 7 o'clock. He was 26.

19 May

On this day in 1921, Christ Church student Michael Llewellyn-Davies drowned in Sandford Lasher, a pool of water downstream of a weir near Sandford Lock. His friend and possible lover Rupert Buxton died with him.

Michael was the youngest boy in the Llewellyn-Davies family, and the favourite of *Peter Pan* author J M Barrie, who befriended the family in 1897. A version of the relationship is portrayed in the 2014 film *Finding Neverland*.

Two paper-mill workers were at the weir, regulating the water for the mill, when they saw the men in difficulties in the pool. Unable to swim (not unusual at the time), they threw in a life-belt, then one ran to Radley College boathouse to get help before telephoning the police. Some students came back with a boat, but it was too late. There was no sign of either Michael or Rupert, and the young men's bodies were not recovered until the following afternoon.

Davies' brothers later acknowledged a suicide pact as a likely explanation, as did Barrie. Davies had a fear of water and could not swim effectively. Dangerous currents in Sandford Lasher had made the pool notorious as a drowning hazard—there were warning signs and a conspicuous 19th-century memorial to previous victims. A witness reported that, when he saw their heads together in the water, the men did not appear to be struggling. And when the bodies were recovered the next day, they were reportedly clasped together.

20 May

On this day in 1908, Iffley mill burned down and has never been rebuilt. Lincoln College had rented the mill to Joe Wilson, the village schoolmaster and lay clerk of St John's College. He lived in the house and sub-let the working mill. That day, Mr Wilson and the miller had closed the mill at midday and travelled by train to Abingdon agricultural show. Returning just after 6pm, the two men admired the ancient mill from the train. An hour later, walking through the streets of Oxford, they picked up talk of Iffley mill being on fire. Neither man could believe it—they had seen no sign of trouble from the train. However, they hurried home and found that the story was true.

The alarm had been raised by a man passing over the toll bridge near the mill. But it was too late. Within minutes, flames had broken through the roof and the whole building was ablaze. Mrs Wilson, who was disabled, was rescued by those first on the scene. The fire brigade soon arrived, but could do nothing except save some furniture from the house.

Hopes that the mill might be rebuilt after the fire were dashed when it became clear that the insurance had lapsed through a misunderstanding when Mr Wilson had sub-let the premises. Now the only reminders of the mill are two millstones, a plaque on a wall and the hundreds of pictures painted by artists over the years.

21 May

On this day in 1947, Oxfordshire-born author Flora Thompson died. Best known for her semi-autobiographical trilogy about the English countryside, *Lark Rise to Candleford*, Thompson was born Flora Jane Timms in Juniper Hill in northeast Oxfordshire, the eldest child of a stonemason and nursemaid. The young Flora's early education was at the parish school in the village of Cottisford where she was described as 'altogether her father's child'. In 1891, at the age of 14, Flora took up a position at the post office in Fringford, a village about 4 miles from Bicester, under postmistress Kezia Whitton.

In 1938 Thompson sent some essays on her country childhood to Oxford University Press. They were accepted and published in three separate volumes, *Lark Rise* (1939), *Over to Candleford* (1941), and *Candleford Green* (1943). In 1945 the books were republished as a trilogy under the title *Lark Rise to Candleford*. The trilogy is a lightly-disguised story of the author's own youth, describing life in a hamlet, a village, and a country town in the 1880s.

22 May

On this day in 1554, Princess Elizabeth was moved from the Tower of London to Woodstock Palace. There she would spend almost a year under house arrest. Crowds cheered her all along the way.

Elizabeth had been imprisoned in the Tower since 18 March on suspicion of being involved in Sir Thomas Wyatt's rebellion against Mary and her proposed marriage to the Catholic Philip I of Spain. Elizabeth was closely interrogated and in danger of execution, but was spared due to her evasive and intelligent responses; she maintained that she had been unaware of the planned uprising. Nothing could be proved, but the degree to which she was privy to the preparations has been questioned by modern scholars. Elizabeth remained

Woodstock Palace

imprisoned as a precautionary measure. Wyatt and his co-conspirators were executed. The rebellion proved disastrous for the Wyatt family, as they lost their title and lands, including the family home, Allington Castle.

On 17 April 1555, Elizabeth was recalled to court to attend the final stages of Mary's apparent pregnancy. When it became clear that Mary was not pregnant, Elizabeth returned to her own home at Hatfield Palace in October. On 6 November, Mary recognised Elizabeth as her heir. On 17 November 1558, Mary died and Elizabeth succeeded to the throne.

23 May

On this day in 1887, Milton-under-Wychwood builder's labourer Robert Upton, 61, battered his wife to death with an iron bar. During the day, he had been working at Shipton Court for local builder Alfred Groves. Having knocked off at 5pm, Upton and some colleagues popped in to the Crown (now the Shaven Crown) for a beer.

When he arrived home at 6pm, an argument broke out between Upton and his 66-year-old wife Emma. Groves' carter Alfred Miles saw Emma burst out of her cottage. 'Here, Alfred, come and hear his prayers [ie, curses],' she called. 'He's going to kill me with an iron bar.' 'All a pack of nonsense,' Miles replied, and Emma returned home. But she was soon rushing across the yard again. Upton himself then erupted out of his cottage brandishing an iron bar and in hot pursuit of Emma. Miles seized the iron bar, whereupon Upton grabbed his wife and punched her. The pair fell to the ground, scuffling, and Upton banged poor Emma's on the ground. Eventually they got up and went back inside.

But then, for a third time, Emma ran out followed by her husband with his iron bar. By this time Alfred Groves was watching too. Upton chased his wife as far as the street, and struck her on the face with the bar. She fell on to her back, her face disfigured and streaming with blood. Upton continued striking her face until Groves rushed over and collared him, saying: 'You've killed her, Robert, at last,' Upton made no reply.

PC King arrived from Shipton and advised Upton that he would be charged with wilful murder. 'Is 'er dead?' the prisoner asked. When told that she was, he replied: 'A bloody good job too.'

Upton was hanged on Tuesday 17 July 1887.

24 May

On this day in 1884, a shocking incident of straw-hat theft took place late at night in St Aldate's. Christ Church undergraduate Spencer J Portal, 20, returned from a drive in the countryside and stopped to talk to friends outside college at midnight. At 12.30 he saw Tom Gate closing, and made a rush to get through. In the same instant, somebody knocked his hat off. Three of Portal's friends gave chase and caught up with labourer Edward Legg in Brewer Street, who was holding the hat (value three shillings).

Legg, who lived in Coach and Horses Yard off Queen Street, asked them whose hat it was, and they accused him of picking it up and running off with it. Legg, on the other hand, claimed that he was simply walking down St Aldate's, came across the hat, and picked it up. When Portal's friends, who included 22-year-old Lord Henry George Grosvenor, overtook him, he gave up the hat.

Portal's father was a manufacturer of paper for banknotes, a trade which was presumably lucrative, since the family lived in Eaton Square with a staff of 17. Spencer J Portal died a baronet in 1955, leaving an estate worth more than £22,000. Grosvenor was son of the Duke of Westminster of Eaton Hall, Cheshire and Grosvenor House, one of the largest private townhouses on Park Lane. The bench, which included the Master of Pembroke College and the Warden of All Souls, chose to believe the University men. Legg was fined two shillings with 18 shillings costs, or seven days' imprisonment in default.

25 May

On this day in 1830, 'one of the best and fairest "mills" [boxing matches] on record'—according to *Jackson's Oxford Journal*—took place near the Four Shire Stone between Chipping Norton and Moreton-in-Marsh. The combatants were Perkins, the 'Oxford Pet', and Alic Reid, the 'Chelsea Snob', and the purse was £100 a-side.

By midday thousands of spectators had assembled to hear a bugle announce the arrival of Perkins. Soon afterwards a carriage-and-four arrived bearing Reid. Perkins was attended by Stockman and Harry Jones, the Snob by Young Dutch Sam and Dick Curtis. Perkins and his team wore dark pink, the Snob and his followers sported crimson. The Oxford Pet weighed in at 10 stone

3 pounds, the Snob at 10 stone 7 pounds. At the commencement of the bout, the betting was 7 to 4 on the Snob. The fight lasted an hour and went to 54 rounds.

Perkins acquitted himself well right up to the 50th round, but by then his right eye was closed up, his left eye swollen and cut underneath. In the 54th round he dropped down from weakness, and his corner gave in. *Jackson's Oxford Journal* was loyal in its verdict on the local man: 'It was impossible for a beaten man to have done more to deserve the respect and approval of his backers.'

26 May

On this day in 1900, Bladon labourer William Franklin, 29, attempted to murder his wife Sarah with a cudgel while she slept in bed. The Franklins' marriage had never been a happy one; Sarah, a gloveress, was somewhat older than her husband at 36, and she already had three children from her first marriage. Together with William and Sarah's own three children, this made eight people crammed in to a two-up, two-down cottage in the centre of a row of three in Providence Place. Or at least it did until 1 May, when the couple buried their 4-month-old baby boy, William, whom they had hastily baptised a few days before. And in the week prior to the murder attempt, Franklin had been bound over to keep the peace in the sum of seven shillings and sixpence following a previous assault on Sarah. This was the unfortunate background to events on that fateful Saturday night. Franklin arrived home and armed himself with a heavy wooden cudgel normally used for crushing potatoes for the pigs. He struck his wife a powerful blow on the back of her head.

Sarah shot out of bed and escaped from the house, taking refuge with a neighbour. She was taken from there to the infirmary at the Woodstock Union workhouse. Franklin, meanwhile, made his escape as far as Cassington. He was discovered on Sunday morning lying outside a barn where he had attempted to take his own life by cutting his throat with a razor. No artery was severed, however, and he was well enough to walk back to Bladon accompanied by Inspector Sorrell of the Woodstock police. The 1901 census finds him a resident in Parkhurst prison on the Isle of Wight, and by 1911 he was living alone in a cottage in his native Middle Barton. Sarah was by that time living back with her mother in Bladon, along with two of her children.

27 May

On this day in 1826, a mob tore down Bicester Town Hall and Shambles. Social unrest among the labouring poor of the area was not unusual. In Bicester, the poor were crowded into two parts of the town known as Crockwell and New Buildings.

In the first decades of the nineteenth century, the owners of the cottages in Crockwell attempted to increase the value of their properties, by subdividing the old buildings and increasing rents. Cottages consisting of at most two or three rooms frequently lacked a single foot of ground attached in which to grow vegetables. In 1831, the Sanitary Committee was moved to remark that the quarters inhabited by the poor were in 'a very unsatisfactory state'.

A severe cholera outbreak carried off 64 souls in the following year. Industry had never really taken off in the area, meaning that there were few employment opportunities outside agriculture. In his *History of the Present Deanery of Bicester, Oxon* (1884), James Charles Blomfield wrote: 'Under all these disadvantages of social evil the town continued its march of progress. The lapse of 160 years had rendered the Town Hall ruinous and unsightly, and the butchers, having established shops in their own houses, had ceased to use the Shambles. These were accordingly pulled down in 1826, but in a very lawless way; a mob being allowed to assault and destroy the old buildings, and to carry away whatever materials any one could appropriate. The Clock and Sundial and Weather-cock were alone preserved.'

In fact, the clock, sundial, and weather-cock had been removed to the house of a watchmaker a few days before, leaving the poor to make what pennies they could out of the remainder. The authorities responded to this 'lawlessness' by appointing a beadle in November the following year. Magnificently garbed in a blue coat with a red collar and cuffs and carrying a staff, he paraded the streets to guard against mischief-makers, and took them before the magistrate where necessary.

28 May

On this day in 1948, Hitler groupie Unity Mitford died, supposedly still with lead in her brain from shooting herself in the head. Unity was the fourth of the

Not a mark on her: Unity Mitford, after supposedly shooting herself in the head

six celebrated Mitford sisters born to Lord Redesdale of Asthall Manor near Burford and his wife Sydney.

In order to get one over on her beautiful elder sister, Diana, who had left her husband for the absurd Oswald Mosley, leader of the British Union of Fascists, dippy Unity determined to attach herself to Adolf Hitler. Weeks of making eyes at Hitler in his favourite café in Munich eventually paid off, and she was invited into his circle. Unity threw herself into the Nazi's propaganda effort, but she was never a match for glamorous Eva Braun.

On the day Hitler declared war on Britain, she was said to have taken the pearl-handed pistol given to her by Hitler to Munich's English Garden and shot herself in the temple. But photographs of Unity on her return to England show no wound to the temple. She was described by her family as 'childlike' as a result of brain damage, and unable even to walk. So how come police reports have Unity careering round the lanes of Oxfordshire, picking up airmen in her car? Were the gunshot story and Unity's dramatic repatriation on a stretcher cooked up by Lord Redesdale to avoid yet another Mitford daughter being interred as a Nazi sympathiser? On the other hand, there are still stories locally of Unity rambling round the lanes hugging a hot water bottle—a bit different from racing around chasing after pilots.

29 May

On this day in 1880, considerable excitement was created in Banbury when the body of a dead baby went missing and some very pleased-looking dogs arrived home.

Two days before, some children were playing by the canal when they spotted a lifeless child in the water. The body was removed to the loft of the Three Pigeons. Early on Monday morning it was brought down to the shed for the doctor to perform a post mortem. As the jury was due to follow later that morning for the inquest, the body was placed on a tea-tray and covered with a sack. An iron pig trough was inverted over the top.

An hour or so later, a man passing along Castle Street noticed a dog emerging from the shed with something in its mouth but, as it was the butcher's dog, he thought no more of it. A little after this, the dog from the Fir Tree Inn arrived home at the yard with something in its mouth too. Distressingly, it was found to be the child's head—and, since the rest of the body was never seen again, this was all the jury had to view when they met at the Three Pigeons at 11am.

The shaken attendees returned an open verdict on the infant, the doctor stating that the child was still-born.

30 May

On this day in 1942, Whitley bomber 4997 took off from RAF Stanton Harcourt as part of Operation Millennium, the first ever thousand-bomber raid. The target was Cologne. Piloted by Flt Lt Pete Daniels and with crew member Bob Pratt, the Whitley was one of 1,047 bombers that took part in the operation, two and a half times more than any previous RAF raid. Fifty-eight were from Polish units. The total tonnage of bombs dropped was 1,455 tons, two-thirds being incendiaries. Two and a half thousand separate fires were started with 1,700 classed by the German fire brigades as 'large'. The action of fire fighters and the width of the streets stopped the fires combining into a firestorm, but nonetheless most of the damage was done by fire and not directly by the explosive blasts. 3,330 non-residential buildings were destroyed, 2,090 seriously damaged and 7,420 lightly damaged, making a total of 12,840 buildings of which 2,560 were industrial or commercial buildings.

The damage to civilian homes, most of them apartments in larger buildings, was considerable: 13,010 destroyed, 6,360 seriously damaged, 22,270 lightly damaged. The number reported killed was between 469 and 486, of whom 411 were civilians and 58 combatants. 5,027 people were listed as injured and 45,132 as 'bombed out'. The RAF lost 43 aircraft (German propaganda claimed 44). Twenty-two aircraft were lost over or near Cologne, 16 shot down by flak, 4 by night fighters, 2 in a collision, and 2 Bristol Blenheim light bombers were lost in attacks on night-fighter airfields.

31 May

On this day in 1879, *Jackson's Oxford Journal* announced the discovery of the Cumnor dinosaur. Workmen at the Chawley brick pits at first tossed the remains onto a dump, but one of them later collected the bones in a sack and they were brought to the attention of palaeontologist Professor Joseph Prestwich who reported them as a new species of Iguanodon.

Prestwich cleaned the jawbone to reveal teeth that were very similar to, although smaller than, those of Iguanodon, a dinosaur which was then much in the news since the discovery eight years previously of 30 or so complete skeletons in a Belgian coal mine. The skeleton represents an animal about 3.5m long and about 1.2m high at the hip; it may be a juvenile. It probably walked mainly on the hind legs, which are longer and stronger than the front pair, though it could drop down onto all fours for ambling and feeding. The jaws have long tooth rows with strongly enamelled, ridged and serrated teeth, evidently intended to deal with vegetation. The holotype fossil of *Cumnoria prestwichii* can be seen in the Oxford University Museum of Natural History.

1 June

On this day in 1854, Oxford's first free public library in Oxford opened in the Town Hall. Free access to information and literature was considered desirable as a way of occupying and improving the minds of a working class with increasing free time as a result of a move off the land and towards shift-work. Victorian middle-class paternalism fostered the creation of libraries, rather than demand from the lower social orders. Campaigners felt that encouraging the lower classes to spend their free time on morally uplifting activities such as reading would promote greater social good.

Oxford's first librarian was Benjamin Blackwell. Judging by a recorded daily attendance of over 400, the library's handsome room on the ground floor of the Town Hall in St Aldate's Street must have been a welcome respite from the workplace, or from an over-crowded family kitchen. In its interior, there was, according to the 1863 *Directory and Gazetteer*, 'a neat little drinking fountain, affording copious libations of *acqua pura*'. During the first year, over 13,000 books were issued for reference, and the metropolitan and weekly newspapers it made available were widely read. The library moved into the new Town Hall in 1897, and to its current home at the Westgate Centre in 1973.

2 June

On this day in 1644, Parliamentarian General William Waller finally succeeded in forcing a passage over the Thames at Newbridge.

During the Civil War, Newbridge was strategically important; there was no other bridge until Radcot, Tadpole Bridge having been built only in 1802. In May 1644 the Parliamentarians hoped to surround Oxford and capture the king. Waller had already been forced back at Newbridge a few days before. In the words of Royalist-supporting newspaper *Mercurius Aulicus*: 'He had before attempted (upon Monday morning) to passe some of his forces over the Thames at a place called Newbridge, in the way betwixt Abingdon and Witney: which were so gallantly received by some of His Majesties Dragooneers, who lay there of purpose to guard that passe, that they were beaten back both with shame and losse before His Majesties Horse which were quartered about Charlbury, and had quickly taken the Alarme, could come in to help them. The shame of which repulse did so vex their Generall that finding in foure dayes no other way to vent his fury, he purposed to revenge himselfe upon Abingdon Crosse… which they most manfully assaulted and pulled downe to the ground.'

By 1 June, Waller had come up with a rather more subtle plan. Newbridge was manned by 90 to 100 Royalist musketeers. Their powder and shot ran out towards the evening on Saturday, so Waller sent a contingent across the river in boats a little way up from the bridge. They were able easily to approach the musketeers from behind and overpower them. Thirty or so Royalists were killed or captured. Royalist Sir Edward Walker recalled that: 'It was not long e'er certain Intelligence was brought that the Rebels of Waller's Army had passed over that Afternoon [Sunday] 5,000 Horse and Foot at Newbridge, and that some of them were advanced within three Miles of that place.'

3 June

On this day in 1900, little Bertie Rose was born in Chapel Lane in Standlake. But by the start of September, baby Bertie had starved to death. His parents William Rose, 40, and Rachel, 45, were charged with neglect at the autumn assizes in Oxford.

Charges of felonious killing and manslaughter had already been thrown out. Neighbour Ann Hughes was present at the birth, and she told the court that the baby was healthy up till mid-July, when Rachel had an epileptic fit. The doctor had advised that the baby be weaned, and so condensed milk was fed to Bertie from then on. Sarah Eaton said that by the end of August the child seemed ravenous. He was never clean.

On 29 August, an NSPCC inspector found Bertie lying on wet and foul-smelling rags in an old pram. The little boy was emaciated, and his bottle contained condensed milk which had gone sour. The inspector gave Rachel ninepence for food for the child, and called the poor-law doctor. Dr Oates said the child was just skin and bones, and not in a fit state to absorb food. The court was told that William Rose was 'partly imbecile' and Rachel was 'of weak mind' and subject to fits.

The jury acquitted the father and found the mother guilty, but recommended mercy on account of the state of her health. Having been remanded in prison for two months, Mr and Mrs Rose were sent home.

4 June

On this day in 1394, Mary de Bohun of Hinton Waldrist castle died. She was the first wife of King Henry IV and the mother of King Henry V.

Hinton Waldrist castle was originally a motte and bailey with a moat. The first castle was built of timber after the Norman conquest of England by the St Valery family, but the Bohuns rebuilt it in stone. Mary was the daughter of Humphrey de Bohun, 7th Earl of Hereford. Mary and her elder sister Eleanor were the heiresses of their father's substantial estates. Eleanor became the wife of Thomas of Woodstock, 1st Duke of Gloucester, son of Edward III. Eleanor and Thomas had the tutelage of Mary, who was being instructed in religious doctrine in the hope that she would enter a convent, and leave her share of the Bohun inheritance to Eleanor and Thomas.

In a plot with John of Gaunt, Mary's aunt took her from Thomas' castle back to Arundel whereupon she was married to Henry Bolingbroke, the future Henry IV. Mary gave birth to her first child, the future Henry V, in 1386, and Prince Henry visited Hinton Waldrist often as a child. But Mary was never queen; she died before her husband came to the throne.

5 June

On this day in 1830, there came the first signs of trouble that eventually led to the Otmoor Riots. As part of the final phase of enclosure, landlords began draining the marshes in 1829. The inhabitants of Beckley, Horton, Charlton, Fencot, Murcott, Oddington, and Noke had the right of grazing cattle, sheep, and horses on common land. Enormous flocks of geese and ducks were also reared. Agricultural labourers watched this vital additional source of income disappearing as the wetland dried.

Nocturnal raids to disrupt the drainage work started in 1829 and, on 5 June 1830, enclosure banks were attacked. Twenty-nine local farmers were charged with breaking the banks of the River Ray and flooding the lands of Sir Alexander Croke. The farmers pleaded that the banks were a public nuisance and they were acquitted.

The people of Otmoor took this as a signal that the whole enclosure was null and void, and that they could destroy fences and re-establish their rights of

Rural unrest in the 1830s

common. On some nights, up to 150 men set out to destroy hedges and stakes with their billhooks. They blackened their faces, wore women's cloaks and tied black scarves over their heads and armed themselves with billhooks, hatchets, pitchforks and staves. Attempts were made to keep the situation under control by stationing Coldstream Guards at Islip, 5th Dragoon Guards at Oxford, and a detachment of the 1st Life Guards at Oddington. Additional policemen were quartered in the villages—except in Charlton where no-one would offer them lodgings.

Everything came to a head on 6 September 1830, when about 1,000 people walked the seven-mile circumference of Otmoor in broad daylight, destroying every fence in their way. The Riot Act was read, and the Oxfordshire Yeomanry summoned. But the protesters refused to disperse and 66 people were arrested, 41 of whom were loaded aboard wagons to be taken to Oxford gaol, escorted by 21 yeomen. The detained men were not restrained so, when a mob attacked the escort with stones and bricks just outside the city, the prisoners escaped.

6 June

On this day in 1914 Barnett House in Oxford, named after Victorian philanthropist Samuel Barnett, was established for the study of contemporary social problems. Barnett and his wife Henrietta both inherited fortunes;

Barnett's family fortune was based upon the mass production of iron bedsteads, his mother's upon shipping, and his wife's upon the manufacture and retail of macassar oil, a popular hair conditioner.

The story of the Barnetts illustrates the extent to which Victorian philanthropy was funded by the rewards of manufacture and trade. They founded the Oxford University Settlement (Toynbee Hall) as a centre of education and 'practicable socialism' in the East End. 'Let university men become the neighbours of the working poor,' wrote Barnett, 'sharing their life... learning from them... and offering in response the help of their own education and friendship.' Where better, then, to start to bridge the gap than with the nation's future leaders among the undergraduates of Oxford? The couple took lodgings in Oxford during Eights Week in 1875.

Soon, among the strawberries and champagne, they had gathered a group of young people keen to experience at first hand life in the slums. From this initiative grew the idea of establishing Toynbee Hall in Spitalfields where generations of students and parishioners took part in programmes of classes, music, and entertainment.

7 June

On this day in 1876 Cowley Barracks opened. Known at first at Bullingdon Barracks because of its position on Holloway Road at Bullingdon Green, the barracks was a response to an increased emphasis on connecting British military forces with their local area as recommended under the Cardwell Reforms.

Twenty acres of land were acquired at a cost of £120 per acre, and the buildings were

Cowley Barracks: the keep

118

erected for £45,000. At first the barracks stood completely isolated in open countryside between the villages of Temple Cowley and Church Cowley. Signs of encroaching development came in the late 1920s with the building of the Bulan Road estate. The barracks closed down completely in 1966. Today the site of the keep has been redeveloped as student accommodation for Oxford Brookes University.

8 June

On this day in 1555 the will of Richard Beauforest of Dorchester was proved in which he gave the abbey church to the parish on condition that the parishioners did not sell or change the 'church implements' without the consent of his executors. Beauforest, a 'great rich man' of the town, had purchased the chancel from the king for £140 when the abbey was suppressed under the Reformation in 1536.

Modern archaeology is overturning old notions that the great Anglo-Saxon kingdom of Wessex always centred on Winchester. In fact, its original heartland lay in the Upper Thames between Dorchester and Abingdon. Landscape analysis has revealed an important routeway linking a great hall complex at Sutton Courtenay with another at Long Wittenham and with the episcopal seat at Dorchester-on-Thames. Dorchester was the seat of a bishopric from 634AD when Pope Honorius I had sent Saint Birinus, its first bishop, to the area to preach Christianity.

A Benedictine monk, Birinus persuaded the West Saxon king Cynegils to allow him to preach. Cynegils was trying to create an alliance with Oswald of Northumbria, with whom he intended to fight the Mercians. At the final talks between the two kings, the sticking point was that Oswald, being a Christian, would not ally himself with a pagan. Cynegils promptly converted and gave Birinus Dorchester-on-Thames for his episcopal see. Alexander, Bishop of Lincoln, founded Dorchester Abbey in 1140.

The church of Dorchester Abbey as it stands today was built entirely by the Augustinian canons, although there are traces on the north side of Saxon masonry, probably part of the ancient cathedral of Birinus. The Anglo-Saxon hall at Long Wittenham has been recreated by the Sylva Foundation on its original site using traditional techniques and methods.

9 June

On this day in 1890, Albert Brassey invited Charlbury residents to tour the grounds of his magnificent 18th-century home at Heythrop Park.

The Brassey family fortune had been amassed by Albert's father Thomas, a railway contractor. Thomas Brassey purchased the house in 1870 and presented it to Albert on the occasion of his marriage. The Brassey family went on to live at Heythrop in considerable style, as a report on the day in *Jackson's Oxford Journal* reveals. Mr Kench of the White Hart in Charlbury took two brake-loads of eager locals to the house where, 'upon arrival at the gardens the party were courteously shown through the splendid vineries, fernery, and peach and orchid houses which excited the admiration of all, and then through the flower garden to the aviary with it gold and silver pheasants, &c. The conservatory was the next attraction, one part of it especially—that assembling a tropical scene with its magnificent tree ferns, creepers, palms, &c., also decorated with beautiful statuary, adding to the grace of the scene. A lovely walk round the pleasure grounds brings the visitor to the new artificial rockery now almost completed, and which forms a most attractive feature, artificial streams falling over boulders of rock forming cascades, terraces planted with ferns and flowers, and a rocky cave which is designed to take the skeleton of a whale brought by Mr Brassey from Iceland. In the grounds are also beautiful lakes and six waterfalls.'

In the 1920s the house passed into the hands of the Jesuits, who sold it in 1969 to NatWest Bank to use as a training college and conference centre. It is currently a luxury hotel, golf and country club.

10 June

On this day in 1312, Piers Gaveston, favourite and rumoured lover of King Edward II, was abducted from the rectory at Deddington. He had been besieged at his castle in Scarborough, and surrendered on 19 May. The terms of the surrender were that the Earls of Pembroke, Warenne and Baron Percy would take Gaveston to York, where the barons would negotiate with the king. If an agreement could not be reached by 1 August, Gaveston would be allowed to return to Scarborough. The three swore an oath to guarantee his safety.

Gaveston was hauled out of bed in Deddington rectory

After an initial meeting with the king in York, Gaveston was left in the custody of Pembroke, who escorted him south for safekeeping, probably intending to arrange a meeting with the king, possibly in his own castle at Wallingford. Breaking the journey at Deddington on Friday 9 June, Pembroke left to visit his wife at Bampton castle, parking Gaveston at the rectory at Deddington, now known as Castle House. (Deddington castle was already in a state of decay, being described in 1277 as 'an old demolished castle' and in 1310 as 'a broken-down castle containing a chamber and a dovecote'.) Gaveston was left with only a small guard at the unfortified rectory. This later gave rise to suspicions, unjustified, that Pembroke had colluded in what happened next.

Early on Saturday morning Gaveston's oldest enemy, the earl of Warwick, 'black dog of Arden' as Gaveston rudely dubbed him, arrived at Deddington with a large force of men. He must somehow have got wind of Gaveston's presence there, suggesting that the stop at Deddington had been arranged at least some days before. Gaveston was led off to Warwick castle, humiliatingly on foot, though to speed things up he was soon plonked on an old nag. At Warwick, Gaveston was condemned to death before an assembly of barons for returning unlawfully from exile. On 19 June, he was taken out on the road towards Kenilworth as far as Blacklow Hill and executed.

11 June

On this day in 1258 King Henry III accepted a new form of government at the Oxford Parliament, also known as the Mad Parliament.

Henry's rule was increasingly unpopular, the result of the failure of his expensive foreign policies and the notoriety of his relatives, as well as the role of his local officials in collecting taxes and debts. The Welsh were in open revolt, and now allied themselves with Scotland—even the English Church had grievances over its treatment by the king. To compound the situation, the harvests in England failed. Within Henry's court there was a strong feeling that the king would be unable to lead the country through these problems.

Back in the spring Henry had asked parliament for yet more money to fight his endless wars and to pay his debts, so the barons, led by the king's brother-in-law Simon de Montfort, Earl of Leicester, took the opportunity to extract a concession from him for a commission of reform to deal with their concerns over the king's methods of governance. The result of the commission was the Provisions of Oxford, which placed power in the hands of a privy council of 15 members, including de Montfort, who were to supervise ministerial appointments, local administration and the custody of royal castles. Parliament, meanwhile, which was to meet three times a year, would monitor the performance of this council. Pressure from the lesser barons and the gentry present at Oxford also helped to push through wider reform, intended to limit the abuse of power by both the king's officials and the major barons.

Henry agreed to the terms, but his success in dividing the barons meant that the project never really got off the ground. In 1261, Henry revoked his assent to the Provisions of Oxford and de Montfort, in despair, left the country.

12 June

On this day in 1844, the Great Western Railway opened its branch from Didcot to a terminus in Grandpont. The line ran into Oxford through the area now occupied by Hinksey Park, along what is now the route of Marlborough Road, and terminated just south of the river.

Work had begun on the line, just under ten miles long, in the previous October, and a mild winter allowed it to be completed and opened to traffic by

The Great Western Railway station at Grandpont in Oxford

June 1844. A station at Didcot was also built to serve the line. Two days prior to the public opening of the railway a special train carried a party of notables, including Brunel himself, from London. The group arrived at Grandpont station at around 2pm and were taken over Folly Bridge by stagecoach to the Angel Inn on the High Street for a celebratory meal.

The opening of the line to the public on 14 June caused enormous excitement; great crowds gathered in areas adjacent to the railway. In Hinksey Field and South Hinksey a special gala day took place with marquees, tents and exhibitions; parties and celebrations went on late into the evening. *Jackson's Oxford Journal* reported that thousands of people watched enthralled as the first public train arrived: '… one of those rampageous, dragonnading fire-devils… arrived at a sufficiently astonishing rate, and though gasping for breath and shining with heat, seemed to have turned not one hair more than was deemed proper by each spectator, even after its long and whirlwind chase.'

13 June

On this day in 1893, writer Dorothy Sayers was born at the Headmaster's House, Brewer Street in Oxford. She won a scholarship to Somerville College, Oxford, and achieved first-class honours in 1915. Women were not awarded degrees at that time, but Sayers was among the first to receive a degree when the position changed a few years later; in 1920 she graduated MA.

Her experience of Oxford academic life eventually inspired her penultimate Peter Wimsey novel, *Gaudy Night* (1935). The issue of women's right to academic education is central to the book's plot. The lecturers of Shrewsbury College are veterans of the prolonged struggle for academic degrees for women, and aware of the disadvantages to this cause of bad publicity. From 1922 to 1931 Sayers worked as a copywriter at a London advertising agency. Her collaboration with artist John Gilroy resulted in the Guinness Zoo advertisements, variations of which still appear today. One famous example was the toucan, his bill arching under a glass of Guinness, with Sayers' jingle:

> *'If he can say as you can*
> *Guinness is good for you*
> *How grand to be a Toucan*
> *Just think what Toucan do.'*

14 June

On this day in 1814, the leaders of the major powers allied against France in the Napoleonic Wars visited Oxford as part of their victory tour following the signing of the Treaty of Fontainebleau and the exiling of Napoleon. The Prince Regent, Tsar Alexander I of Russia and king Frederick William III of Prussia, believed that, with Napoleon banged up on Elba, the whole business was done and dusted, and they could afford to relax and swagger about a bit. The Prince Regent, particularly, was convinced that he personally had vanquished the Emperor, not Wellington—even though he was the only one of the three leaders never to have set foot on a battlefield.

Arriving at midday, the Prince Regent alighted from his carriage on Magdalen Bridge and proceeded up the High Street and on to the Divinity School on foot, with well-wishers crowded into every vantage point on pavements, in windows and even on rooftops. At around 1pm the Tsar and his sister arrived at Merton, the king of Prussia at Corpus Christi, and the Prussian Prince and Field-Marshal Blucher at Christ Church. After a quick snack, all the guests assembled at Christ Church to meet the Prince Regent. The party was conducted by the Chancellor on a tour of all the notable buildings of the University. At 7pm, a magnificent dinner was served in the Radcliffe Camera.

In order to allow the public to view the proceedings, a temporary staircase had been built to reach an upper window. The window had been converted into a doorway in to the gallery from where the people of Oxford could gaze down upon the splendours below. At 11pm the guests emerged into streets illuminated by lanterns and candles, creating what was then the unusual site of a city lit up against the night sky. On the following day the three triumphant rulers were awarded honorary degrees. At the very same time, rumours were beginning to circulate on Elba that Napoleon was making arrangements to leave the island. On 1 March 1815, he landed in France.

15 June

On this day in 1824 Lord Churchill's' gamekeeper James Millin, 30, was murdered by poachers in the Wychwood Forest. On the previous Whit Monday William James, a known poacher, had been accused by assistant keeper Bayliss of taking venison from the forest. When Bayliss was unable to appear in court on the due date, James Millin's brother Joseph went in his stead. The charge was dismissed.

In the ensuing weeks, William James was heard muttering darkly against Joseph Millin to the effect that he would as easily shoot Millin's head off as he would that of a fly. Pittaway was heard to say that he wouldn't mind doing the same. In the event, they killed Joseph's brother instead. James was found by his brother Joseph at around 9pm, lying on his back in Hensgrove Coppice, still alive but bleeding profusely from the thigh. Joseph saw William James and Henry Pittaway loitering about nearby. James Millin asked for water, and was then carried to South Lawn Lodge where he died at 11pm that evening.

The next day, Joseph Millin went back to the spot where he had discovered his brother, and found scorch marks from gunpowder in the bushes a few yards from where his brother lay. Two lead bullets were also located. Ten days after the shooting, Joseph Millin went to Pittaway's house and found a gun 'screwed just below the lock—a poacher's gun', he said. At the murder trial on 29 July, 30 witnesses were called, but James and Pittaway declined to speak. They were found guilty and hanged on 2 August, and buried in the same grave at Taynton the following day. William James, who probably fired the shots, was 48, Henry Pittaway was 27. Both were married men with families.

16 June

On this day in 1685, an army officer came to Oxford from London, accompanied by a drummer, recruiting troops. Five days previously, Charles II's illegitimate son James, Duke of Monmouth, had landed with three ships at Lyme Regis in Dorset at the start of what became known as the Monmouth Rebellion.

Protestant Monmouth hoped to seize the throne from his Catholic uncle James II. He published a *Declaration for the defence and vindication of the protestant religion and of the laws, rights and privileges of England from the invasion made upon them, and for delivering the Kingdom from the usurpation and tyranny of us by the name of James, Duke of York*. The king's Foot Guards at Whitehall had been sent to deal with the threat, so replacements were sought in the regions. From Oxford they took between 30 and 40 volunteers—'the rusticks and tallest', according to antiquary Anthony Wood. Abingdon men were less inclined to fight for James—the town yielded only four volunteers. Three days later, the militia comprising a regiment of foot and a troop of horse met in Oxford. They left for Somerset at about 4am on 21 June, a Sunday, going via Dorchester and Abingdon.

Those suspected of sympathising with the rebels were rounded up and kept in the castle, including Thomas Hord of Cote near Bampton, Thomas Beard of Fritwell, and Rob Pawling, a Headington mercer. The rebellion failed, and Monmouth was beheaded for treason on 15 July 1685.

17 June

On this day in 1646, a ceasefire between Royalists and Parliamentarians was agreed at Unton Croke's house in Marston. Soldiers from the opposing armies made their way with all speed to the various city gates to get drunk together.

Unton Croke, the local grandee, made his manor house available to General Fairfax as his HQ in 1645. Cromwell himself is known to have visited the house at that time and is likely to have made other visits later as he was constantly present around Oxford during the siege. Terms respecting the ancient rights of Oxford and safeguarding the departing Royalist garrison were also agreed.

On the 20th the treaty was formally signed by Fairfax and Royalist Sir Thomas Glemham, governor of Oxford, in the Audit House at Christ Church.

Unton Croke's house at Marston near Oxford

Two days later King Charles I's nephews, Prince Rupert and Prince Maurice, were allowed to leave the city with 300 gentlemen. On 24 June the first 3,000 of the Royalist garrison marched out of the city with full military honours, as agreed. They were disarmed and disbanded at Thame and issued with passes from Fairfax guaranteeing their safety and liberty.

Although 2,000 passes were issued over a few days, a number of people had to wait their turn. Fairfax placed guards on the Bodleian Library to protect it against looting. On 25 June, the keys of the city were formally handed over to Fairfax; with the larger part of the regular Oxford garrison having left the day before, he sent in three regiments of foot soldiers to maintain order. The evacuation subsequently continued in an orderly fashion, and peace returned to Oxford.

18 June

On this day in 1879, Russian novelist Ivan Sergeevich Turgenev received an honorary doctorate at the Sheldonian. He was not just the first Russian novelist, but seemingly the first novelist of any nation to be so honoured.

A frequent visitor to England, Turgenev had many friends at Balliol—the college which took the lead in obtaining the doctorate for him. The Master of

Turgenev went down a storm with the ladies

Balliol, who entertained the reform-minded Turgenev, reported that the novelist gave him 'a terrible account of Russia: 26 or 28,000 of the best of the youth of the country in prison or on their way to Siberia—constitutionalists turning nihilists in their despair'.

Others stress his extraordinary charm. One memoirist recalls the impression the author made on her friend Mrs Evans, wife of the Master of Pembroke College: 'He was entertained on the eve of the ceremony at Pembroke College… The presence of the tall Russian amongst the University guests, his whole personality, made a great and sudden impression even on those to whom he was just a name. He spoke readily and with great cordiality; his English was exceedingly good, and the amenity of the foreign guest was felt by all… All the circumstances of that Commemoration have passed away from Mrs Evans's recollection. Only Tourguénieff remains, his look of power, and especially his wonderful eyes, which flashed as he spoke; these stay and cannot fade from the memory of anyone who conversed with him.'

19 June

On this day in 1509, a quarry in Headington was leased to provide stone for the new buildings at Brasenose College, and so this is the date which the college keeps as its foundation. Before the foundation of Brasenose College part of the site was occupied by Brasenose Hall, one of the medieval Oxford institutions which began as lodging houses and gradually became more formal places of learning. In 1333 a group of rebellious students attempted to migrate from Oxford to Stamford in Lincolnshire, and one supposedly took the door-knocker from the Hall. This bronze knocker, which some say gave the college its name, now hangs in the college's dining hall.

The college still observes a custom on Shrove Tuesday every year which goes back to the days when the assembled company was gathered around braziers in Hall, with smoke floating around in the open timber roof. Like most large private institutions and households, the college brewed its own beer and each year an undergraduate would write verses in praise of the new brew of Brasenose ale, usually well sprinkled with topical references to current events and to members of college. The verses were recited by the butler when he presented a brew of warmed beer with spices and apples. The oldest surviving verses date from the early 1700s and the sequence is almost complete from 1815. The verses came to an end when the college brewhouse was demolished in 1889, but the custom was revived in 1909, although the beer was no longer homemade.

20 June

On this day in 1852, kindly John Davey, 64, allowed some Irish travellers to sleep in his shed at Bridge House in Dorchester, providing straw for their beds.

During the night four men, evidently the worse for drink, came upon the sleeping wayfarers and attacked Margaret Donovan 'in a shameful and disgusting manner'. When Mrs Donovan's husband Dennis and their friend Patrick Bryant endeavoured to rescue her, they were subjected to a violent beating.

When news spread of the incident the following day, it caused a sensation throughout the town, and the four men disappeared. However, two of them—John Higgins and George Greenaway—were swiftly traced to London and brought back to answer the charge against them. On the 26th, the magistrates at Oxford fined each man £5 or two months' imprisonment for each of the three assaults, meaning a total of £15 or six months in gaol for each man. Neither man could find £15, so both went to prison. The other two men involved in the attack were never identified.

21 June

On this day in 1867, workman William Miller of Boar Street, 48, was called in to investigate why the water was 'bad' in the new well at the Queen's Hotel on

Abingdon market square. A lighted candle was lowered repeatedly down into the well, and always went out at the same point—where the walls broadened out from the narrow neck. No damage could be seen to the walls of the well, but there were fragments of something floating on the surface of the water.

Miller said he would go down and remove them, since the well might not be opened again for a while. Having collected the floating objects, Miller was on his way back up the ladder when his hands began to shake. He turned blue around the mouth and eyes, and dropped like a stone into the water without uttering a word. A rope was immediately lowered down to him but, although he managed to grasp it, his hands had lost all strength and could not hold on.

William Wiblen, an employee of the hotel's landlord, was then let down the well by the same rope. When he got to the point where the candle had always gone out, he felt a tingling sensation in his eyes and a feeling of helplessness. He was pulled back up without delay.

Wiblen reported that Miller's head was out of the water, so he could not have drowned. After a few more attempts, the body was retrieved. That afternoon the inquest jury returned a verdict that the deceased was killed by inhaling 'carbonic acid gas' (carbon dioxide). Miller left a pregnant widow, Sophia, and six children, and all but one of the jurors surrendered to Mrs Miller their shilling fee.

22 June

On this day in 1964, the Rolling Stones grudgingly played the Magdalen College Commemoration Ball. The band was little known when the booking was made in 1963, but by the time of the ball they had charted with *Come On*, *I Wanna Be Your Man* (written by John Lennon and Paul McCartney) and *Not Fade Away*. The Rolling Stones were obliged to fork out £1,500 in return air fares from America to honour a booking made for a fee of £100.

Guests at the ball had to push their way to the marquee through crowds of young girls chanting, 'We want the Stones', alternating with screams. Fans clambered over the walls and scampered around tripping over guy ropes trying to evade the police. To one officer they sang 'We Love You, Policeman,' and 'We Love You, Sergeant' as he stolidly carried on with his duties. After trying to mob two lesser-known groups, including Oxford's Falling Leaves,

Mick fires up the boys at the Magdalen College Commemoration Ball in 1964

the teenagers missed the Rolling Stones completely. They had slipped past the crowd one at a time, mingling with the ordinary guests.

So disgruntled was the band about being forced to honour their one-hour booking that they ungraciously spent the first 40 minutes tuning up. Bass player, Bill Wyman, had to use one of the Falling Leaves' amplifiers because his own had packed up. Brian Jones was reportedly zonked out of his mind. They were hissed and booed at first, which apparently delighted them. But when the ever-professional Mick Jagger snapped into action, they all did. By that time the tent was so tightly jammed with people that it was standing room only—no room for dancing.

23 June

On this day in 1880, a terrific thunderstorm storm raged over the village of Over Norton. Edwin Betteridge, a 37-year-old loom-tuner at the blanket mill of Messrs Bliss, spent the evening laughing and joking with his neighbours. At twenty minutes to ten he popped round to George Payne's beerhouse in Payne's Square on Choicehill Road where his wife Elizabeth had sought company during the storm. Just as he reached Payne's doorway, he was struck by lightning and dropped to the ground. Baker Thomas Jarvis and another neighbour, Mrs Hayden, wife of the blacksmith, carried him into Payne's, where Mrs Hayden attempted to revive him. But within minutes he died with his head resting on Mrs Hayden's arm. Surgeon Mowbray Jackson examined the body the following morning and found scorch-marks extending from Betteridge's left ear all the way down his back and reaching as far as both legs.

His widow Elizabeth was left with two children, Mary Ann, 8, and Ernest, 6. The little family moved to Chipping Norton and found a home in King's Head Yard. Elizabeth took up work as a weaver.

24 June

On this day in 1832, cholera broke out in Oxford. A warning was posted up in the early summer: 'If any one is seized with sickness, slight vomiting, and purging, a burning heat at the stomach, with cramp in various parts of the body, and a feeling of cold all over, it probably is the Cholera'.

A temporary hospital was built at Pepper Hill, and Bartlemas at Cowley became a house of recovery. A House of Observation was established in St Aldate's, to which those in danger were encouraged to go whilst their homes were fumigated. A notice of 2 August bade them: 'Look to Godfrey's Row—look to Bull Street—and learn from their afflictions a lesson profitable to yourselves. Like you, they tarried too long in the midst of disease, and, sooner than quit their habitations, many sickened and died.'

Insanitary conditions including open drains were recognised as the principal cause. Chloride of lime was recommended as a disinfectant and a quantity was purchased from High Street druggist R T Jones and distributed to the various parish authorities in the city. A leaflet was addressed 'To the Dwellers in narrow Courts and Alleys, and all other confined situations' by 'A Well-wisher to the Poor Man's Health'. It urged people to 'White-wash your Houses. Put an end to foul smells. Throw Lime or Lime-water into or upon the matters that produce them; and as we may expect close and sultry weather, make every thing sweet and cleanly, and without loss of time'.

By the end of November there had been 184 cases in Oxford, with a mortality rate of 52 per cent.

25 June

On this day in 1879, the grist mill at Little Clanfield was sold to the Ecclesiastical (later Church) Commissioners. Since the 1640s, or even earlier, the mill had been in the hands of the Blagrove family, many of whom were resident millers grinding corn into flour and animal feed. A tenant secured repairs in 1769, when the mill buildings were allegedly near collapse.

In 1879 John Blagrove retired and moved out, along with his two spinster sisters, and William Baston and his family moved in from Hardwick near Ducklington. In 1879 the Little Clanfield mill drove two pairs of stones, increased to three by 1895 when steam was introduced to supplement inadequate water power during dry periods.

During the early 20th century trade diminished, and in 1925 the mill was refitted as a straw-rope factory.

26 June

On this day in 1851, Joseph Caudwell, 41, aimed out of the window of his house on Folly Bridge and shot graduate Alexander Henry Ross, 22, with a blunderbuss, injuring the Christ Church man in the neck, ear, hand and foot.

The remarkable castellated house at 5 Folly Bridge, originally known as North Hinksey House, was erected in 1849 for money-lender and debt-collector Joseph Caudwell. Caudwell had made his fortune from lending small sums at interest to undergraduates at the University, men who by definition were under-age. Unsurprisingly, 'Caudwell's Castle' soon attracted unwanted attention from high-

Caudwell's Castle

spirited University men, such as those who tried on that June night in 1851 to up-end the cannons that sat on the forecourt.

Ross was taken back to his lodgings for medical attention. An hour later, some of Ross's fellow students went to the house and broke a window. At his subsequent trial Caudwell was found not guilty after his counsel made much of the malicious intent of the students who 'after luxuriating at a cricket club supper at the Maidenhead, smoking cigars and drinking beer, sallied forth, and in order to fill up or rather to kill time, proceeded to this man's house for wanton mischief...'.

The following day, Caudwell was found guilty of perjury in a separate case of money-lending and sentenced to seven years' transportation. He did not appear in court, although he was seen in Oxford during the day. In anticipation of the verdict, he transferred all his property in to the hands of his son Francis and disappeared. He died in Boulogne in 1893.

27 June

On this day in 1870, nine-year-old Julia Ann Crumpling of New Yatt was tried for stealing a pram from Mr and Mrs Edmund Smith of Witney, who had left it outside her front door in the High Street.

Scullery maid Annie Sherborne encountered Julia with the pram and claimed that the girl said: 'Just look at the perambulator my mother has bought from Mrs Bew for 12 shillings; put your baby in it and let it have a ride.' Evidently a suspicious Sherborne informed the authorities because a while later Sgt Morgan arrived and asked where the perambulator had come from. Julia claimed that her mother had bought it in Witney on the previous day.

This story was not believed, and the court ordered that she be detained in gaol for seven days in order that the chaplain might have an opportunity of talking with her. Thereafter she would be released on condition that her father promised to send her to school and look closely after her future conduct. Julia was placed in the prison's B Wing that housed women and teenagers. She would have been allowed one change of clothes a week and one bath. Interestingly, Julia's father John Crumpling, 51, was tried on the same day for receiving stolen goods, but the verdict was 'bill ignored', meaning that he was discharged for lack of evidence.

28 June

On this day in 1962, Sir Albert Richardson, architect, opened Vivien Greene's dolls' house museum at the Rotunda, Grove House, Iffley Turn. Mrs Greene had married novelist Graham Greene at St Mary's Catholic Church, Hampstead, in 1927, but the couple separated formally in 1948. After the family home in London was bombed during the war, Mrs Greene and her children removed to Oxford. At a local auction she came across a miniature, derelict Regency town house which she bought for £5 and took home on the bus with her.

As war raged and her marriage disintegrated, she restored and furnished the dolls' house, and began collecting others. After the marriage ended, she travelled the world to add to her collection, and in the 1960s Greene gave her the money to build the Rotunda as a dolls' house museum incorporating the spiral staircase from the St James's Theatre in London. The world-famous museum housed more than 40 antique dolls' houses dating from 1668 to 1886, some up to 6ft tall. The closure of the museum was announced in September 1998, when Mrs Greene explained that, at 94, she could no longer cope. The collection was auctioned off in London in the same year.

Sir Albert Richardson opens Vivien Greene's dolls' house museum in 1962

Cropredy Bridge

29 June

On this day in 1644, Charles I and General Sir William Waller came up against each other at the Battle of Cropredy Bridge. To avoid being surrounded in Oxford the king had marched his army out of the city, and the two armies eventually found themselves facing each other on opposite banks of the River Cherwell.

On the morning of 29th, Waller ordered his troops to cross the river at Cropredy Bridge and attack the rearguard of the Royalist army. It was an opportunistic strike, typical of Waller's style, against a Royalist army strung out in line of march. The battle extended over several miles, involving Slat Mill Ford as well as Cropredy Bridge, and extending across to the Northamptonshire border at Hay's Bridge near Chipping Warden. The Royalist dragoons were soon overpowered, but in crossing the river the Parliamentarian troops had also become vulnerable. The Parliamentarians were eventually beaten back across the river, abandoning eleven guns.

Now short of supplies and under cover of darkness, the Royalist army slipped away taking the captured guns with them. The Royalists had suffered just a few casualties, whilst Waller lost 700 men, including many deserters. Though the engagement itself was indecisive, the repercussions proved a massive setback for the Parliamentarian cause. Demoralised and dejected, the Parliamentarians now realised that part-time troops serving far from home were not going to win this war. The New Model Army was formed and took to the field for the first time the following year.

30 June

On this day in 1860, 'Soapy Sam' Samuel Wilberforce, Bishop of Oxford, spoke against Darwin's theory of evolution at the Oxford University Museum of Natural History. Fellow of the Royal Society Wilberforce—son of the abolitionist William Wilberforce—criticised Darwin's theory on scientific grounds, arguing that it was not supported by the facts, and he noted that the greatest names in science were opposed to the theory.

Nonetheless, Wilberforce's speech is generally remembered today only for his inquiry as to whether it was through his grandmother or his grandfather that Darwin-supporter Thomas Huxley considered himself to be descended from a monkey. Huxley is said to have replied that he would not be ashamed to have a monkey for his ancestor, but he would be ashamed to be connected with a man who used his great gifts to obscure the truth. The popular view was and still is that Huxley had got the better of the exchange.

However, historians agree that this story of the debate between Wilberforce and Huxley was a later fabrication and that it is impossible to know the precise details of the debate. 'Reports from the time suggest that everybody enjoyed himself immensely,' claimed Scottish explorer David Livingstone, 'and all went cheerfully off to dinner together afterwards.'

1 July

On this day in 1163, King Henry II summoned a Grand Council of bishops, barons and other magnates to his hunting lodge at Woodstock, the medieval forerunner of Blenheim Palace. The prime purpose for the council was for Henry to receive, in front of and witnessed by his vassals, homage from the Prince of Wales and Malcolm IV, King of the Scots. It was also at this Council that Henry proposed that the *auxilium vicecomitis* (Sheriff's Aid), raised by all sheriffs in the land, monies hitherto kept by them, should be paid over directly into the king's treasury and exchequer. Prior to his appointment as archbishop of Canterbury, Becket had been Chancellor at the king's Exchequer for several years.

It is almost certain that he would know intimately and specifically what rights the king did or did not have to raise taxes, and in what circumstances. So Becket opposed the proposal on the grounds that it was contrary to established custom.

A row ensued; it was the start of a major feud that would end with Becket's death in 1170.

2 July

On this day in 1631, Sir William Pope, Earl of Downe, died at Wroxton Abbey. Downe was responsible for initiating the building of the impressive house at Wroxton that still stands today. He built the 17th-century Jacobean manor on the foundations of a 13th-century Augustinian priory which was destroyed during Henry VIII's 1536 Dissolution of the Monasteries. Downe appears to have got little further than completing the central block, leaving the north wing unfinished at his death (the south wing was added in the mid-19th century).

While it is not clear why Sir William left the house incomplete it may be that the complications of the leasehold structure devised by his uncle discouraged too great a financial investment.

3 July

On this day in 1361, Princess Mary, daughter of Edward III, was married at Woodstock Palace at the age of 16 to John IV of Brittany, 22, (traditionally John V in Britain). The marriage was intended by Edward to create an alliance in support of his renewed claim to the French throne. The accounts for the wedding dress created by her tailor John Avery survive.

A gift from the king, the dress comprised a tunic and a mantle made from two types of cloth of gold: Racamatiz of Lucca and *baldekyn d'outremer*. The mantle must have been unusually long because seven pieces of cloth (45 ells, or about 68 feet!) were needed to make it. It was lined with 600 trimmed minivers (squirrel furs), a present from the king of France, and 40 ermine. Her situation did not change after marriage since she and her husband remained at the English court. Plans were made for when the couple to leave England and take up residence in Brittany as the recognised Duke and Duchess.

However, within a few months, Mary developed 'a lethargic disease from which it was impossible to rouse her', and she died sometime before 13 September 1361 without ever setting foot in Brittany or reaching her 17th birthday. She was buried in Abingdon Abbey in a tomb commissioned by Queen Philippa. Mary's husband referred to her as 'my late dearest companion'. They had no children.

4 July

On this day in 1931, Oxford Zoo opened on the site now occupied by Thames Valley Police headquarters in Kidlington. Animals were given by the London, Berlin, Bristol and Dublin zoos as well as many individual collectors, although some expected at the opening failed to arrive because of an outbreak of foot-and-mouth disease. The *Oxford Times* reported: 'During the last few days, exhibits have been arriving almost hourly and they have settled down in a way that suggests they have been lifelong inmates. Yesterday, a camel, lion, jackal and two wolves had been put in their quarters and the lion was at once so at home that he enjoyed a long sleep, from which he refused to be awakened by the incessant tapping of workmen's hammers. A family of baboons consists of father, mother and three sturdy youngsters, one of which was gravely grooming his grey-bearded father.'

Rosie the elephant was arguably the most famous animal at Oxford Zoo, but Hanno the lion was a favourite too. There were also monkeys, kangaroos, llamas, bears, rabbits, guinea pigs, birds and fish. The zoo became a popular weekend haunt for Oxfordshire people in the 1930s. On the first Sunday, more than 2,000 people flocked to the zoo. Admission was sixpence for adults and thruppence for children. The zoo had a short life. It closed in September 1936, and in 1937 the whole collection was moved to Dudley Zoo.

Rosie the elephant, star of Oxford Zoo

Execution of Catholics in 1589

5 July

On this day in 1589, Catholic priests George Nichols and Richard Yaxley, along with lay helpers Thomas Belson and Humphrey Pritchard, were hanged for celebrating mass at the Catherine Wheel Inn in Magdalen Street East.

Initially all four were sent to the Bridewell prison in London where Nichols and Yaxley were hung by their hands for up to 15 hours to make them betray their faith, but without success. The two priests were later moved—Nichols to the Tower of London, and Yaxley to the Gatehouse. On 30 June 1589 all four were ordered back to Oxford for their trial. The priests were condemned for treason, and the laymen for felony, and they were executed at the Holywell gallows, situated where Broad Street, Longwall Street, and St Cross Road meet. The heads of the priests were set up at Oxford Castle, and their quarters on the four city gates. The Catherine Wheel inn was demolished in two stages in 1720 and 1826 in order to expand Balliol College.

6 July

On this day in 1577, the Black Assize broke out in Oxford, a pestilence which claimed the lives of at least 300 people, including the Lord Chief Baron of the Exchequer, Sir Robert Bell, and the Lord High Sheriff, Sir Robert D'Oyly of Merton. The outbreak was so-named because it was believed to be associated with a notorious trial at the assize court at Oxford Castle that year.

Catholic bookseller Rowland Jenkes was tried and found guilty of distributing

Popish books. He was sentenced to have his ears nailed to the stocks, from which he was at liberty to cut himself free. His response to this was to place a curse on the courtroom and city.

Most of the fatalities in the subsequent contagion were said to be adult males, including some members of the jury. This encouraged the belief that Jenkes's curse was the cause. It seems more likely that these people died from 'gaol fever', or typhus, a bacterial infection spread by lice. It is common in the unsanitary, overcrowded prison conditions where prisoners often had to wait for the judge to arrive to hear their case. When the prisoners were finally brought up from the cells in front of the judge, typhus would spread from the gaol to the court, and hence into the general population.

A mass burial of some 60–70 people between the castle and the prison was excavated by archaeologists in 2004. The skeletons date to the right period, and most of the individuals are male, suggesting that at least some of them may be connected with the 1577 epidemic. From the mid-14th century until the second half of the 19th century, Oxford was regularly visited by plague, cholera, smallpox and typhoid fevers.

7 July

On this day in 1733, Handel debuted *Athalia*, his new oratorio specially written for the occasion, at the Sheldonian Theatre in what was one of the few great events in the musical history of the 18th-century University. Tickets were five shillings, a copy of the great man's book ('not worth one penny', according to the irascible Oxford diarist and antiquary Thomas Hearne) would have set you back one shilling.

The composer's trip to Oxford coincided with the so-called 'Oxford Act', the University's annual graduation ceremony for masters of arts and the higher doctorates—now known as the 'Encaenia'. But if Handel himself was offered an honorary doctorate, he declined.

At that time the Act usually involved a short season of dramatic performances given by one of the London theatre companies. However, the presence in 1733 of Handel and 'his lowsy Crew', as they were famously dubbed by Hearne, caused all available accommodation to be snapped up, and the actors were denied access to the city. They were obliged to perform in Abingdon instead.

Gill & Co ironmongers at Carfax

8 July

On this day in 2010, Gill & Co, Oxford ironmongers in High Street, shut down after 480 years' trading.

King Henry VIII was on the throne when Gill & Co became the country's first ironmongers in Oxford in 1530. The independent shop had been in business ever since, trading six days-a-week through the reigns of 20 monarchs and 76 prime ministers.

It originally opened in 1530 off Cornmarket. Surviving the English Civil War, two world wars, two depressions and three recessions, Gill & Co finally hung up its pots and pans, beaten by the recession and the onward march of out-of-town superstores like B&Q and Homebase.

Gill & Co originally provided ironware for local residents, and through the centuries it stocked chimney-sweep brushes, scythes, iron nails and hay rakes. It tried to move with the times and in its final years the shelves boasted a range of household items including tools, tin tacks, lightbulbs, compost, charcoal and rat repellent.

The shop operated from a number of different locations in and around the High Street over the years, including the Crown Inn passageway and 4–5 High Street, before moving to its final base 50 years ago. It was a great favourite of college handymen.

On the positive side, Gill & Co still enjoys a flourishing trade in Chipping Norton.

9 July

On this day in 2010, Russian agent Sergei Skripal landed at RAF Brize Norton as part of a spy swap between the United States and Russia. At the time, much of the media focus was on Anna Chapman, the glamorous young wife of a British psychologist, who was among ten deep-cover operatives being sent back to Russia in the same exchange.

But on 4 March 2018, Skripal, a former Russian army officer and double agent for MI6, was found alongside his daughter Yulia, 33, both slumped on a bench near a shopping centre in Salisbury. The 66-year-old and his daughter had been poisoned with a nerve agent called Novichok, in what is believed to have been a Russian assassination attempt. Both Sergei and Yulia survived the attack. On 30 June 2018, a similar poisoning of two British nationals in Amesbury, seven miles from Salisbury, involved the same nerve agent. Charlie Rowley found the nerve agent in a perfume bottle and gave it to Dawn Sturgess, who sprayed it on her wrist. Sturgess fell ill within 15 minutes and died, but Sturgess survived. British police believe this incident was not a targeted attack, but a result of the way the nerve agent was disposed of after the poisoning in Salisbury.

Chapman and nine other sleeper agents were charged with 'carrying out long-term, deep-cover assignments in the United States on behalf of the Russian Federation'. The ten Russian agents returned to Russia via a chartered jet that landed at Vienna, International airport where the swap was effected.

Spy Anna Chapman

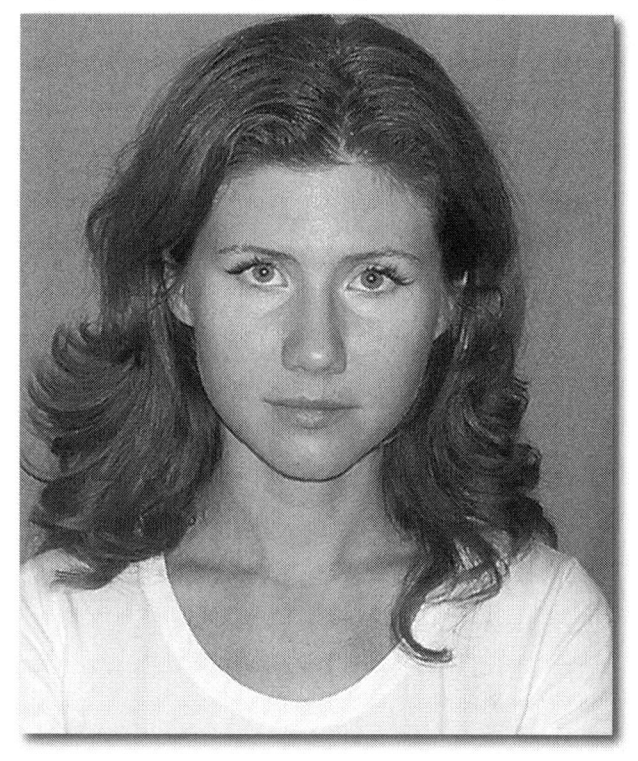

Human dissection

10 July

On this day in 1815, Shillingford butcher James Bannister was executed for cutting his wife Charlotte's throat. He had also attempted to cut his own throat, but failed. It was not the first time he had attempted suicide, and financial problems may have been the cause. Bannister, the owner of 71 acres with accompanying properties in Shillingford, Warborough and Benson, had gone bankrupt.

Part of his punishment was that his body would be used for anatomical dissection, a fate worse than death itself according to prevailing religious belief. But the 18th century had seen important changes in British medicine. The old trade of barber-surgeon had been slowly transformed into a science based on research carried out in the dissecting room.

The Murder Act of 1752 permitted that the bodies of murderers be dissected after death to contribute to medical knowledge that would benefit the living. After the criminal was hanged, medical students would be there as the criminal was taken down from the gallows and would argue over who would dissect the body, making the anatomist as feared as the executioner himself.

With the passing of the 1832 Anatomy Act the legal acquisition of bodies for dissection was expanded to include the unclaimed bodies of those dying in hospitals and in the workhouse. For the poor it only intensified the fear and shame of dying in the workhouse.

11 July

On this day in 1918, Venetia Burney was born in Headington. At the age of 11, she is said to have suggested the name Pluto (Roman God of the Underworld with the handy ability to make himself invisible) for a newly-discovered planet.

Burney was the granddaughter of Falconer Madan, librarian at the Bodleian. Falconer Madan's brother, Henry Madan, science master of Eton, had in 1878 suggested the names Phobos and Deimos for the moons of Mars. On 14 March 1930, Falconer Madan read in *The Times* of Clyde Tombaugh's discovery of a new planet, and mentioned it to his granddaughter Venetia. She suggested the name Pluto, the Roman God of the Underworld who was able to make himself invisible. Falconer Madan forwarded the suggestion to astronomer Herbert Hall Turner, who cabled his American colleagues at Lowell Observatory. Clyde Tombaugh liked the proposal because it started with the initials of Percival Lowell who had predicted the existence of Planet X, which they thought was Pluto because it was coincidentally in that position in space.

On 1 May 1930, the name Pluto was formally adopted for the new celestial body. Whether Burney was really the first person to propose the name has been doubted on plausibility grounds, but she is credited as such.

12 July

On this day in 1756, *Pirates of the Caribbean* character John Carteret, 2nd Baron Granville, was awarded a DCL by diploma from Christ Church. He was almost the only English nobleman of his time who spoke German, which allowed him to converse with and gain the trust of King George I who spoke no English. This only served to exacerbate the wrath of his enemy Robert Walpole. On 18 October 1744 Carteret became 2nd Earl Granville on the death of his mother. His first wife died in 1743, and in April 1744 he married Lady Sophia Fermor, daughter of the Earl of Pomfret, a fashionable beauty and the toast of London society, who was younger than his own daughters. Granville's ostentatious public displays of affection were ridiculed by Horace Walpole (son of Sir Robert) as 'the nuptials of our great Quixote and the fair Sophia' and 'my lord stayed with her there till four in the morning. They are all fondness—walk together, and stop every five steps to kiss.'

13 July

On this day in 1832, the people of Banbury turned out to celebrate the Great Reform Act. Also known as the Representation of the People Act, the legislation introduced wide-ranging changes to the electoral system of England and Wales.

Before the reform, most members represented boroughs only nominally. The number of electors in a borough varied widely, from a dozen or so up to 12,000. Criteria for qualification for the franchise varied greatly between boroughs, from the requirement to own land, to merely living in a house with a hearth sufficient to boil a pot. The Act met with significant opposition, especially in the House of Lords, but it was eventually passed mainly as a result of public pressure. The Act granted seats in the House of Commons to large cities that had sprung up during the Industrial Revolution, and removed seats from the 'rotten boroughs'—those with very small electorates and usually dominated by a wealthy patron. The Act also increased the electorate from about 400,000 to 650,000, making about one in five adult males eligible to vote.

The right to vote for the member for Banbury was extended from the 12 aldermen and 6 capital burgesses of the borough to all the 'ten-pound householders' of the parish which included Neithrop, Calthorpe, Wykham, Hardwick, Easington, Grimsbury, and Nethercote. A procession representing mainly local trades and extending nearly half a mile paraded through the town during the day, followed by sports and games. The celebrations concluded in the evening with illuminations.

14 July

On this day in 1877, Count Gleichen's statue of King Alfred the Great was unveiled at Wantage by the Prince and Princess of Wales. Alfred was born in the royal estate of Wantage between 847 and 849.

After the kingdoms of Northumbria, East Anglia and Mercia had fallen to the Vikings, Wessex under Alfred was the only surviving Anglo-Saxon province. Alfred nearly succumbed to the Vikings as well, but kept his nerve and won a decisive victory at the battle of Edington in 879. Further Viking threats were kept at bay by a reorganisation of military service and particularly

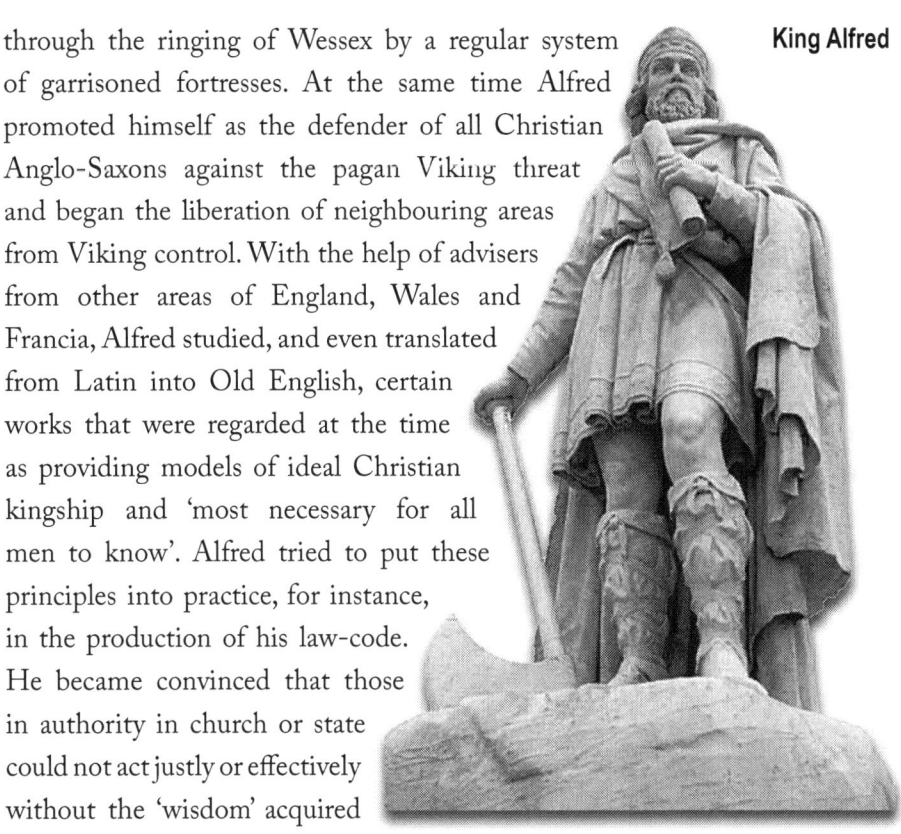

King Alfred

through the ringing of Wessex by a regular system of garrisoned fortresses. At the same time Alfred promoted himself as the defender of all Christian Anglo-Saxons against the pagan Viking threat and began the liberation of neighbouring areas from Viking control. With the help of advisers from other areas of England, Wales and Francia, Alfred studied, and even translated from Latin into Old English, certain works that were regarded at the time as providing models of ideal Christian kingship and 'most necessary for all men to know'. Alfred tried to put these principles into practice, for instance, in the production of his law-code. He became convinced that those in authority in church or state could not act justly or effectively without the 'wisdom' acquired through study. He set up schools to ensure that future generations of priests and secular administrators would be better trained, as well as encouraging the nobles at his court to emulate his own example in reading and study. This interest in learning made him the obvious choice to be chosen retrospectively as the founder of Oxford University when that institution felt the need to establish its historical credentials in the 14th century.

15 July

On this day in 1661, the Committee of Privileges in the House of Lords pronounced that, 'in the eye of the law', Nicholas Vaux had been the legitimate 3rd Earl of Banbury, even though the circumstances of his birth strongly suggested otherwise.

The 1st Earl, William Knollys, was 84 when Nicholas was born in January 1631. His first marriage of over 30 years to Dorothy Brydges had produced no children, although Dorothy already had two sons from her first marriage.

Following Dorothy's death, William married 19-year-old Lady Elizabeth Howard in 1605. A daughter, Catherine, was born in 1609 but died in infancy. For the next 18 years, Elizabeth produced no further children until 1627, when she bore a son named Edward.

In 1631 Elizabeth gave birth to Edward's younger brother Nicholas at the house of Edward Vaux, 4th Baron Vaux of Harrowden. Her husband William died in the following year. His will was proved on 2 June 1632 (his two 'sons' were not mentioned), and within a month Elizabeth was married to Edward Vaux. Vaux was not a popular man within an establishment still nervous about Catholic scheming. He was suspected of involvement in the Gunpowder Plot. Elizabeth, too, was suspected of Papist sympathies. Unsurprisingly, therefore, following the death of Nicholas's elder brother Edward, the House of Lords was resistant to the idea of allowing Nicholas, whom they considered to be the illegitimate son of the Catholic Vaux, into their ranks. Nicholas had even been brought up 'Vaux', not 'Knollys', and Edward Vaux settled the whole of his estates on Nicholas, speaking of him as 'now Earl of Banbury, heretofore called Nicholas Vaux' to the total exclusion of his own lawful heirs.

However, the Committee reminded doubters that: 'by the Common Law of the Land, if the Husband be within the four Seas, and the Wife hath Issue, no proof is to be admitted to prove the Child a Bastard'. Hence the 1661 ruling cleared the way for Nicholas's son Charles to sit in the House as 4th Earl of Banbury.

16 July

On this day in 1697, the body of Lenthall family steward John Prior was found hidden in the grounds at Burford Priory.

Prior's deceased employer William Lenthall had been rather unlucky in his choice of wife. Catherine Hamilton was famously promiscuous, and the marriage was a deeply unhappy one. When William died in 1686 he left his estate in the care of two trustees, his steward John Prior and his friend Sir Edmund Fettiplace, to be held for his eldest son John. In the meantime, Catherine married again, this time to her cousin Charles Hamilton, 5th Earl of Abercorn. He and Catherine supposedly wanted to gain control of the Burford estate before young John Lenthall came of age, but Prior put up a spirited opposition to their attempts. At least, that was the story that circulated following the discovery of Prior's body.

On 16 July, Earl Abercorn was tried for murder in Oxford, but he was soon acquitted. One outraged observer of the trial wrote: 'The murder was clear. Yet, the jury being bribed, he was brought in not guilty. They were also drunk.' Poor John Prior is buried at the church and commemorated on a stone in the chancel. His burial entry in the parish register reads 'Mr John Prior, Murdered and found hid in the Priory Garden, was buried April 6th'.

However, Thomas Phillips' *Oxfordshire Monumental Inscriptions* (1825) gives a different explanation for the murder: 'This John Prior was steward to some Gentleman, and having advanced money to his employer, had the tythes secured to himself, which was supposed to have been the cause of his death.'

John Lenthall succeeded to his father's estate, married and had a family. Burford Priory remained in the Lenthall family until 1828.

17 July

On this day in 1581, Jesuit preacher Edmund Campion was arrested at Lyford Grange near Wantage.

Merchant's son Campion was admitted to St John's College, Oxford, by its founder Thomas White, where he became an outstanding lecturer in Rhetoric. In 1566 Queen Elizabeth offered him Royal patronage, having been deeply impressed by a lecture he delivered in Latin during her visit on the subject of Natural Science. However, his leanings towards the 'old religion' resulted in his grant being revoked. He wrote a pamphlet arguing against the validity of the Anglican Church and 400 copies were found on the benches of St Mary's, Oxford, in June 1581. It caused a sensation, and the hunt for Campion was on.

On his way to Norfolk, he stopped to preach at Lyford Grange. He was captured by a spy named George Eliot and taken to London with his arms pinioned and wearing a paper hat inscribed 'Campion, the Seditious Jesuit'. He was kept imprisoned for some months, being questioned in front of the Queen and later tortured. He was eventually tried at Westminster and condemned to death for conspiring to incite sedition and dethrone the monarch. He was hung, drawn and quartered at Tyburn on 1 December 1581. Campion was beatified by the Roman Catholic Church in 1886 and canonised in 1970.

18 July

On this day in 1290 the Jews in Oxford were expelled by King Edward I. The earliest Jews had arrived in Oxford from France in 1070s and soon developed a thriving community in the city and surrounds. Archaeological excavations suggest that the Jewish Quarter centred on the medieval tower of Carfax. Edward's initiative was, of course, a money-making wheeze.

The king was short of cash and needed to impose a tax on his knights. To make this more palatable, he cancelled all their debts to Jewish money-lenders all over the country. Edward seized Jewish property for himself, and the knights' debts were wiped out. Many Jews emigrated to Scotland, France and the Netherlands, and as far as Poland which, at that time, protected them. By this time, thanks to the punitive measures already imposed by the king, there were very few Jews left in Oxford anyway. Those who stayed were mainly elderly widows and, since they probably converted and adopted Christian names, they disappear from the record. The Jews were allowed to leave with their chattels only, so any outstanding property was confiscated. Much of it went to the Bishop of Wells and subsequently became the property of Balliol College.

19 July

On this day in 1893, blacksmith William Widdows, 37, of Fisher's Lane in Charlbury, was ordered at the petty sessions to have his children vaccinated. A second order was made in September 1894 and another in March 1895. Prosecution was postponed for six months to give Widdows time to mend his ways; Widdows was evidently a committed anti-vaccination parent.

Although the law had made it compulsory for infants to be vaccinated against smallpox since 1853, it was the poorer part of society that was particularly targeted. Despite the falling death rate, the compulsory element of the Act caused uproar in Victorian society. Non-complying parents faced a fine of 20 shillings, which could be charged repeatedly. Working-class families resented the fact that wealthier parents could easily pay the fine and avoid vaccination. Poorer parents even risked confiscation of their household possessions if they couldn't pay, and some mothers and fathers were imprisoned for disobeying the Acts. The legislation seemed to sanction intrusion not only into working-class people's lives but also their bodies. In 1885, a demonstration took place in Leicester that attracted a crowd of around 80,000 people. The demonstrators marched with images of a child's coffin, labelled 'another victim of vaccination'.

As for the Widdows family however, the clan does not seem to have suffered. The family thrives in the area to this day.

20 July

On this day in 1869, Henry Gardner, manager of John Towle's farm at Horspath, set a rabbit trap among the oats. Early on the following day it had gone, and so had labourer George Hinton. A few days later publican Leonard Massey of the Crown and Thistle at Shotover Hill said that Hinton and some others visited his pub and offered a rabbit trap as a pledge for the beer they drank. Instead, Massey gave one of the men a shilling for five traps—but not Hinton. Hinton was charged with the theft of Gardner's trap, but no evidence was offered connecting him directly with the crime, so he was discharged.

It is hardly surprising that Henry Gardner did not want to get on the wrong side of his employer, John Towle (below). Farmer, paper manufacturer, alderman, justice of the peace and former mayor of Oxford, Towle was a somewhat cussed character, always ready to challenge authority and custom. On hearing that the Great Western Railway was coming to Oxford, he erected a paper house on the site of the proposed railway embankment, perhaps to get compensation or perhaps just to make life difficult for the railway company.

Houses with tarred paper roofs were not unusual, but Paisley House had paper walls as well as a paper roof. When Towle built it in 1844 it was only two-roomed, but it grew over 30 years into a substantial five-bedroom villa with a veranda and conservatory. It was occupied until 1988.

John Towle: fully paid-up member of the Oxford awkward squad

21 July

On this day in 1683, the name of James, Duke of Monmouth, was erased from the buttery records at Christ Church.

King Charles II's illegitimate son had lodged in the college in 1665 during the outbreak of plague in London. But in 1683 Monmouth was implicated in the Rye House Plot to murder the king. The plot arose as a result of concern among some members of Parliament, former republicans and sections of the Protestant population of England that the king's relationship with France under Louis XIV and the other Catholic rulers of Europe was too close. Anti-Catholic sentiment, which associated Roman Catholicism with absolutism and tyrannical rule, was widespread, and focused particularly on the succession to the English throne.

While Charles was publicly Anglican, he and his brother were known to have Catholic sympathies. These suspicions were confirmed in 1673 when James was discovered to have converted to Roman Catholicism. The plan was to conceal a force of men in the grounds of Rye House in Hertfordshire and ambush the king and the duke as they passed by on their way back to London from the races at Newmarket. The royal party was expected to make the journey on 1 April 1683, but a major fire in Newmarket on 22 March destroyed half of the town and the races were cancelled. The king and the duke returned to London early, and the planned attack never took place.

As the obvious beneficiary of the plot, Monmouth was highly suspect figure. He was obliged to retire to the Dutch Republic, where he continued to plot rebellion.

22 July

On this day in 1938, the potential kidnapper of Lord Nuffield was sentenced to seven years' penal servitude.

Experienced blackmailer Patrick Boyle Tuellman posed as a journalist and arranged a meeting with Lord Nuffield, renowned Oxford businessman and philanthropist who built up the Morris Motors car company from a small bicycle business. Tuellman then held out a piece of paper threatening to shoot Nuffield if he raised the alarm and ordering him to walk to his car. Tuellman and his accomplice, Arthur Ramsden, planned to bind Lord Nuffield in chains, then drive him to a yacht at Pin Mill, Suffolk, where they would force him to write three letters at gunpoint. One would be addressed to his secretary, saying he had been called away for a week, another would be to his bank, authorising the payment of £100,000 to a Dr Webb, and a third would be a letter of credit Tuellman could present to the bank to prove he was Dr Webb.

The plot was foiled when Ramsden betrayed the plan to Oxford City Police. The force briefed Nuffield and set up a sting to catch Tuellman in the attempt. Lord Nuffield took a keen interest in the preparations and insisted on attending every meeting. On 28 May police ambushed Tuellman in Cowley in his car. Officers found him to be in possession of two automatic pistols, ammunition and items of disguise. Birmingham Assizes tried Tuellman and on 22 July convicted him. He served seven years' penal servitude.

23 July

On this day in 1821, the Prince Regent's former mistress Frances Villiers, Lady Jersey, died at Middleton Park near Bicester.

Although apparently happily married to George Bussy Villiers, 4th Earl of Jersey, when he was 34 and she was just 17, beautiful, spiteful Frances had many lovers including William Cavendish, 5th Duke of Devonshire, the husband of Frances's friend Georgiana. Frances, already a grandmother, became mistress of the Prince of Wales in 1793. Determined to establish her own supremacy over the Prince's primary mistress, the Catholic Maria Fitzherbert, Frances urged the Prince to make a legal marriage with a woman she could control.

Princess Caroline of Brunswick could never hope to compete with the dazzling charms of Lady Jersey. But the public loved Caroline; she was cheered whenever she appeared in public. The Prince and Lady Jersey were booed—and worse. Rotting vegetables were among the missiles aimed at the Prince. In Brighton in 1796 Frances was burned in effigy, and when her London house was pelted with stones, she became genuinely frightened.

Former friends of her own class began to drop her too. She was shunned by society, but the long-suffering Earl stood by her throughout. To the considerable surprise of society, Frances was devastated at her husband's death in 1805. She died four days after the coronation of her former lover, King George IV.

24 July

Thomas Baltzar

On this day in 1658, hard-drinking German violinist Thomas Baltzar astonished a musical gathering in Oxford with his virtuosity. Among the regulars was antiquary Antony Wood who described his 'very great astonishment' at the Lubecker's technical mastery. He saw Baltzar 'run his fingers to the end of the finger-board of the violin, and run them back insensibly, and all with alacrity and in very good tune, which [I] nor any in England saw the like before'.

At a subsequent meeting was John Wilson, professor of music at the University, who, according to Wood, after hearing Baltzar play: 'did, after his humoursome way, stoop down to Baltzar's feet to see whether he had a huff on [hooves], that is to say, to see whether he was a devill or not, because he acted beyond the parts of man.' Following the Restoration of the monarchy, Baltzar entered Charles II's service as a leader of the king's private music ensemble at an annual salary of £110, a high figure for the time.

25 July

On this day in 1218, Henry III granted a charter permitting a market in Adderbury: 'It is commanded the Sheriff of Oxfordshire that he cause Peter de Rupibus, bishop of Winchester, to have a market every week on Monday at his manor of Edburgebur', so that it be not to the injury of the neighbouring markets. Witness the Earl [of Pembroke] at Bannebir' the 25th day of July.'

As the king was only ten years old at the time, clearly somebody must have been acting for him. Who could it be? Surprise, surprise—greedy Peter de Rupibus (otherwise known as Peter des Roches) was the boy's guardian, and the Earl of Pembroke was gallant William Marshal, regent and protector for Henry during his minority.

A market was a valuable asset for a town, so the two members of the king's ruling council would appear to have cooked up this development between them. Once a charter was granted, it gave local lords the right to take tolls and also afforded the town some protection from rival markets, as demonstrated here. When a chartered market was granted for specific market days, a nearby rival market could not open on the same days.

Prior to 1200, markets were often held on Sundays, the day when the community congregated in town to attend church. Some of the more ancient markets appear to have been held in churchyards. Most people lived on farms situated outside towns, and the town itself supported a relatively small population of permanent residents. Farmers and their families brought their surplus produce to informal markets held on the grounds of their church after worship. By the 13th century, however, a movement against Sunday markets gathered momentum, and the market gradually moved to a site in town's centre and was held on a weekday—Monday in the case of Adderbury. By the 15th century, towns were legally prohibited from holding markets in churchyards.

26 July

On this day in 1893, 27-year-old thatcher James Lapworth was charged with the murder of seven-year-old Beatrice Alice James and five-year-old Emily Ethel Judd, both of Little Faringdon between Lechlade and Kelmscott.

On the previous Saturday the girls had gone out into the fields to play. When they failed to return home, their parents went out looking for them. As there was still no sign of them by nightfall, the police were sent for and search parties worked through the night. It wasn't until the following morning that Emily Judd's father found his daughter's body in the river Leach. She had been thrown in alive.

Beatrice James' body was found in a dry ditch half a mile away, her neck slashed. She had also been stabbed, and an attempt to rape her had been made. Lapworth, who grew up in a cottage between Langford House and the school but now lodged in Wharf Lane, Lechlade, had spent the morning downing five pints of ale at the Swan in Southrop. He had been spotted in Little Faringdon on the day of the murders, but not with the girls. At 5am on the following Tuesday, he was arrested at his sister's house at Cerney Wyck near Cirencester. His clothing had bloodstains on it, as had his pocket knife and handkerchief. Lapworth was sent to Oxford Castle on the evening of 26 July and charged.

On Saturday 5 August, the case against Lapworth was heard at the Burford Petty Sessions. Several witnesses described having seen Lapworth in the local area (he did live and work there, after all), very near to where the bodies were found. Lapworth called William Deering, landlord of the Temperance Hotel at Lechlade, to describe how he had seen the bloodstains on Lapworth's clothes as far back as May. Lapworth argued that this was due to having tripped over a step about three months earlier, making his nose bleed.

At the trial, on 21 November 1893, the jury took just three minutes to acquit James Lapworth of murder, arguing that the case against him was purely circumstantial—he was in the wrong place at the wrong time.

Nobody else was ever charged with the murder of Emily Judd and Beatrice James as they played in a meadow on that summer afternoon.

27 July

On this day in 1469, William Herbert, 1st Earl of Pembroke, was beheaded on the porch of Banbury church. Herbert supported the Yorkist cause during the Wars of the Roses.

In 1461 Herbert was rewarded by King Edward IV with the title Baron Herbert of Raglan (having assumed an English-style surname in place of the Welsh patronymic 'ap William'), and was invested as a Knight of the Garter. Soon after the decisive Yorkist victory at the Battle of Towton in 1461, Herbert replaced Jasper Tudor as Earl of Pembroke. He fell out with Richard Neville, Earl of Warwick, 'the kingmaker', in 1469 when Warwick turned against the king. At the battle of Edgecote Moor the supporters of Warwick defeated the forces of King Edward IV, and the Earl of Pembroke and his brother Sir Richard Herbert were captured.

Pembroke's fate was sealed, but many pleaded for Sir Richard on account of the chivalry he had displayed in the field, including the earl. 'Let me die for I am old,' Pembroke is supposed to have said as he laid down his head, 'but save my brother which is young, lusty and hardy, meet and apte to serve the greatest prince of Christendom.'

But his captors, mindful of Warwick's inevitable desire for vengeance following the death of his cousin Sir Henry Neville at Edgecote, carried on with their business, executing eight others as well as the Herbert brothers. Sir John Clapham, one of Warwick's squires, carried out the actual beheading of Pembroke. The Yorkists returned the favour in the following April, when Clapham was captured in the English Channel, taken to Southampton, and executed.

28 July

On this day in 1982, the last ever general market was held at Oxpens. It had moved to Oxpens Road in St Thomas's parish from Gloucester Green in 1932. Livestock were driven through the streets from Oxpens to the abattoir at Eastwyke Farm, off Abingdon Road. Youngsters with sticks would turn out to help staff make sure the animals did not stray.

In later years, a stalls market was held alongside the cattle market, with fruit, vegetables and all sorts of other merchandise on sale. When the cattle market closed in 1979, the stalls market was moved to one half of the site, and demolition men moved in to dismantle the pens in the other half, ready for work to begin on extensions to the Oxford College of Further Education, now City of Oxford College. Traders often complained that the Oxpens site was out on a limb so in 1982 the market returned to its historic site in Gloucester Green, but with no animals.

29 July

On this day in 1842, Henry Fox Talbot took the earliest-known photographs of Oxford. As early as 1800 Thomas Wedgwood of the famous pottery family had already made photograms—silhouettes of leaves and other objects—but these faded quickly. In 1827, Joseph Nicéphore de Niepce had produced pictures on bitumen, and in January 1839, Louis Daguerre displayed his 'Daguerreotypes'—pictures on silver plates—to the French Academy of

First ever photograph of the High, by Fox Talbot

Sciences. Three weeks later, Fox Talbot reported his 'art of photogenic drawing' to the Royal Society. His process based the prints on paper that had been made light sensitive, rather than bitumen or copper-paper.

Fox Talbot went on to develop the three primary elements of photography: developing, fixing, and printing. Although simply exposing photographic paper to the light produced an image, it required extremely long exposure times. By accident, he discovered that there was an image after a very short exposure. Although he could not see it, he found he could chemically develop it into a useful negative. The image on this negative was then fixed with a chemical solution. This removed the light-sensitive silver and enabled the picture to be viewed in bright light. With the negative image, Fox Talbot realised he could repeat the process of printing from the negative. Consequently, his process could make any number of positive prints, unlike the Daguerreotypes. He called this the 'calotype' and patented the process in 1841. The following year he was rewarded with a medal from the Royal Society for his work.

30 July

On this day in 1871, gardener Edward Roberts, 31, carried out his threat to murder laundress Ann Merrick, 37, of Witney.

Roberts had developed a passion for Ann, with whom he lodged, but her affections were engaged elsewhere. Also in the household were Ann's mother Esther, 70, and another lodger, labourer John Godfrey, 66. On the previous night heated words were exchanged between Ann and Roberts. He threatened that, if she would not consent to marry him, he would make sure nobody else should have her.

On Sunday morning, while Ann's mother was at church, Roberts and Godfrey sat smoking pipes by the fire after breakfast. At about 11.30am, Ann was kneeling down, scrubbing the floor. Roberts went into the pantry and returned with his hands behind him. Stepping up behind Ann, he raised a hatchet with both hands and struck her head, slicing off a piece of skull—according to the *Witney Express*—'about the size of a five shilling piece'. Godfrey rushed to fetch a neighbour. Roberts also left the house and handed himself in at the police station, saying: 'I be come to give myself up.' When interviewed, Roberts explained: 'I loved that girl as I loved my life, and I hope her soul's in heaven… See what jealousy will do; jealousy has done this.'

Ann Merrick died of her wound, and a ballad of questionable taste detailing the horrible incident enjoyed considerable success at that year's Witney Feast. Edward Roberts was executed on 23 March 1872.

31 July

On this day in 1718, two young lovers were struck by lightning at Stanton Harcourt. John Hewit, a 25-year-old labourer, and Sarah Drew, an 18-year-old milkmaid, had just become engaged.

Poet Alexander Pope was staying in the tower at Stanton Harcourt manor at the time; and he recorded the tragic incident on the day. 'Between two and three o'clock in the afternoon, the clouds grew black, and such a storm of thunder and lightning ensued that all the labourers made the best of their way to what shelter the trees and hedges afforded,' he wrote. 'Sarah was frightened, and fell down in a swoon on a heap of barley; John, who never separated from her, having raked together two or three heaps the better to secure her from the storm. Immediately after was heard so loud a crash as if the heavens had split asunder.

'Everyone was now solicitous for his neighbour, and they called to one another throughout the field. No answer being returned to those who called to the lovers, they stepped to the place where they lay. They perceived the barley all in a smoke, and then spied the faithful pair; John with one arm about Sarah's neck, and the other held over her, as if to screen her from the lightning. They were struck dead, and stiffened in this tender posture. Sarah's left eye was injured, and there appeared a black spot on her breast. Her lover was blackened all over; not the least sign of life was found in either. Attended by their melancholy companions, they were conveyed to the town, and next day were interred in Stanton Harcourt churchyard.'

Pope composed the epitaph which was engraved on a stone in the parish church of Stanton Harcourt.

> 'Near this place lie the bodies
> Of John Hewit and Sarah Drew
> An industrious young man
> And virtuous young maiden of this parish;
> Who, being at harvest work (with several others),
> Were in one instant killed by lightning,
> The last day of July, 1718.
> Think not by rigorous judgment seized
> A pair so faithful could expire;
> Victims so pure, Heaven saw well pleased.'

1 August

On this day in 1931, Annie Kempson, 58, was battered and stabbed to death and robbed of a few pounds at her home, Boundary House, in St Clement's, Oxford. Her body was discovered two days later by her brother after Annie failed to arrive at a friend's house as expected.

Scotland Yard was called in, and over 300 people were interviewed. An autopsy put the time of death at around 10am on Saturday and this was supported by the fact that there were breakfast things out on the kitchen table and her bed was unmade. A delivery boy got no answer when he tried to deliver some shoes to Annie at around 11am. In the house the police discovered a business card bearing the name of door-to-door salesman Henry Seymour, 39. He became the sole suspect and was arrested in Brighton on 15 August.

At his trial in October, Seymour admitted that he had been in Oxford on

Queueing to get in to the trial of Henry Seymour

the Friday and had been staying in the Greyhound Hotel in Aylesbury all the preceding week. This was confirmed by the landlord. He had missed the last bus back to Aylesbury on the Friday night and had stayed with a friend, leaving at 9.30am on the Saturday morning. This friend testified that she saw him with a hammer and chisel, although he said it was a hammer and screwdriver. Seymour caught the 11.03am bus back to Aylesbury. Witnesses confirmed that he was indeed on the bus.

The defence introduced a number of witnesses who testified to seeing Annie alive *after* 10.30am on the Saturday. William Law saw her in Pembroke Street at 11.20am. John Woodward served her in his shop between 12 and 1pm. Frederick Taylor, who had known her for 20 years, saw her at 12.30pm and Kate Barron, who had known Annie all her life, saw her at 3pm.

The prosecution could offer no witnesses who had seen Seymour at Annie's home on the Saturday. Other than his business card, there was no physical evidence linking him to the crime. No murder weapon was ever found. Even so, it took the jury just 38 minutes to return a guilty verdict. Seymour's appeal was denied, and he was hanged in December 1931.

2 August

On this day in 1940, a Fairey Battle took off from RAF Benson in the early hours for a cross-country training exercise, but crashed into a hill at Ewelme. The crew included Richard Ormonde Shuttleworth, founder of the Shuttleworth Collection of vintage aircraft and vehicles in Bedfordshire, who was killed at the age of 31.

He began to collect and restore vintage cars, and first took part in a London to Brighton Veteran Car Run in 1928. The injuries suffered in a serious crash caused him to retire from motor racing. Shuttleworth became interested in aviation and earned his pilot's licence. He collected old aircraft, repaired them for flight at workshops at Old Warden, Bedfordshire, and flew them at air displays.

When the Second World War broke out Shuttleworth joined the RAF Volunteer Reserve (RAFVR). He was selected to join the Aircraft Crash Investigation Branch; he was training with No 12 Operational Training Unit RAF at RAF Mount Farm near Dorchester when the fatal crash took place.

3 August

On this day in 1765, the tomb of one Bowden, a London butcher, was split in half by lightning during a terrible summer storm in Bicester.

Lightning struck the tower, damaged the belfry and the bells, broke into the body of the church, tearing up part of the floor in the south aisle which shattered most of the lower windows, leaving the building 'full of smoke, accompanied with a suffocating sulphurous stench'. This explains why there is almost no medieval stained glass left; the occasion of the repair-work may also have been taken to remove the mullions and tracery in the remaining windows in order to lighten the interior.

The damaged chimes were mended in 1766 at the cost of £47. Only one medieval stained-glass window remains from that 18th-century storm. A note at the front of the parish register reads: 'Saturday August the 3d. Hear was a verry Dreadfull Thunder and Litening which took the Ball of from the Weather Cock and Shatered the Pinacoll of the Same and took some of the Ruff of the Tower With the Lead, and tore the Arch of the Bell window Down and Split the frame that the Speak Bell hangs to and the Stock of the Great Bell and then decended Down to the Second Loft and tore the Chimes all to pieces[?] and then to the Bellfree and took Every Pane of Glass out of the Window and Patishon from the Arch And Drove Down in the Middle of the Church and there Came Down into the Church and Broke a pavement under the Gallery and this Asended and Shattered Most of the Lower Windows of the Church.'

Bowden's tomb, surrounded by iron rails at the end of the chancel, was at last repaired 40 years later.

4 August

On this day in 1845, British sailing ship *Cataraqui* sank in Australian waters, claiming 400 lives. Ninety-two people from Oxfordshire were among those who perished, mostly poor people hoping to start a new and better life. They included 43 from Tackley, 15 from Stonesfield, 9 from Kiddington, 4 from Wootton and others from Chesterton, Stoke Lyne, Fringford, Fritwell and Great Haseley. The ship, which left Liverpool four months earlier, was just two days from Melbourne when it hit rocks in a gale at 4.30am, broke in half and went down off the south-west coast of King Island in the Bass Strait.

Only nine people—eight crew and one passenger—survived Australia's worst peacetime marine disaster. They managed to reach King Island, where they shared salvaged provisions with survivors of another wreck in the same waters. After five weeks, they were rescued and taken to Melbourne.

Wreck of the *Cataraqui*

5 August

On this day in 1301, Edmund of Woodstock, son of Edward I, was born at Woodstock Palace. Edward was 62 at the time of Edmund's birth.

Though not resident in his sons' household, Edward I had taken great interest in the princes' upbringing. Before he died, the king had promised to provide Edmund with substantial grants of land. In August 1306, Edward I signed a charter promising Edmund land worth 7,000 marks a year, and in May 1307, another 1,000 marks was added to this. He probably intended to give the earldom of Cornwall to Edmund; it had been left vacant after Edward I's cousin Edmund died without children in 1300. On 7 July 1307, before Edmund had turned six, King Edward I died, leaving Edmund's half-brother to succeed as Edward II.

When Edward II came to the throne, he went against his father's wishes by granting the earldom of Cornwall to his favourite, Piers Gaveston. Edward nevertheless did take steps to provide his half-brother with an income. In May 1321, Edmund received the strategically important Gloucester Castle, and further grants followed his creation as Earl of Kent on 28 July 1321. Edward II's close relationship with Gaveston had been a source of conflict at Court, and Gaveston's execution by a group of rebellious barons in 1312 had brought the country to the brink of civil war. As Edmund came of age, he became an important member of the circle around his brother.

But in 1330, having plotted against his nephew Edward III, Edmund of Woodstock was sentenced to death. It was almost impossible to find anyone willing to perform the execution of a man of royal blood, so a convicted murderer beheaded Edmund in exchange for a pardon for himself.

6 August

On this day in 1854, the first death occurred in that year's outbreak of cholera in Oxford. The victim was a 32-year-old butcher's wife Emma Jessop who lived at 14 Clarendon Place off Walton Street; she died in ten hours and left a husband Richard and a 4-year-old daughter, Betsy.

The city had been visited by cholera twice in living memory, with epidemics in 1832 and 1849. In 1854, of 317 known cases, 129 resulted in death. Deaths in the colleges and halls, plus the county gaol and the infirmary, were notably low. (The Radcliffe Infirmary declined to receive cholera cases, and nursing at home was provided for the poor.) Women were more badly affected than men. Deaths outside the city occurred in Lechlade, Brize Norton, Abingdon,

Harwell, Brookhampton, Little Milton, Albury, Banbury, and Little Bourton.

An enquiry was undertaken into the causes, both physical and moral, of the epidemic, and chief surgeon Sir Henry Acland, physician to the Radcliffe Infirmary, published his report on 1 May 1856. A more efficient system of drainage was recommended, as well as a general purification of the city's water courses. Sanitary arrangements of the poor, particularly with regard to the siting of privies, also came under suspicion. 'In short', concluded Sir Henry, 'faulty dwellings, faulty ventilation, foul streams, inadequate drainage, are by united testimony to be found even in this City of Palaces.'

Emma's widower Richard Jessop remarried to the daughter of a college servant in 1856. At 32 in 1883, Betsy Jessop married from 49 Walton Street to baker Joseph Hale. Both of her sons came home from the First World War. She died aged 91 in 1942, still living at 49 Walton Street.

7 August

On this day in 1940, the Luftwaffe photographed Witney RAF Training Depot, and their intentions were unlikely to be friendly. Built by the Ministry of Defence and opened in March 1918 as an RFC training depot, the station closed and lay dormant until 1930 when civil aviation commenced.

The airfield and runways were hidden from aerial view, by camouflaging the ground to look like hedges and fields (evidently not very well camouflaged, judging by the Luftwaffe photograph). Springfield Oval was built nearby to house personnel from the base. Used during World War II as a relief landing

Hurricanes and Spitfires were repaired at RAF Witney

ground for RAF Brize Norton, the station went on to play a vital role as a repair unit during the Battle of Britain.

Spitfires and Hurricanes were flown or transported there after being damaged or shot down. Indeed, many types of aircraft were repaired by de Havilland engineers before being rushed back into service. Range Road is so-named because it is sited near to where butts were set up so that pilots could test-fire a plane's machine guns. Another role upon the outbreak of the World War II was the conversion of many of the civil De Havilland Dragon Rapides which were impressed into service with the RAF and Royal Navy. Referred to in military service by the name De Havilland Dominie, the type was employed for radio and navigation training, passenger transport and communications missions; hundreds of additional Dominies were also constructed during the war. The unit closed in 1946, and Smiths Industries established their first factory there.

The site is now an industrial estate on the B4047 Burford Road between Minster Lovell and Witney. World War I and II buildings still survive, and are in constant use even today.

8 August

On this day in 1854, an anti-slavery meeting was held in Charlbury. The speaker at the packed Grammar School Room was the Irish Catholic Father Theobold Mathew.

Mathew had spent some time in the United States, where he had disappointed his anti-slavery friends by keeping quiet on the subject. But in England he campaigned to persuade the American church to follow the example of the Quakers and refuse membership to slave owners. He described the cruelties inflicted on slaves, and the risks taken by those helping runaways. Mathew felt sure that many of his audience would have read Harriet Beecher Stowe's novel of 1852, *Uncle Tom's Cabin*, and wished they could do something to help. He offered them a chance to 'give practical effect to their benevolent feelings' by aiding the Anti-Slavery Missionary Society. The society published 3,000 copies of its own paper every week, urging the religious bodies of America to abandon their alliance with 'Slave Power'. At the close of the lecture, which lasted nearly two hours, a collection for the promotion of the cause was taken at the door, and several copies of the newspaper were purchased.

9 August

On this day 1986, residents in New High Street in Headington woke up to find that a shark had apparently crashed nose-first through the roof of broadcaster Bill Heine's house at number 2. An Oxford landmark was born.

An American who studied law at Balliol College, Heine was running two Oxford cinemas at the time, but from 1988 he became better known as a Radio Oxford presenter. When pressed by journalists to provide a rationale for the shark, he explained: 'The shark was to express someone feeling totally impotent and ripping a hole in their roof out of a sense of impotence and anger and desperation… It is saying something about CND, nuclear power, Chernobyl and Nagasaki.'

Oxford City Council tried to get rid of the shark on the grounds that it was dangerous to the public, but engineers pronounced it safe. The council then attempted to invoke the Town and Country Planning Act. Heine declined their offer to display the sculpture in a public building such as a swimming pool. On 23 January 1990 he submitted a planning application, but this was refused, with Andrew Adonis (now Lord Adonis) the only Oxford city councillor voting in favour of it. Heine appealed to the Secretary of State for the Environment, then Michael Heseltine. Heseltine's inspector came out in favour of the applicant, and in a letter dated 21 May 1992 the Secretary of State declared: 'Any system of control must make some small place for the dynamic, the unexpected, the downright quirky. I therefore recommend that the Headington shark be allowed to remain.'

10 August

On this day in 1677, records antiquary and diarist Anthony Wood: 'Mr John Haslem [was] caught with Price's wife at an ale house in Blew Boar Lane by proctor Wyght; turned out of his butler's place.' Henry Price was landlord of the Blue Boar, so presumably this was the ale house in question.

The 'Blewebore Inn' dated back at least to the mid-13th century, and was once owned by King Henry III. In 1553 William Tresham, sub-dean of Christ Church, undertook building works in the alley where Blue Boar Lane now runs, and hence the lane at that time bore his name. The wall on the south side was long called Dr Tresham's Wall. In 1614 it was called either Tresham's or New Lane, then Blue Boar Lane by the mid 1600s, and Bear Lane in 1751. It was known as Blue Boar Street in 1772.

John Haslem went on to have three children with Mrs Price. Henry Price died 1705, and was buried at Merton. He is described in the parish register as being 'formerly cook of Christ Church', so perhaps his humiliation was too great for him to remain at the Blue Boar Inn. The inn closed in around 1818 and the building was demolished in 1893 to make way for the Town Hall, later the Oxford Public Library, now the Museum of Oxford.

11 August

On this day in 1908, Winston Churchill proposed to Clementine Ogilvy Hozier at a house party at Blenheim Palace. Churchill had already proposed marriage to three other women during his twenties, all of whom refused, although all of them remained his friends. He met Clementine, ten years his junior, at a party, the Crewe House ball, in 1904 but the meeting wasn't a success. Unusually for Churchill, he was tongue-tied and they hardly spoke. The two met again at a dinner party in 1908, to which Clementine had been invited at the last minute

Winston Churchill and Clementine Hozier during their engagement

to fill a gap at the table. This time they got on rather better. Clementine was an earnest Liberal and supporter of greater rights for women. Impressed by her beauty, her intelligence and her ability to talk politics Churchill began an ardent courtship. He persuaded his cousin the Duke of Marlborough to invite her to a small house party.

After failing to appear in the morning and almost blowing his chance, Winston took Clementine for a walk in the afternoon to the Rose Garden. While the pair sheltered from a shower in the Temple of Diana, Churchill asked Clementine to marry him. The wedding took place just a month later and they were married for 56 years, until Churchill's death in 1965.

12 August

On this day in 1952, Oliver Butler, 23, became the last man to be hanged at Oxford. He had been convicted of the murder of his girlfriend, Rose Meadows, 21. Rose was found strangled in a field near her home at Horley near Banbury. The couple had met at the Northern Aluminium factory in Banbury where they both worked. Butler was already married but Rose's mother could see that he really loved her daughter and she let him move in with them.

Around noon on 19 May 1952, Rose and Butler went for a walk together. At 3.30pm Butler went to a railway signal box and asked the signalman to call the police, as he had strangled his girlfriend. A tearful Butler told police that Rose taunted him that one day he would go back to his wife and she would meet another man. He put his hands round her throat, allegedly to frighten her, but she laughed and dared him to strangle her. He did.

At his trial in July, Butler claimed Rose's death was an accident and that he had confessed to police while he was still overwhelmed with grief. The jury found him guilty.

13 August

On this day in 1894, Kate Bennett of Grimsbury near Banbury committed suicide at the age of 21 by swallowing carbolic acid. She had been staying with her friend Mary Ann Harris in Howard Street off the Iffley Road in Oxford.

Mrs Harris had gone out, leaving Kate in charge of her 4-year-old daughter

Mabel. Upon her return, she found Kate unconscious on the floor of her bedroom. The doctor sent for a stomach pump, but the young woman died before it arrived.

She had been in low spirits since the death about a month before of her fiancé, 21-year-old Jack Rostron from Manchester. Kate explained in her last letter that she could not go on without him.

She wrote to Mrs Harris: 'Hoping you will forgive me for what I have done, but I could not bear it any longer, and there is things I hope you will do and will see that they are done. First let Mr Rostron know, and Mrs Bennett, and see that my ring is buried with me for poor Jack's sake. And I should like that new nightdress put on me. You will know, that flannel one. When you find me it is in my box. Let my box and all my things go to Manchester. Thanking you for your kindness to me and my poor Jack, as he was all I had to live for. Hoping you will all think as well as you can of me, so good-bye for ever.'

14 August

On this day in 1856, eccentric geologist and palaeontologist William Buckland died in Islip. While living at Corpus Christi in 1824 he wrote the first full account of what would later be called a dinosaur.

Buckland preferred to carry out his field-work wearing an academic gown, and he was known occasionally to lecture on horseback. He would bring his presentations to life by imitating the movements of the dinosaurs under discussion. Buckland's passion for scientific observation and experiment extended to his home, where he had a table inlaid with dinosaur coprolites (fossilised poo). The original table-top is exhibited at the Lyme Regis museum.

He claimed to have eaten his way through the animal kingdom. He reported that the most distasteful items were mole and bluebottle fly; panther, crocodile and mouse were among the other dishes noted by guests. The raconteur Augustus Hare claimed that: 'Talk of strange relics led to mention of the heart of a French king preserved at Nuneham in a silver casket. Dr Buckland, whilst looking at it, exclaimed: "I have eaten many strange things, but have never eaten the heart of a king before," and, before anyone could hinder him, he had gobbled it up, and the precious relic was lost for ever.'

The heart in question is said to have been that of Louis XIV.

15 August

On this day in 1637, the future Dean of Christ Church, Samuel Fell, wrote to Archbishop William Laud complaining about the excessive number of alehouses in Oxford. It was a typical example of what Laud considered to be Fell's over-estimation of his authority as head of a college.

Fell received several severe reprimands in 1639. As promoter of a new examination for the bachelor of arts degree, Laud was incensed by Fell's re-examining of Christ Church men *after* the public exercise. He wrote calling him 'a sudden, hasty, and weak man, and most unlike a man that understands government'.

On the outbreak of the Civil War, Fell became a conspicuous Royalist and, after serving the office of vice-chancellor in 1645 and 1646, was reappointed in 1647. In this office Fell led resistance after the Parliamentary victory. Soon after his reappointment the Parliamentary visitors came to Oxford. Fell was summoned before them on 29 September 1647, but he declined to attend. He was taken into custody and called before the Committee of Parliament in November. He was ordered to quit his Oxford lodgings, but he did not do so. Eventually soldiers under the newly-imposed chancellor, Pembroke, removed Margaret Fell and her children in April 1648.

Fell retired to Sunningwell, where he died in February 1649, reportedly of shock on hearing of the king's execution.

16 August

On this day in 1914, the Third Southern General military hospital for the territorial force was officially opened at the Examination Schools in the High Street with a dedication ceremony attended by the Bishop of Oxford. The first patients arrived on 13 September.

The hospital eventually had at least ten different branches in Oxford, with wards occupying both university and city buildings. The Examination Schools had 346 beds, including 94 for orthopaedic cases and 25 for what were described as 'nerve cases'. While the site was being prepared, Magdalen College School had accommodated the wounded until the pupils returned in late September 1914.

Somerville College had 262 beds for officers; the poets Robert Graves and Siegfried Sassoon were both patients there. Other sites in Oxford itself included the Cowley Road workhouse infirmary, the Oxford Masonic Buildings, New College, Radcliffe Infirmary, the town hall, University College, and the Oxford Eye Hospital. The Third Southern General Hospital also had responsibility for another 1,000 beds in local auxiliary and Voluntary Aid Detachment (VAD) hospitals including the University of Oxford VAD Hospital, which opened in the district nurses' hostel.

The Wingfield Convalescent Home in Headington was converted into a 20-bed military hospital. By 1916 wooden huts were added to provide another 75 beds, and the Oxford Orthopaedic Hospital was set up in huts in the grounds. This hospital eventually became the present Nuffield Orthopaedic Centre. High Wall in Pullen's Lane, Headington was also used for officer casualties during the First World War.

17 August

On this day in 1694, recorded antiquary Antony Wood: 'About 1 or 2 in the morning the Magdalen Hall plate was stolen. The thieves broke open Magdalen College gate leading into the grove, and then by force wrenched open a bar out of the window of the buttery.'

Thus began a lamentable tradition that continues to this day. In February 2013 the Dean was forced to act after decanters, crystal punch-bowls, side-plates and expensive silverware disappeared during dinner. A letter sent to the Junior Common Room said: 'Over the past few months we have invited all first-year undergraduates to dine in the New Room as our guests. At each dinner several decanters, stoppers, and other items of college property have been removed without permission… Often, as tonight, it has been obvious what has been happening, but we have turned a blind eye… on the assumption that these items would be returned quickly and safely.'

JCR president Millie Ross issued an appeal for the items to be returned, saying that such activity is fine as a harmless prank, but might jeopardise student inclusion in such dinners in future. However, first-year English student Frank Lawton responded: 'Other than the small matter of it technically being theft, it seems to be a great and noble tradition.'

18 August

On this day in 1783, at around 9.15pm on a clear, dry evening, a huge fireball meteor was seen by the startled residents of Oxfordshire. The meteor entered the Earth's atmosphere over the North Sea, then whooshed over the east coast of Scotland and England and across the English Channel. It finally broke up over south-western France or northern Italy.

Tiberius Cavallo, an Italian natural philosopher, reported: 'Some flashes of lambent light, much like the aurora borealis, were first observed on the northern part of the heavens, which were soon perceived to proceed from a roundish luminous body, whose apparent diameter equalled half that of the moon, and almost stationary in the same point of the heavens… This ball at first appeared of a faint bluish light, perhaps from appearing just kindled, or from its appearing through the haziness; but it gradually increased its light, and soon began to move, at first ascending above the horizon in an oblique direction towards the east. Its course in this direction was very short, perhaps of five or six degrees; after which it directed its course towards the east… Every object appeared very distinct; the whole face of the country… being instantly illuminated.'

The meteor was visible for around 30 seconds, and a rumbling noise, 'as it were of thunder at a great distance', was heard some ten minutes after the meteor appeared. Other accounts noted red and blue colour tints in the fireball.

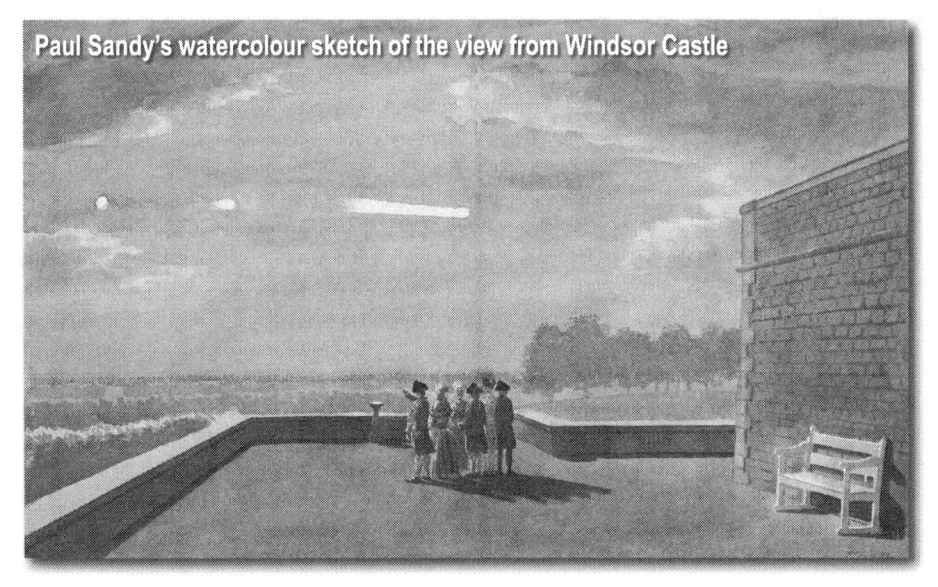

Paul Sandy's watercolour sketch of the view from Windsor Castle

19 August

On this day in 1880, a fatal gun accident near Bampton resulted in the death of labourer David Haines during harvest. Haynes was one of a team of seven harvesting corn, a job which went on into the evening. Fellow labourer Robert Bridges recalled that when Haines's job was finished, he tucked his scythe under his arm and made off towards the lane where a cart was waiting, promising to give Bridges a ride home too. Suddenly, a gun went off and Haines clutched his side, gasping: 'I am shot.' He sank to the ground, murmuring: 'I am dying.' Haines was taken home in the cart and died a short while after.

Embury Wenman, a baker in Bampton Market Place, said he had taken the gun to the field to scare the rooks off his corn. He loaded the gun after he got to the field. Haines had just finished his work and was standing about ten yards off. 'I put the gun under my arm,' said Wenman. 'The hammer was down on the cap and I was putting it at half-cock when it went off and shot Haines.' The inquest jury returned a verdict of 'accidental death'.

Haines, who was 37, was buried on the following Sunday. The coffin was followed to the church by the numerous Haines clan and many friends. He was a well-respected and popular man who had worked for the Wenman family for ten years. He left a wife, Ann, two small daughters, and a son of seven weeks.

Embury Wenman, the man who fired the fatal shot

20 August

On this day in 1605, Sir Anthony Cope entertained James I and Queen Anne for a day and a night at Hanwell Castle near Banbury. Sir Anthony was MP for Banbury in seven parliaments (1571–1583 and 1586–1604), and then represented Oxfordshire from 1604 until 1614.

He was imprisoned in the Tower of London in 1587 for presenting to the Speaker of the House of Commons a Puritan revision of the *Book of Common Prayer*. However, the Queen's displeasure with Cope does not appear to have lasted long, because she knighted him in 1592–93.

Sir Anthony appears to have been much in favour with James, who appointed him his first high sheriff for Oxfordshire upon his accession in 1603. Sir Anthony then retired from public life to his seat at Hanwell, where he is recorded to have kept 'a hospitable house in the old English style'.

King James I made Sir Anthony a baronet on 29 June 1611. He was called out of retirement to serve in James's second parliament in 1614. He died soon after its dissolution in the same year.

21 August

On this day in 1942, a mid-air, night-time crash occurred over Chipping Norton. Eight aircrew died when a Vickers Wellington bomber collided with an Airspeed Oxford trainer in the early hours of the morning.

The Airspeed Oxford was on a pilot-training flight from No 6 Advanced Flying Unit, Little Rissington, whilst the Wellington was on a night-training flight from No 15 Operational Training Unit based at Harwell. The Wellington lost its entire starboard wing and engine over the Castle Mound and caught fire immediately. Shedding burning wreckage, it glided down, skimming rooftops, before finally crashing into what is now Redrobe Cottage (then Yew Dell) in Church Street.

The occupants of the house escaped through the kitchen window. The nose came to rest touching the side of the house and the tail rested across the garage roof and adjoining walls. This was the only portion to remain intact. The crew of six were killed. The aircraft had no bombs on board, but ammunition from the four Vickers machine guns exploded for some considerable time after the plane landed. The fire was extinguished with chemical foam by the Chipping Norton fire brigade assisted by fire crews from the local airfield. The remains of the aircrew were recovered and taken to the mortuary at the workhouse, now Cotshill.

The training aircraft disintegrated and came down at Cott's Farm, Over Norton, killing both members of the crew. The cause of the crash was thought to have been the darkness of the night at a time when on-board radar was still in the early stages of development.

22 August

On this day in 1959, Ron Atkinson made his playing debut for Headington United FC.

After beginning his career as a ground staff boy at Wolverhampton Wanderers, he was signed by Aston Villa from works team BSA Tools at the age of 17, but never played a first-team match for them. He was transferred to Oxford United (then called Headington United under manager Arthur Turner) in the summer of 1959 on a free transfer. There he played alongside his younger brother Graham, and rapidly rose to captain. He went on to make over 500 appearances in all competitions as a wing-half for the club, earning the nickname 'The Tank', and scoring a total of 14 goals.

He was United's captain through their rise from the Southern League to the Second Division, achieved in only six years from 1962 to 1968, an impressive feat. He was the first-ever footballer to captain a club from the Southern League through three divisions of the Football League. Atkinson still holds the club record for appearances.

23 August

On this day in 1880, 11-year-old Henry Harris was slashed in the throat with a fagging hook (a small, sharpened hook used to cut crops and straw close to the ground).

It was a Saturday evening, and Henry and his brother John, 14, had been on a cart-ride to Abingdon. They were returning home to College Row in the company of a friend James Tinson, 14. James recounted what happened: 'I was with Henry and his brother in the lane on Saturday evening, between 6 and 7. John Harris had a fagging hook in his right hand, and was chopping the hedge as they walked along. I saw Henry struck by the hook; his brother did not know that Henry was so near to him, and the hook caught his throat.'

John told James to fetch the father of the two boys. Meanwhile he dragged his brother to the step of the nearest cottage. The Harris's neighbour George Stacey saw Henry and John at about 6.40pm. Henry was lying on Dixon's doorstep, bleeding from the throat. John explained to Stacey: 'I was cutting the hedge with the hook, and it caught Henry who was behind me, and I could not help it.' And Henry gasped: 'No, Johnny, you could not help it.'

Mr Harris, 61, arrived to find his son Henry, his throat bound with cloths. At the direction of the surgeon, Mr Lyon, Henry was taken home. After the family reached home, Mr Harris asked Henry what had happened. 'Johnny was cutting the hedge, and I was running behind and was cut by the hook. John did not try to do it.' Mr Lyon arrived just before 8 o'clock and, while he was trying to ascertain the depth of the wound in Henry's neck, the boy suddenly vomited, turned over, and died. The next day, poor John was speechless with grief. It was yet another blow for the family; Mrs Harris had died two years before, aged 48.

24 August

On this day in 1665, William Paule, bishop of Oxford died in Chinnor. He began life as one of 16 children of a London butcher, and ended it having had three rich wives. He attended All Souls College, and became rector of Brightwell Baldwin in 1632. That year he resigned his fellowship at All Souls and made the first of his three advantageous marriages that, together with his close ties to the City of London, help explain his subsequent wealth and advancement.

Mary was the daughter of Sir Henry Glemham of Glemham, Suffolk, and Anne, daughter of Thomas Sackville, first earl of Dorset. Following Mary's death in 1633 a dispute between Paule and his sister-in-law, Lady Dorchester, over the latter's promise to pay £600 into a trust for Paule and his wife, was referred to Archbishop Laud and Lord Keeper Thomas Coventry, who reported in February 1634 that the viscountess offered to pay £250. The outcome of this is unknown, but in January 1635 Paule married Alice, daughter of Thomas Cutler of Ipswich and Anne Dandy. This marriage too was brief: Alice died in November the same year. Within weeks Paule married Rachel, daughter of East India merchant Christopher Clitherow, lord mayor of London.

Through the influence of Gilbert Sheldon, his former warden at All Souls, and 'being esteemed wealthy, and knowing in secular affairs' as the antiquary Anthony Wood put it, Paule was in the autumn of 1663 elected bishop of Oxford. Sheldon hoped that Paule would use his ample means to rebuild the episcopal palace at Cuddesdon. But, although Paule's will reveals that he had already bought timber for the project which he bequeathed to his successor, the ever-shrewd businessman Paule died before anything further could be achieved.

25 August

On this day in 1878, Mrs Anne Hindrey of 67 Cardigan Street in Oxford discovered that a pair of check trousers belonging to her husband William were missing. She asked lodger Charles Henry James, 37, who had arrived on the first day of the Port Meadow races, if he knew anything about the matter, and James claimed the trousers had been among a bundle of clothes he had taken to Cowley and sold. He promised to bring them back, begging: 'For God's sake, don't say anything about it. I will pay you for them.'

When charged before the mayor, James insisted that Mrs Hindrey had actually sold the trousers to him for four shillings, claiming that she had originally wanted five shillings and sixpence. At the police court James repeated the Cowley story, but after he was sentenced to two months' hard labour, he came up with an alternative version, claiming that his sister had given him the trousers, and that he now intended to lay a charge against Mrs Hindrey. Charles James was a petty conman who had recently been convicted at Abingdon of posing as a Church of England clergyman and obtaining a communion service by false pretences. He is probably the same Charles James who was jailed in the spring of 1863 convicted of 'frequenting a place of public resort called the Cheltenham Race Course on the 13th April 1863 with intent to commit felony'.

26 August

On this day in 1959, a small car was launched in Oxford as the Morris Mini Minor and the Austin Seven. It would become the best-selling car in history.

Designer Alec Issigonis, born in 1906, was a talented engineer who worked from 1936 for Morris Motors Ltd. There he worked on a number of cars, including the Morris Minor. In 1955 he was recruited by the British Motor Corporation to design a family of new models. Development on the smaller of these took priority when fuel rationing was introduced due to the Suez Crisis. It wasn't until 1961 that it was renamed the Austin Mini, and eight years after that Mini became a marque in its own right.

Issigonis's design broke the mould, with its transverse-engine, front-wheel-drive layout and incredibly compact dimensions. Allowing 80 per cent of the area of the car's floorplan to be used for passengers and luggage, the Mini revolutionised the small car. Production ran until 2000. The last Mini (a red Cooper Sport) was built on 4 October 2000 and presented to the British Motor Industry Heritage Trust in December of that year.

A total of 5,387,862 cars had been manufactured, nearly 1.6 million of which were sold in Britain, although the majority of these were sold at least 20 years before the Mini's demise, meaning that the majority of those sold had been scrapped before the end of the original Mini's production life.

27 August

On this day in 1327, Thomas Cobham, Bishop of Worcester, died, and his books became the property of the University, forming the nucleus of its great collection.

Cobham had decided in 1320 to build on the collection of books already available to serve the small number of schools situated round the University Church of St Mary the Virgin. He planned to construct a library above the church of Convocation House and to pay for all its furniture and fittings. However, the inefficient administration of his funds meant that the building was still unfinished at Cobham's death seven years later, and his creditors instituted foreclosure proceedings on the manuscripts in his collection. His death meant that the project could not be completed.

The dispute with the University authorities lasted about ten years, until 1337, whereupon work was resumed on the building of the library Cobham had originally envisaged. Construction work was completed some 30 years later, in 1376, but the furniture and fittings—-mainly desks—were not delivered until 1410.

28 August

On this day in 1718, Sir Edward Longueville, 56, broke his neck at Bicester races in King's End Field. His father Sir Thomas had apparently suffered the same fate, though not at the races.

Much of Bicester's prosperity in the 18th and 19th centuries was due to the races. Later they were held at Northbrook in Kirtlington parish, on Bucknell Cow Common, or on Cottisford Heath. They were an important social event and brought much trade to the town. Erasmus Philipps wrote in 1721 of the 'Plate Balls'—dances held in the Black Boy Inn, celebrating the award of the various trophies.

Philipps described the distinguished company there, which included leading members of London society, 'Martha of the Cocoa Tree' (possibly a courtesan) among them, as well as Oxfordshire gentry. By an astonishing coincidence, Philipps also died as a result of a fall from his horse: on his way home from Bath in 1743 his mount was startled by some pigs and threw him. Phillips was tipped into the River Avon and drowned.

29 August

On this day in 1636, King Charles I, Queen Henrietta, and Charles's nephew 17-year-old Prince Rupert of the Rhine visited Oxford. They were staying at

Woodstock, and were entertained at St John's College by Archbishop Laud. In the fullness of time, both king and host would be executed.

Young Rupert was already a soldier with battlefield experience. At the age of 14 he fought alongside the Protestant Frederick Henry, Prince of Orange, and the Duke of Brunswick at the Anglo-German siege of Rheinberg, and by 1635 he was acting as a military lifeguard to Prince Frederick. Rupert went on to fight in the Thirty Years War. By the end of this period, Rupert had acquired a reputation for fearlessness in battle, high spirits and considerable industry. He is probably best remembered today for his role as a Royalist commander during the English Civil War. He had considerable success during the initial years of the war, his drive, determination and experience of European techniques bringing him early victories.

As the war progressed, though, Rupert's youth and lack of maturity in managing his relationships with other Royalist commanders ultimately resulted in his removal from his post and ultimate retirement from the war.

30 August

On this day in 1625, King James I made his first visit to the now-lost Tudor mansion of Rycote. The great mystery surrounding Rycote is—for whom was it built?

Rycote frequently hosted royalty, including Henry VIII during his honeymoon with the doomed Katherine Howard, but to date no documentary evidence concerning the precise date of the mansion's construction has been discovered. Historians have differed in their interpretation of the mansion's architectural styling with suggested construction dates ranging from the early 1500s to the 1550s. The Tudor mansion, therefore, can have been commissioned by one of only three individuals: Sir Richard Fowler, Giles Heron or John, Baron Williams of Thame.

Channel 4's *Time Team* concluded that the mansion was built for Sir Richard Fowler. Citing the Tudor antiquary John Leland's claim that Fowler was 'very onthrift [ie, extravagant]'; they argued that the mansion had bankrupted Fowler and necessitated its sale to Sir John Heron in 1521. However, documentary evidence suggests that Fowler was already in financial difficulties at the beginning of the 16th century and may not have possessed the wealth to build such a lavish residence. Some architectural historians date the styling of the mansion to the 1520s, in which case the mansion was almost certainly built for Giles Heron who inherited Rycote upon the death of his father Sir John in 1522. Other evidence suggests that the mansion dates from the mid-sixteenth century and was therefore the work of John, Baron Williams of Thame. Williams acquired Rycote from Giles Heron in 1539. A clause in Williams's 1559 will, respecting the new lodging, and the old without the moat at Rycote' may support this.

31 August

On this day in 1984, a Cyberman invaded the Children's Bookshop in Broad Street, Oxford. One of Doctor Who's most terrifying foes landed in Oxford to mark 21 years since the science fiction series started in 1964.

Script writer for the popular BBC series, Terrance Dicks, was there to mark the release of a birthday-special for the programme entitled *The Five Doctors*. Members of the Oxford Doctor Who Appreciation Society were also at the event. The Cybermen are a species of emotionless, space-faring cyborgs who convert human beings (or other similar species) to join and populate their ranks.

The First Doctor, played by William Hartnell, opposed these Cybermen when they attempted to drain the Earth's energy to make way for Mondas' return to the solar system; in this encounter, Mondas absorbed too much energy from Earth, destroying it and all Cybermen on Earth. The adventure took its physical toll on the Doctor, forcing him to regenerate for the first time, becoming the Second Doctor, played by Patrick Troughton.

A Cyberman meets his match

1 September

On this day in 1979, newly-established Green College, Oxford, took over the 18th-century Radcliffe Observatory on the Woodstock Road. The Grade I listed building, modelled on the ancient Tower of the Winds in Athens was built at the suggestion of Thomas Hornsby, the Savilian Professor of Astronomy at the University, after he had used his room in the Bodleian Tower to observe the transit of Venus across the Sun's disc in 1769.

The transit was a notable event which helped to produce greatly-improved measurements for nautical navigation. The observatory was begun in 1772 with funds from the trust of John Radcliffe, whose considerable estate had already financed a new quadrangle for University College as well as the Radcliffe Library (now the Radcliffe Camera) and the Radcliffe Infirmary.

The building was a functioning observatory from 1773 until its owners, the Radcliffe Trustees, sold it in 1934 to Lord Nuffield, who then presented it to the Radcliffe Hospital. In 1936, Lord Nuffield established the Nuffield Institute for Medical Research there. In 1979, the Nuffield Institute relocated to the John Radcliffe Hospital and the observatory was taken over by Green College.

A rural setting for the Radcliffe Observatory in 1832

2 September

On this day in 1687, vicar Francis Stanier of Banbury granted licences for certain parishioners to be touched by James II for the King's Evil. The church register at Wardington records that John Davis of Williamscott obtained a certificate for his 7-year-old son Richard, William Meacock for his son James, 10, and Isabell [illegible] for herself.

The custom of touching was first adopted in England by Edward the Confessor and in France by Philip I. In England the practice was attended with great ceremony; from the time of Henry VII sufferers were presented with especially touched coins to be worn as amulets or charms. The custom reached its zenith during the Restoration; Charles II is said to have touched more than 90,000 victims between 1660 and 1682. The royal touch was most commonly applied to people suffering from scrofula or the King's Evil, better known as tuberculosis, and exclusively to them from the 16th century onwards. The disease rarely resulted in death and often went into remission on its own, giving the impression that the monarch's touch cured it.

James II was very sceptical about the ritual but nevertheless indulged in it. The last royal healer in England was Queen Anne, who touched 200 victims in 1712. The exiled James II's Jacobite heirs claimed the ability until the 1780s.

3 September

On this day in 1991, a national outbreak of rioting reached the Blackbird Leys estate. At the start of the 20th century Oxford acquired an industrial working class. From small beginnings emerged the Morris car factory in Cowley, employing some 20,000 people by the 1970s. Council planners saw the 'final solution' to the housing shortage in the development of large estates on the eastern and south-eastern fringes of the city. Blackbird Leys was one response.

Most of the men worked in the car factory and around half the population in the sixties had moved from elsewhere for employment. The estate was built for families and in the 60s one quarter of its population was under five years of age, another quarter of school age. All these youngsters inevitably turned into teenagers. The 1977 Housing (Homeless Persons) Act, alongside the unanticipated impact of Mrs Thatcher's right-to-buy legislation and the halting of council new-build, ensured that 'vulnerable' tenants came to form a large part of new tenancies. Tenants in such urgent need of housing were far more likely to be housed in less popular estates with a more rapid turnover of occupants, such as Blackbird Leys.

At the same time the 80s' collapse of the manufacturing economy hit the estate's economic mainstay—the car industry. The rate of unemployment on the estate peaked at 20 per cent, and 50 per cent for those aged 16 to 19. All this came to a head in September 1991. 'Hotting', the theft of cars followed by displays of driving prowess on the estate's streets, had become a local sport for some of Blackbird Leys' youngsters. A police crackdown was met by resistance when up to 150 youths stoned riot-geared police officers. It may or may not be significant that the thrill-seeking and oppositional nature of the unrest was expressed by means of the car—the very thing that had brought many families to Blackbird Leys in the first place, and the industry that was now offering an uncertain future.

4 September

On this day in 1588, Robert Dudley, Earl of Leicester, died at Cornbury Park. He had recently been appointed commander of Elizabeth's forces to face the threat of Spanish invasion from the Netherlands.

He had assembled a force of 4,000 militia at West Tilbury in Essex to defend the Thames Estuary against any incursion up-river toward London. In a PR masterstroke, he arranged for Queen Elizabeth to visit Tilbury to announce his appointment and to rally the troops. The Queen's speech on 9 August 1588 has gone down in history. The ageing Leicester had been suffering from a recurring stomach ailment, but matters of state had taken priority. Now he was at last on his way to Buxton to take the waters, but he never made it. He was taken ill at Cornbury and died there.

Elizabeth I was devastated by the death of the man she referred to as her 'eyes', or 'Sweet Robin'. It was reported that she shut herself in her chamber for days and refused to speak to anyone. It got so bad that William Cecil, Lord Burghley, gave the order for her doors to be broken down. She kept the farewell letter Dudley wrote to her in a special casket which she kept at the side of her bed. It was found there when Elizabeth died 15 years later in 1603.

5 September

On this day in 1666, worshippers at St Martin's church, Carfax, erupted into Cornmarket Street in fear of their lives. Some claimed they could smell smoke, others burning pitch.

News had by this time reached Oxford that London had been alight for three days since Sunday, and by Tuesday an east wind had carried the resulting clouds of smoke over Oxford, darkening both the sun and the following night's moon. Rumour and suspicion swept the city. 'The fier did so much affrighten the nation that all townes stood upon their own defence day and night,' reported *Jackson's Oxford Journal*, 'and particularly Oxon, every one being soe suspicious that no sorry fellow or woman could pass but they examined him; no gun or squib could go off but they thought it a fatal blow.'

It turned out that the immediate cause of the alarm at St Martin's was a butcher calling 'Hyup! Hyup!' to his oxen as he drove them through Carfax. And no malevolent fire-starter was required to rid Oxford of the 11th-century church of St Martin; the city fathers declared it unsafe in 1820 and demolished it, leaving only the 13th-century west tower. The rebuilt church was opened in 1822, but demolished in 1896 to make way for traffic.

6 September

On this day in 1851, six people were killed and eight injured at Bicester in one of the earliest major train crashes. A special excursion train laid on for the Great Exhibition left Euston Station at 5pm carrying 200 passengers home. At Bletchley the driver, William Carrier, was told not to stop at Bicester but to carry on straight through to Oxford.

However, no one told Charles Bruern, the stationmaster, at Bicester about this. Expecting the train to stop he had the points switched to move the train over to the platform. When the train steamed through at full speed the points couldn't handle the force and the train was derailed. The first three coaches overturned and, being largely wooden, smashed to pieces. The engine came to rest about two feet from the stationmaster's house.

Cries for help and screams of pain came from the mangled wreckage. Sawing through so many timbers meant that it took three hours to rescue

Bicester station

all the trapped passengers. London cheesemonger William Bolton, who was seriously injured in the accident, gave a harrowing account of his experience: 'I felt a considerable rocking... I heard a cracking, but before that I heard a long whistle, and remarked on it to my brother; I did not hear any voice calling out. The carriage fell over with a crash like thunder, and I became insensible; I was underneath the carriage, and was sawn out, which I am told occupied about three and a half hours; I found, as soon as I became sensible, that my face was towards the ground, and my legs over some man who asked me to assist him, but I could not, because I was suffering under extreme pressure across the lower part of the back and my thighs; it was quite dark, and I could not see who the man was that I was lying upon.'

Five people were killed outright in the accident, including 14-year-old William Carrier, son of the driver. William Bolton's cousin Joseph Luckett, also a cheesemonger, died from his injuries the following day.

7 September

On this day in 1876, Oxford Military College was established as a private, all-male boarding school in Cowley. Prince George, Duke of Cambridge, was patron.

The buildings, which had been used previously by the Cowley Middle Class School, were purchased for the college in July 1876. A 16th-century manor house stood on Oxford Road near the corner with Hollow Way. The campus consisted of school buildings, playing fields, and a central parade square.

The school drew its cadets, aged from 13 to 18, from the UK and the colonies. Candidates, whether sons of officers or not, were prepared for commissions in the military, or for any profession or business. Classical studies were combined with a military curriculum. Instruction was given in military riding, infantry drill, lance, sword, carbine drill, swimming and gymnastics.

The college was declared bankrupt in 1896. Its 88-acre (36ha) site later housed Morris Motors (1912–25) and the Nuffield Press (1925–1992). The main college building, the manor house, was demolished in 1957. The remaining buildings were used by the Nuffield Press until the mid 1990s, after which they were converted into residential flats.

8 September

On this day in 1157, Richard I was born, probably at Beaumont Palace in Oxford. He was the third of five sons of King Henry II of England and Duchess Eleanor of Aquitaine.

With two older brothers, Richard was never expected to inherit the crown. Henry II's eldest son, William, died of a seizure at Wallingford Castle in 1156 aged three. The next brother, Henry 'the Young King', died aged 28, during the course of a campaign in Limousin against his father. Six years after Henry the Young King's death, Henry II died, and Richard succeeded.

Richard 'the Lionheart' has become a national hero, but in fact he spent only around six months in England during his entire reign. He treated England as a piggy-bank to fund his crusades as well as the enormous ransom paid to the Holy Roman Emperor as a result of his capture on his way home. Beaumont Palace became a monastery, but at the Reformation most of the structure was dismantled and the stone reused in Christ Church and St John's College. The last remnants were destroyed in the laying out of Beaumont Street in 1829.

9 September

On this day in 1890, the milkwoman called as usual at the almshouses on Church Green in Witney. Hearing groaning from within Sarah Gould's

Witney almshouses

cottage, she alerted neighbour Leah Fowler who fetched her son Moses. Moses Fowler, a gardener, propped a ladder against an upstairs window and gained entry. He found elderly widow Mrs Gould lying on her side at the bottom of the stairs, a pool of blood under her head. Moses unlocked the door and let in his mother, his brother Ezra (also a gardener) and neighbours Mrs Mumford and Mrs Smith. Sarah was put to bed and the doctor sent for.

Sarah managed to explain that she went to the top of her stairs to shake a wasp out of her clothing and accidentally tumbled all the way back down. Poor Sarah died at 12.30pm that afternoon. The inquest later that day at the Fleece Inn at Witney heard that Sarah suffered three wounds to her head and face as well as a fractured arm. She was a much respected member of the community, and left 8 children, 43 grandchildren, and 15 great-grandchildren.

10 September

On this day in 1912, a Royal Flying Corps Bristol Coanda monoplane crashed at Wolvercote. On board were Lt Edward Hotchkiss, 28, and Lt Claude Albemarle Bettington, 30. Taking-off from Larkhill, Salisbury Plain, Wiltshire at 7am, they flew directly to Port Meadow.

On their approach for landing a quick-release catch holding a strap opened at 2,000 feet and the strap fractured a flying wire which whipped about, tearing a hole in the starboard wing. The fabric stripped off and control became impossible; the aircraft crashed into the ground at Godstow Road, Lower Wolvercote, 120 yards (110 metres) short of Port Meadow. Bettington was flung to his death from the aircraft and Hotchkiss perished in the impact.

The incident resulted in a five-month ban on the flying of all monoplanes by the military wing of the RFC. The crash site, opposite the Trout Inn pub in Wolvercote, is now known locally as 'Airman's Bridge'.

11 September

On this day in 1940, a run of the film *Babes in Arms* starring Judy Garland and Mickey Rooney at the Majestic Cinema in Botley Road was suddenly interrupted. The wartime government acquired the premises to house evacuees escaping German bombing raids in London.

The premises originally opened in November 1930 as the Oxford Ice Skating Rink, with a ballroom, two cafes and a restaurant as well as the rink. In the summer of 1933 it was temporarily converted into the Rink Cinema, with seating provided for 1,500. It opened in July 1933 with *The Viennese Waltz* and closed in October 1933 with Evalyn Knapp in *Bachelor Mother* and Laurel & Hardy in *Beau Chump*, and reverted to an ice skating rink for the winter season. On 2 April 1934 it re-opened as the Majestic Cinema with an enlarged seating capacity for 1,900. A new raked floor had been installed and a small balcony had replaced an earlier raised viewing area. The opening film was *I'm No Angel* starring Mae West.

The building was used to shelter evacuees until January 1941. Local people hoped it would re-open as a cinema, but it wasn't to be. The building was used as a hostel, then a Frank Cooper marmalade factory. In later years it became an MFI furniture store. It was demolished in the 1980s and purpose-built retail units were constructed on the site which were occupied by MFI and Halfords.

12 September

On this day in 1881, an inquest took place on the strange death of a month-old baby after just five days in Chipping Norton workhouse.

The baby's unmarried mother, Mary Ann White, 22, had been living in her

Chippy workhouse

brother's household at Charlbury as 'housekeeper'. Ambrose White was an unlikely man to be enjoying the luxury of a housekeeper; he was a simple agricultural labourer with a wife, a 2-year-old and a new baby of his own, so it seems probable that Mary Ann had been taken in by him because of her desperate situation.

On Wednesday 7 September Mary Ann and her baby were brought to the workhouse by Ambrose's wife Sarah. The master, William Webb, thought she looked well, if a little weak, which he put down to her confinement. Matron Mrs Webb thought Mary Ann 'very strange in manner'. Nurse Eliza Haynes was instructed to keep a close eye on mother and baby. She said she noticed nothing unusual, except that Mary Ann sometimes refused food. One of Mary Ann's dormitory companions Sarah Smith stated that on the Sunday Mary Ann had said several times that she wished her baby were dead because she had so little milk to give it. Early on Monday morning, Sarah Smith found the baby lifeless beside Mary Ann.

Mary Ann announced that she had killed the child. She said the same to Dr Hutchinson—and claimed that she meant to do it. The post mortem revealed that the child had been suffocated. In the second half of the 19th century childbirth was believed to be a common cause of a form of insanity: puerperal mania. 'If she killed the child,' declared Hutchinson, 'an uncontrollable influence seized the woman at the time; her mind hanging in the balance, the balance went the wrong way.' The condition was known as. But the coroner pointed out that there was no evidence whatever that Mary Ann killed her baby, and the jury returned the rather less sensational verdict of 'death from suffocation'.

The King' Head in Park Lane, Woodstock (now closed)

13 September

On this day in 1884, a report appeared in *Jackson's Oxford Journal* giving interesting insights in to the glove-making industry of Woodstock. The case of James Harper and the Goddens reveals a lot about how the trade worked. Harper was both a glove manufacturer and the landlord of the King's Head in Park Lane—not an unknown combination in the town, where glove-making had often been combined with other trades.

For some reason Harper lost his head in the summer of 1884 and stole two pairs of gloves, value nine shillings, and two pairs of tranks (the unstitched pieces of a glove), value five shillings and sixpence, the property of glovers Josiah Godden and his son Harold.

Harold Godden explained before the bench: 'It is the custom of the trade to have the gloves sewn by women in the villages. The work is carried backwards and forwards between the gloveresses and the manufacturers by carriers.' The gloveress would be expected to turn round the finished gloves in about a week. Carrier Ann Partlett had collected the week's work from the Goddens on 5 June, and then popped in to the King's Head for a glass of beer. While she was there, the gloves disappeared from her basket.

James Harper, licensee of the King's Head since 1875 and member of the parish church restoration fund committee in 1876, said while in custody: 'I can't think how I came to do it. It was an unguarded moment.' He was gaoled for 12 months. Following his disgrace, Harper moved to Chiswick, where he evidently prospered in the manufacturing of gloves. He died 1898, leaving over £3,000.

14 September

On this day in 1264, Walter de Merton formally completed the foundation of the House of Scholars of Merton, later Merton College. He appears to have owed his education to the Augustinian canons of the priory at Merton in Surrey. He not only took its name himself but also explicitly conferred it upon his college. In 1236 there was a parliament at Merton Priory, and Henry III frequently visited the house. It seems that on one of these occasions Walter de Merton entered the king's service; his career was under way.

He acquired a substantial plot of land in Oxford, including the church and churchyard of St John the Baptist and several houses between St John's Lane (now Merton Street) and the south wall of the city, and established his scholars there. They had previously been lodged in Bull Hall, in Pennyfarthing (later Pembroke) Street. On a journey back from Oxford in 1277, while fording the river Medway, Merton fell from his horse and died of his injuries two days later.

15 September

On this day in 1673, a Monday, vintner Anthony Hall's election as Oxford mayor resulted in a riot. Hall's election was popular with the townspeople, but not with the scholars of the University.

According to antiquary Anthony Wood, Hall's speech of thanks on the town hall balcony advised his audience that, though he could speak neither French nor Spanish, if they would accompany him to the Bear he would prove that he could speak English—ie, he would treat everyone to a beer. This glibness was greeted by hisses from the scholars, whereupon the townsmen attacked them. The scholars 'made some resistance by flipping them on the cheek', reports Wood, and in the evening fighting broke out and continued throughout Tuesday and Wednesday. A scholar of Brasenose College had his arm broken, and another received a head wound. The fighting went on for over a week, and would have gone on longer 'had not the vice-chancellor and proctors bestirred themselves for the appeasing of it'.

So what was the objection of the scholars to the election of Anthony Hall as mayor of Oxford? According to Hearne, another Oxfordshire diarist (albeit a blinkered one), Hall was 'a Man of no Industry, it being common with him to lye abed 'till very near dinner time, and to drink very freely of the strongest liquors'. Not at all like the scholars at the University, then.

16 September

On this day in 1942, a Wellington bomber crashed at Lower Farm in Milton-under-Wychwood. The Vickers Wellington MkIII BJ728 had taken off from RAF Chipping Warden for a night navigation exercise.

At around 6.10am, over the town of Conway in Caernarvonshire, the starboard engine failed. The pilot announced that he was going to make a precautionary landing at RAF Little Rissington. However, the port engine then faltered too, and at 7.10am the aircraft came down at Lower Farm and burst into flames. Five of the crew perished.

Meanwhile, 17-year-old Ron Dale had spotted the Wellington in trouble in the skies over the village. Hearing the plane plough into the ground, he ran to the wreck, vaulting fences along the way. When he arrived, he saw the 23-year-old tail-gunner Armstrong Lyon trapped in the burning aircraft, engulfed in flames. The teenager grabbed the airman by both arms and hauled him to safety.

Realising that the flames were about to ignite the fuel tank, the sergeant shouted to Ron to flee from the plane. As the pair raced away from the wreckage, the plane exploded. The two men then stood together in a ditch smoking cigarettes while waiting for the ambulance to arrive—'Doc' Lyon missing a boot and trouser leg and with severe burns to his leg and face.

Six weeks after the crash Sgt Lyon returned to Milton-under-Wychwood to thank Mr Dale for saving his life, but the teenager was out at work. Lyon never saw him again.

Armstrong 'Doc' Lyon

17 September

On this day in 1881, an inquest was held at the Case is Altered Inn at Neithrop near Banbury in to the death of Hannah Bennett, 41, a mother of seven.

John Bennett, a gardener, had come home to Bath Cottages on the Tew Road and had his supper between 8 and 9 o'clock in the evening. After the meal he had gone out into the back yard to tidy up. Hearing a noise in the house, he went inside to find his wife lying on the floor near the stairs. Thomas, the couple's 14-year-old son, was desperately trying to extinguish the flames which were consuming his mother's face. Hannah had been putting her 9-month-old baby Frank to bed, and fallen down the stairs carrying a paraffin lamp. The fall knocked Hannah unconscious, and she never came round again. She died the followed evening. The jury gave a verdict in accordance with Dr Edward Warey's diagnosis of compression of the brain.

In the following year, John remarried to domestic servant Mary Ann Bailey. The couple moved to Handsworth in Staffordshire. John died in 1915. Thomas married and made his living as a house-painter. He died aged 41. Baby Frank served in the First World War and survived to come home, but he does not appear to have married and also died relatively young at 43.

18 September

On this day in 1607, the King's Arms opened at 40 Holywell Street, Oxford, the back part of the present pub. The site was originally occupied by buildings erected by Augustinian friars in 1268. After the Dissolution of the Monasteries in 1540, the land passed to the City of Oxford.

The lease book of Oxford Council for 1607 shows that 'Thomas Franklyn has licence to set up an inn with the sign of the King's Arms'. The name refers to King James I who was involved with Wadham College immediately to the north. The following year, there was plague in Oxford, and it may have struck at this inn, for the council record for 30 July 1608 states: 'It is agreed that some two women shalbee procured to goe into Francklin's howse to bury the mayde that is now dead, and that they shalbee kept with sufficient dyet and mayntenaunce either in that howse or in some cabin that shalbee buylt; and moreover that order shalbee taken for erecting of cabins as necessitie shall

The King's Arms in the 1940s: spy Kim Philby was a regular

requier in place convenient as may bee gotten.' In the 17th century, the King's Arms was a popular location for plays; it was a coaching inn by 1771.

Graham Greene identified the King's Arms as the pub where he and Kim Philby, among other intelligence officers, shared drinks around 1944. Greene was said by Philby to have been a practical joker in the comfortable confines of the pub. It was around this time that Philby wanted to promote Greene, but the author rejected the idea and resigned.

19 September

On this day in 1903, the South African War Memorial was unveiled in St Clement's to commemorate those who died serving with the 1st Battalion, Oxfordshire Light Infantry in the Second Boer War, 1899–1902. Listed on the plinth are the names of the 33 men killed in action and the 109 men who died of disease.

It was unveiled by the Bishop of Oxford in the former churchyard of St Clement's Church (now the site of the Plain roundabout). Between 4,000 and 5,000 people attended the ceremony. There was no statue on top of the plinth on the day; the 1st Battalion were under orders for India, so the ceremony took place while it was still unfinished so that they could be present.

The plinth is Portland stone and stands about nine feet high. The monument shows a soldier in pith helmet and South African campaign uniform, holding his rifle in the ready position. Lt General Green Wilkinson said that the memorial was 'a sacred possession, and would be handed down for many years in the City of Oxford amongst the beautiful buildings and historic houses'. The Mayor said that it would 'be always prominent before the citizens'.

No, it wouldn't. The memorial was removed to Cowley Barracks in the 1950s, then in the 1960s to the Territorial Army Centre at Slade Park in Horspath Driftway, Headington and subsequently in 2009 to the Territorial Army Centre in Abingdon.

20 September

On this day in 1948, the Morris Minor was launched. The idea of a practical, economical, and affordable car for the general public was conceived as early as 1941, and the model was originally christened the 'Mosquito'.

Although a governmental ban existed on civilian car production, Morris Motors' vice chairman, Miles Thomas, wanted to prepare the ground for new products to be launched as soon as the war was over. Chief engineer Vic Oak had already brought to Thomas' attention a promising junior engineer, Alec Issigonis, who had been employed at Morris since 1935 and had frequently impressed Oak with his advanced ideas about car design in general. With virtually all resources required for the war effort, Thomas nonetheless approved the development of a new family car that would replace the Morris Eight.

Issigonis' overall concept was to produce a practical, economical, and affordable car for the general public that would equal, if not surpass, the convenience and design quality of a more expensive car. In later years he summed up his approach to the Minor: 'People who drive small cars are the same size as those who drive large cars and they should not be expected to put up with claustrophobic interiors.'

Thomas ensured that the project remained as secret as possible, both from the Ministry of Supply and from company founder William Morris, Lord Nuffield, who was still chairman of Morris Motors, and was widely expected to look unfavourably on Issigonis' radical ideas. The Morris Minor was the first British car to sell over a million units. Production ceased in 1971.

Debby did Bicester in 1982

21 September

On this day in 1982, a tornado tore through Bicester causing injuries to residents and damage to buildings. A former tropical storm called Hurricane Debby was the cause.

Debby struck Bermuda on 16 September, then travelled across the Atlantic Ocean. Leaving Newfoundland at midday on 19 September, it reached the Bristol Channel on 21 September. A tornado formed which struck Bicester at around 9.30am. Within minutes a swathe of damage 1,200 metres long and 100 metres wide was left in its wake. Several people were injured, but none seriously.

The most extensive damage occurred in Hertford Close in north-east Bicester, where eight houses and bungalows lost ridge and roof tiles. The trail of destruction then moved through Murdock Road, where two buildings had their roofs lifted, causing cracks in the walls. At Elm Farm Dairy on the corner of Arkwright Road the canopy was ripped from a milk float, and in a nearby office building a window was literally sucked outwards. A lorry trailer was lifted and carried over a fence. The entire roof of an engineering workshop was elevated into the air and deposited on an adjacent roof. Several staff were taken to hospital and treated for shock.

On the Launton industrial estate a boundary wall was toppled on to a family sheltering behind it. The family was taken to hospital and treated for minor injuries. Across the road from this wall the entire roof of the Oxfam warehouse was lifted and damaged, a corner of the warehouse collapsed, and a wall bulged outwards by a foot. Sixty staff had to be evacuated. By the time the tornado reached the Telford industrial estate its ferocity was abating. It caused minor roof damage to two buildings and bowled some wooden sheds over.

22 September

On this day in 1592, Queen Elizabeth I began a six-day visit to Oxford, staying at Christ Church. Upon her arrival, she was greeted by a student got up as Apollo, who addressed the esteemed visitor in poetic verse. A committee had been constituted on 9 August 'concerning her Majesty's entertainment'. All the colleges were assessed in proportion to their income, and at Christ Church the sum of £31 2s 2d was spent 'in stage & towards plaies'. (This was considerably less than the £150 they had been obliged to fork out during her 1566 visit, and later complained about.) The Queen was now 59 and seems to have been content with a reasonably decorous timetable. Only two plays were performed, both comedies, one in Latin. One morning there was also a 9am divinity lecture, but we are not told whether the Queen was present.

On the morning of her departure Elizabeth sent for the heads of houses and, according to antiquary Anthony Wood, 'spake to them her mind in the Latin tongue. And among others there present she schooled Dr John Rainolds for his obstinate preciseness, willing him to follow her laws, and not run before them.' During Elizabeth's previous visit to Oxford in 1566, he had dressed up as a girl to play Hippolyta in a performance of *Palamon and Arcite* as part of an elaborate entertainment for the Queen. She had rewarded him with eight gold angels. But he was now becoming an increasingly strident Puritan, and recalled this youthful role with embarrassment. He came to share Puritan objections to the theatre, being particularly critical of cross-dressing roles. The Queen suffered from no such scruples.

23 September

On this day in 1663, Charles II travelled from Cornbury Park to visit Oxford. He arrived accompanied by his queen, Catherine of Braganza, at 6pm, both on horseback. The royal train was greeted with great ceremony, processions of burgesses and University officials, and the gift of a black plush-covered bible adorned with silver-gilt fixings. The exhausted royal party, who had actually commenced their day in Cirencester before heading to Cornbury Park for lunch, then collapsed into their lodgings at Christ Church.

Next morning the king was up early for a visit that did not include Queen

Barbara Villiers

Catherine—to his primary mistress Barbara Villiers, Lady Castlemaine, at the lodgings of Dr Richard Gardiner, a canon of Christ Church.

Anthony Wood's account in his diary of this visit to his mistress finish with eight illegible words that were scored through. But all becomes clear when we remember that, four days later, Barbara gave birth to her third child by the king, Henry FitzRoy, 1st Duke of Grafton. Oxford was Barbara's preferred resort to give birth again in 1665, when the plague was raging in London. She travelled with the royal Court to Oxford, and in December 1665 at Merton, she gave birth to George, her fifth and last child with Charles. In consequence, a rude ditty in Latin (and translated into English to facilitate the widest-possible understanding), was posted on Lady Castlemaine's door. Even a reward of £1,000 did no yield the name of the offending poet.

24 September

On this day in 1880, young Samuel Coleman lost his life while preventing a train crash on the track at Grimsbury near Banbury. Two years earlier he had been attracted to a career with the Great Western Railway.

Samuel, aged 19, and two others were engaged in building a fog hut on the line. Fog huts were small sentry-box style structures providing shelter for a 'fog man' who monitored visibility on the line. For this, Samuel and his colleagues were obliged to carry half-hundredweight planks across the rails. At about 2pm Samuel set down a plank in order to pop back to speak to the men in the hut. At the same moment, a fully-laden coal train approached and, spotting the wood on the line, the driver shut off the steam, reversed his engine, hauled on the brake, and flung sand on the rails for added grip. When the train was just three yards away from the obstruction, Coleman rushed forwards to remove it.

He was struck on the back of his neck and shoulder and thrown into the four-foot way (between the rails). The whole train passed over him and carried him some distance on the ashpan of the engine. The train was saved, but Samuel was picked up, unconscious, with severe lacerations to his face, and his nose partially severed. He was wounded on the shoulder, and at the base of his skull was a fracture. He died at the Horton Infirmary the next day.

25 September

On this day in 1941, a Wellington Z8354 crashed into Jarn Mound on Boars Hill. The crew of six were all killed. The Wellington was from the overseas delivery unit at RAF Hampstead Norris near Newbury. It was on its way to Malta, and it is not clear why the Wellington was so far off its route. The opening of a new front in North Africa in June 1940 increased Malta's already considerable value. British air and sea forces based on the island could attack Axis ships transporting vital supplies and reinforcements from Europe. The Axis resolved to bomb or starve Malta into submission.

From June 1940 to November 1942 Malta endured a siege while the air forces and navies of Italy and Germany fought for control of the island against the RAF and the Royal Navy. Malta was one of the most intensively-bombed areas during the war. But Allied convoys were able to supply and reinforce Malta, while the RAF defended its airspace—though at great cost in materiel and lives. The accident report states that Wellington Z8354 had lost an engine and, in the early hours of the morning, was circling to land at Abingdon.

The crash crater can still be seen to this day just inside Stockwells Field in Sandy Lane. The incident made the national press when a young German who was living nearby filmed the wreckage and was arrested. He was deported for spying. Wreckage was still being picked up at the crash site in 2006.

26 September

On this day in 1142, King Stephen captured Oxford Castle with his cousin and rival monarch Empress Matilda inside, and a three-month siege began.

Queen Matilda flees

During the period now known as the Anarchy (1135–1153), these two grandchildren of William the Conqueror contested the throne hotly. Having recently raised a large army in the north, Stephen surrounded Matilda at Oxford. He believed that all he needed to do to win the war decisively was to capture Matilda herself.

Oxford was a secure town, protected by walls and the river Isis, but Stephen led a sudden attack across the river, leading the charge and swimming part of the way. Once on the other side, the king and his men rampaged into the town, trapping Matilda in the castle.

Oxford Castle was a powerful fortress so, rather than storming it, Stephen decided to settle down for a long siege. One freezing night just before Christmas, Matilda, supposedly disguised against thick snowfall in a white cloak, somehow snuck through enemy lines. She fled across the frozen river and made her way to the safety of Wallingford Castle which was held by a close supporter. The war continued for the next 13 years.

27 September

On this day in 1884, John William Rose, 22, murdered his drunken and abusive father at the family home in Bridge Street, Witney. John's mother Hannah explained how her husband had come home from work at 6pm that day. By 9.30pm she and her two sons and four daughters were all upstairs in bed. Her husband was drunk. Mr Rose came upstairs and words were exchanged; he had for some time been obsessed by an unfounded suspicion concerning Hannah's fidelity. Hannah attempted several times to go to her daughters' room to sleep, but Mr Rose continually called her back. This went on until 1.30am. Eventually he announced that, if she did not get out of the house at once, he would beat her brains out against the wall. He went downstairs to fetch his knife, saying he was going to slit his wife's throat and throw her downstairs. Returning upstairs, Mr Rose, 54, a powerfully-built man, seized Hannah by the neck and dragged her to the top of the stairs. She screamed: 'Murder!' and her daughter Charlotte cried out: 'Oh! He's murdering mother!' At this point John William appeared in his doorway carrying a revolver. A sickly lad, he always slept fully-clothed in case there was an incident just such as this one. When a warning shot had no effect on his father, John William shot Mr Rose dead. Rushing out of the house to fetch a doctor, he encountered his father's employer, and exclaimed: 'Father was murdering mother, and I have shot him; oh dear, where shall I get a doctor?' He immediately surrendered his weapon. The court heard that Mr and Mrs Rose had lived happily together for 27 years, but that recently drink had taken hold of Mr Rose. Until that unfortunate development, relations between father and son had been perfectly cordial. The jury took five minutes to find John William not guilty of murder.

28 September

On this day in 1683, an earthquake was felt in Bicester at 7am. It appears to have extended as far north as Burford, north-west to Long Hanborough, west to Brampton, south to Abingdon, and east to the Thames, making a circuit of about 70 miles. It was also detected at Burford, Watlington, Brill and other places in Berkshire. A sound resembling prolonged thunder, extended to Dorton in Buckinghamshire. The *ignis fatuus* ('Will of the Wisp', or ignited methane) had been seen often some days before the earthquake. Reported seismologist Robert Mallet: 'A man who was fishing in the Cherwell at Oxford perceived the boat to tremble under him and the little fish showed signs of alarm.' Apparently the most violent effects were 'the throwing down of a tin vessel, and setting in motion a bed upon castors'. A few days later, on 9 October, an aftershock was felt at Oxford. Mallett describes it as being 'very feeble at Oxford, but violent farther north', ie, in Derbyshire and Staffordshire.

29 September

On this day in 1327 (or possibly 1328), Joan of Kent, known to history as the Fair Maid of Kent, was born in Woodstock. In 1340, at the age of 12, Joan secretly married 26-year-old Thomas Holland of Upholland, Lancashire, without first gaining royal consent. Shortly after the wedding, Holland left with the English expedition into Flanders and France. The following winter (1340 or 1341), while Holland was overseas, Joan's family arranged for her to marry William Montacute, son and heir of the first Earl of Salisbury. The 13-year-old Joan said nothing about her alliance and married Montacute, who was her own age. Joan did not reveal her existing marriage because she was afraid Holland would be executed for treason.

When Holland returned around 1348, he confessed the secret marriage to the king, and appealed to the Pope for the return of his wife. Montacute kept Joan confined until, in 1349, the Pope sent her back to Thomas Holland. Following Holland's death, Joan married Edward, the Black Prince—also born in Woodstock—son and heir of King Edward III. The French chronicler Jean Froissart called her 'the most beautiful woman in all the realm of England, and the most loving'.

She was the mother of King Richard II of England. Richard commissioned the Wilton Diptych, completed in the 1390s, upon which Joan is depicted as the Madonna (above).

30 September

On this day in 1932, Sarah Jane Cooper, creator of Oxford Marmalade, was buried in Wolvercote cemetery. Sarah Jane Gill married Frank Cooper, an

'Italian warehouseman' (high-class grocer) in 1872. The Coopers began their married life at 31 Kingston Road but soon moved to the High.

Sarah made her first batch of marmalade in the kitchen there in 1874 and some was sold in the couple's shop at 83 and 84 High Street. The Scottish fashion for lighter breakfasts including marmalade had arrived in Oxford not long before. The Coopers were the first in Oxford to market a homemade recipe with wholesome ingredients—just Seville oranges and sugar. It was sold in white stoneware jars made for them by Malings of Newcastle. Cooper's Oxford Marmalade became an essential part of college breakfasts.

Demand followed Oxford men to all parts of the Empire and the firm enjoyed royal patronage. In 1903 Frank Cooper Ltd opened a new and architecturally-striking factory at Park End Street, near the station. The High Street shop remained open until 1919. The Coopers moved home from there in 1907 to 155 Woodstock Road. Sarah Jane seems to have retired gracefully when the new factory opened but her husband was actively involved in the business until his death in 1927.

1 October

On this day in 1946, Mensa, an international organisation for people with a high intelligence quotient, was founded at Lincoln College, Oxford.

Roland Berrill, an Australian barrister, and Dr Lancelot Ware, a British scientist and lawyer, had the idea of forming a society for very intelligent people, the only qualification for membership being a high IQ. It was to be non-political and free from all other social distinctions such as race and religion.

Mensa's requirement for membership is a score at or above the 98th percentile on standardised IQ or other approved intelligence tests. Mensa's constitution lists three purposes: to identify and to foster human intelligence for the benefit of humanity; to encourage research into the nature, characteristics, and uses of intelligence; and to provide a stimulating intellectual and social environment for its members. However, Berrill and Ware were both disappointed with the resulting society. Berrill had intended Mensa as 'an aristocracy of the intellect', and was unhappy that a majority of Mensans came from humble homes, while Ware expressed disappointment that so many members spent so much time solving puzzles instead of world problems.

2 October

On this day in 1326, Queen Isabella 'of France' reached Oxford following her invasion of England. In 1325 she had been sent to France by her husband King Edward II to negotiate a peace treaty with her brother Charles IV to conclude the War of Saint-Sardos, but she turned against Edward and refused to return. Instead, she allied herself with the exiled Roger Mortimer who had become her lover, and invaded England with a small army in 1326.

Edward had become unpopular partly because of his blind favouritism, firstly for Piers Gaveston and then for the Despenser family. Isabella and Mortimer left Paris in the summer of 1326, taking her son Prince Edward (the future Edward III) with them, and travelled north-east into Holy Roman Empire territory to William I, Count of Hainault. Isabella betrothed Prince Edward to Philippa, the daughter of Count William, in exchange for a substantial dowry. She then used this money to raise a mercenary army. Count William also provided eight ships and various smaller vessels as part of the marriage arrangements.

After the invasion, Edward's regime collapsed and he fled to Wales, where he was captured in November. The king was forced to relinquish his crown in January 1327 in favour of his 14-year-old son, Edward III, and he died in Berkeley Castle on 21 September, probably murdered on the orders of the new regime.

3 October

On this day in 1885, *Jackson's Oxford Journal* reported the latest episode in the tumultuous incumbency of Rev George Moore of the parish of Cowley. Under the heading 'Stormy Vestry Meeting', the newspaper said: 'A meeting of the parishioners was held on Thursday evening se'nnight, under the presidency of the Vicar, the Rev G Moore.

'At the outset the proceedings were of a disorderly nature, a question being raised as to the regularity of the meeting. Mr W Plowman, as churchwarden, asserted his right to call a vestry without the consent of the Vicar, which the Vicar immediately disputed. Personalities [insults] were then freely indulged in, and some time was spent wrangling about the allotments, the money received therefrom, who possessed it, and what had become of it, and ultimately the meeting broke up without coming to any definite result.' This was actually a reasonably peaceful meeting by Rev Moore's standards. A forceful and opinionated character convinced of his own rightness, he was physically attacked at a vestry meeting at Easter 1887 by a man who claimed the vicar had buried his two baby daughters 'like pigs'.

As well as being a clergyman, Rev Moore was also a farmer, landlord, and horse dealer, and some felt these interests took priority over his religious duties. He collected rents owed from his perch high in his trap. Arriving at the cottage in question, he would lean over, run his whip along the fence, and call out: 'Rent!' Any poor soul who could not afford to pay that week was thus sure to be exposed to humiliation. The murky nature of Rev Moore's vestry accounts caused much ill-feeling. On the other hand, he was a powerful preacher, eliciting laughter and tears in equal measure. His harvest festivals were famous for miles around, and had to be split over two Sundays. Of course, one could reserve a front pew seat—for a small fee.

4 October

On this day in 1784 an Oxford pastry cook named James Sadler flew a hot air balloon from Oxford to Woodeaton near Islip. He drifted off from the fields by Merton College early in the morning, and rose about 3,600ft into the air. He flew for about 30 minutes and made it six miles to Woodeaton. The townspeople brought Sadler back to the city a hero, unharnessing the horses and dragging his carriage all around Oxford for hours. The *London Chronicle* declared that: 'Sadler is known from the humble cabbage-seller to the mightiest of lords.'

James Sadler

Sadler, who worked in the family business, The Lemon Hall Refreshment House in Oxford, had designed and built his own balloon and basket, manufactured his own hydrogen and served as his own pilot. The first English aeronaut had become an overnight celebrity, inspiring all sorts of balloon memorabilia, and remained so for much of his life. Here was a man who was flying in a balloon at up to 94mph (151km per hour), when people were only used to speeds as fast as a horse.

Ballooning was expensive. Sadler would put his balloons on display before flying them, charging money to fund his flight. Such was the lack of information about the skies that some people thought you could use a paddle to row in the sky. Sadler had been warned he might collide with Heaven, and that sky dragons might come and attack him. They didn't, but he did crash into hills, and plunge into both the Irish Sea and the Bristol Channel.

5 October

On this day in 1883, an astute Bicester police officer spotted a runaway criminal from London and detained him. A telegram had been received from London CID that morning, desiring the Bicester police to keep a sharp look-out for Oxford-born John Alexander Searle who had absconded with £70 belonging to his father Henry, a comfortably-off tailor in Norwood.

At about 2pm Supt Bowen noticed Searle driving past the police court on his way to Heyford station. Having met Bowen on a previous visit to the area, Searle leaned over to shake hands with the officer. Bowen clasped Searle's proffered hand and promptly arrested him. On Searle's person he found three £10 notes, £9 in gold, and 15s and sevenpence halfpenny in coins. A post office savings book revealed that £20 had been deposited in Oxford that morning. Searle was frog-marched back to London.

Father and son evidently came to terms because, a couple of years later, they were both in court for a joint enterprise remedying a distressing matter concerning John's sister. Miss Searle had been working as a governess to the children of commercial traveller Charles Williamson at his house in Norwood Road. She had produced an illegitimate child by Williamson, at which development the Searles felt entitled to extract a promise from Williamson that a similar mischance would not recur.

But a second child did appear, at which the Searles went to the Williamson home, knocked Williamson about, and generally trashed the place. John was bound over for 12 months in the sum of £50.

At Christmas 1886, John was again in court, this time at Marylebone, standing witness for his future brother-in-law Sydney Whitworth following a night of overly-boisterous carol singing. A fracas had broken out, culminating in Sydney thumping a policeman. John got his brother-in-law off by attesting that the officer had not identified himself as such when he grabbed Sydney.

6 October

On this day in 1899, the death occurred of Felicia Skene, philanthropist, prison reformer and writer of the Victorian era.

Daughter of a Scottish lawyer, Felicia Skene enjoyed a cosmopolitan upbringing in Scotland, France and Greece where she moved in court and diplomatic circles. The family later lived at Frewin Hall, and Felicia embraced charitable works in St Thomas's parish. She collaborated with physician Sir Henry Acland during the cholera and smallpox epidemics of 1854.

The first woman in England to be appointed a prison visitor, she pleaded for prisons to be places of reform and believed in individual counselling. She played the harmonium and organ in the prison chapel and would meet released prisoners at the prison gates at 6am to provide breakfast and other practical assistance. She rescued prostitutes and promoted the idea of a more liberal regime in penitentiaries. Whilst enjoying the friendship of respectable society figures, she kept open house for the destitute. Her personal humility was nicely demonstrated by her remark in old age: 'I am like the Martyrs' Memorial: everyone knows me and no-one is interested in me.'

Philanthropist Felicia Skene

7 October

On this day in 1920, women were at last allowed to take degrees at Oxford. Women had studied at Oxford since the 1870s, but until 1920 they were not admitted as full members, and were not even entitled to claim the degrees they had earned.

By this time, four women's colleges had been established at Oxford: Lady Margaret Hall, Somerville, St Hugh's and St Hilda's. Their students were allowed to attend University lectures, and to sit examinations equivalent to those taken by men. However, the University authorities did not permit them to graduate.

For a while, an unsatisfactory solution was found. Between 1904 and 1907, the so-called 'Steamboat Ladies' could travel to the more liberal University of Dublin, which would award them their degrees. This changed in October 1920 with a new statute. It operated retrospectively: women who had previously earned their degrees could return to Oxford, be formally 'matriculated' as University members and go through graduation.

Full equality between the sexes took much longer. A quota limiting the total number of women remained in place until 1957. What's more, the colleges and halls that make up the University remained single-sex well into the 1970s, and some beyond. St Benet's Hall was the last to go fully co-educational, in 2015.

8 October

On this day in 1644, a dreadful fire raged in Oxford, caused by a soldier roasting a stolen pig.

According to antiquary Anthony Wood, writing in the third person: 'It began about two of the clock in the afternoon in a little poore house, on the South side of Thames street (leading from the North gate to high bridg) occasion'd by foot-soldier's roasting of a pigg, which he had stol'n. The wind being verie high, and in the North, blew the flames Southward very quick and strangly, and burnt all houses and stables (except S. Marie's coll.) standing between the back-part of those houses, that extend from the North gate to S. Martin's church on the East, and the houses in the North Baylie, called New inn lane, on the West: then all the old houses in the Bocherew [Butcher's Row, or modern Queen

Street] (with the Bocherew it self) which stood between S. Martin's church and the church of S. Peter in the Baylie; among which were two which belong'd to A[nthony]. Wood's mother, besides the stables and back-houses belonging to the Flowr de Luce, which were totally consumed, to her great loss, and so consequently to the loss of her sons, as they afterwards evidently found it.'

The massive increase in population resulting from the establishment of King Charles' Civil War Court in Oxford strained the city's resources to breaking point. A fortnight after the fire, the situation was so bad that the city council drew up a strongly worded 'petition comprehending our pressures and grievances' to the Lords Commissioners. It is clear evidence of the growing disillusionment of Oxford citizens occasioned by overcrowding, hunger, expense of fortifications and disease. The petitioners described how 'by the late lamentable fire very many inhabitants whose estates consisted of houses, household stuff, wares and goods are utterly ruined, amongst which eight common brewhouses and ten bakehouses were burnt besides many malthouses, malt, wheat, wood and other provisions, who must all be relieved by the other inhabitants, especially those who are allied and friends unto them'.

9 October

On this day in 1880, 16-year-old servant girl Elizabeth Neville was charged with theft from Edward Prescott's draper's shop in Park Lane, Woodstock. Her sister Anne, 20, a chambermaid at the Bear, and her mother Alice were both charged with receiving the stolen goods. Also involved in the scheme were William Styles, 34, and his step-son William Green, 19.

The town of Woodstock was awash with rich visitors in the late Victorian period—the high watermark for lavish entertaining at Blenheim Palace. Guests at balls and shooting parties were well-served in the town with the luxury goods they required. Seeing all these beautiful things was too much for young Elizabeth. Silk scarves and handkerchiefs, cashmere stockings, kid gloves, an opera cloak, shawls, lace tippets, and embroidery, tablecloths, blankets and towels all found their way out of the back of Mr Prescott's shop and into the hands of 11-year-old Martha Styles.

Other parcels went to Elizabeth's sister Anne at the Bear, and some items were sent home to the girls' mother Alice in Ratley. Elizabeth told her mother and sister that the goods were either already paid for, or that the cost was to be deducted from her wages.

Both families, Nevilles and Styles, were under pressure. Alice Neville was a widow; at the age of 46 she still had a daughter aged 13 at home, as well as an illegitimate granddaughter aged 2. For the Styles it was even worse. In his early 20s, farm labourer William had become involved with a gloveress nine years his senior, Emma, possibly Green, who already had three sons. To these, William and Emma added six children of their own—a heavy burden on a farm labourer of 34.

Elizabeth was sentenced to three months' hard labour, and returned to live with her mother upon her release. She found work as a servant. Having received a glowing character reference from landlord Henry Pratt, Anne was acquitted, and returned to her job at the Bear. Styles received one month's hard labour; his step-son was acquitted. Alice Neville received a severe warning from the bench.

10 October

On this day in 1880, a gun accident in Bicester resulted in the death of 26-year-old Joseph Whitton, son of a Fringford shepherd. Apparently Whitton had only recently come to Bicester from Birmingham, looking for harvest work. He had lodged with a butcher named Joseph Leach in New Buildings, Bicester.

He and his companion, convicted poacher Edward Gomm of Charlbury, set out at 3.30pm that day on an expedition. Whitton, a farm labourer, took with him an old gun, loaded with powder and shot, broken and carried in his pocket. After walking as far as Bucknell, they turned round and returned at about 7pm.

Just at the entrance to the town, Whitton accidentally dropped the gun. It went off, and the charge penetrated his abdomen, forcing his intestines to protrude.

Whitton reeled back and fell, calling to Gomm to run for help. Whitton's brother-in-law was fetched, and carried him to his home in New Buildings, where Dr Drinkwater alleviated his sufferings to the best of his ability. But Joseph Whitton died at 4am on the following morning.

The next day an inquest was held at the Plough Inn, possibly the pub now known as 'Jacob's Plough'. The jury reached a verdict of 'accidental death'.

11 October

On this day in 1880, an inquest at Sibford Gower heard how 75-year-old labourer's widow Anne Aris had burst into her neighbour Sarah Young's cottage in Burdrop on the previous Wednesday 'all in flames'.

Between 11 and 12 o'clock, Mrs Aris had been chatting quite normally with Sarah, and then gone indoors and lit the benzoline lamp which her son Benjamin had brought her the night before. She was in the habit of sitting very near to her open fire, and it seems that some oil had splashed from the lamp on to her apron and caught alight. She rushed round to Sarah's cottage completely aflame. Sarah called to carpenter William Poulton and his son Lewis who were working next door. They came at once, and William Poulton threw a bucket of water over Mrs Aris which at last extinguished the flames. But the front of her dress was already burnt off.

Asked what had happened, Mrs Aris explained that her apron had caught alight, and the more she tried to put it out, the more it blazed. She did not say exactly how her apron came to be in flames, but she vowed to be very careful how she handled a benzoline lamp in future, should she live. However, she did not think she would live, and she was right. After lingering for two painful days, poor Mrs Aris perished at last.

Burdrop, part of the parish of Swalcliffe until 1841

12 October

On this day in 1655, a young woman poisoned herself for love of Catte Street bookseller Joseph Godwin.

Antiquary Anthony Wood reported in the third person: 'A handsome maid living in Catstreet, being deeply in love with Joseph Godwin, a junior fellow of New Coll., poyson'd herself with rats-bane. This is mention'd because it made a great wonder that a maid should be in love with such a person as he, who had a curl'd shag-pate, was squint-ey'd and purblind [partially blind], and much deform'd with the smal pox. He was the son of a father of both his names who was a bookseller at the upper end of Catstreet in Oxford; and, before he had been translated to Winchester school, had been in the same forme with A. Wood at New Coll. school.'

The lovelorn maid in question may be Ann Roger, an apparently-single woman who was buried the following day at a 12th-century church on Queen's Lane, north of the High Street. It is now deconsecrated and houses the college library of St Edmund Hall. Joseph Godwin, born 1633, had been admitted a fellow of New College at the age of 19 in 1652, awarded the equivalent of a doctorate in 1658, and then vacated his fellowship. His father, also Joseph Godwin, died in 1673, leaving his entire estate to his son, including the bookshop. There are numerous references to purchases from Godwin in Wood's records.

13 October

On this day in 1909, vandals set fire to the famous 'Joe Pullen's Tree', a landmark at the top of Headington Hill. To be fair, the elm was already a shadow of its former self, having been much chopped about in the 230 years or so since the Rev Josiah Pullen planted it in about 1680.

From 1656 until his death in 1714, Pullen was vice-president of Magdalen Hall, then still situated in the grounds of Magdalen College. Nearly ten years after Pullen's death, diarist Thomas Hearne described how Pullen loved the walk to the top of Headington Hill: 'Upon the Top of Heddington Hill, by Oxford, on the left Hand as we go to Heddington, just at the Brow of the Branch of the Roman Way that falls down upon Marston Lane, is an Elm that is commonly call'd and known by the Name of Jo. Pullen's Tree, it having been planted by the Care of the late Mr. Josiah Pullen of Magdalen Hall, who used to Walk to that place every day, sometimes twice a day, if tolerable Weather, from Magdalen Hall and back again in the Space of half an Hour.'

The elm soon became famous. When, in November 1795, there was a terrible storm throughout the entire country, the *Gentleman's Magazine* reported that 'Joe Pullen, the famous elm, upon Headington hills, had one of its large branches torn off and carried to a great distance'. Around the beginning of 1847 there was an attempt to chop the tree down, but an outburst of popular indignation stayed the woodsman's axe. More storm damage occurred in 1851, and then in 1887 the weight of snow brought some branches down, so the larger limbs were removed. In 1894 rot had set in, so the tree was cut down to a stump, and the base was protected by a brick collar. Arsonists finished off the job in 1909.

14 October

On this day in 1905, readers of the *Oxford Times* of 14 October 1905 were offered a startling headline to savour over their breakfast : 'FOX-HUNT IN CORNMARKET STREET. Considerable stir was caused in Queen-street and Cornmarket-street on Thursday morning by the appearance of a fox, which came from the direction of Castle-street and was pursued by a number

A fox causes a rumpus in Cornmarket Street in 1905

of men and boys to the shop of Mrs Andrews, milliner, Cornmarket-street, which it entered. It's intrusion caused some alarm among the assistants, who sought refuge in the window, much to the amusement of the spectators. It was eventually caught by means of a wire snare by Mr Gooch and Mr Mayo, and taken away in a sack. Subsequently it was found that Reynard was a pet belonging to Mrs Mouat of Montalt House, Paradise-street, whence he escaped.'

In the accompanying illustration, the adventurous fox is indeed shown wearing a collar—as no feral fox would deign to do. His owner Mrs Mouat was a Kensington doctor's widow. She lived in some comfort in a big house in Paradise Street with her three sons and her widowed sister, plus a cook and a domestic servant. Her son John was a medical student at the University. Mr Gooch was probably Horace Gooch, 19, also a medical student, lodging in St Clement's. It seems reasonable to suppose that he was a friend of John Mouat's, present in Paradise Street at the time of the fox's break for freedom. Mr Mayo was probably painter Richard Mayo, 37, of 4 New Road.

15 October

On this day in 1881, an inquest was held at Ascott-under-Wychwood on the body of 12-year-old John Pratley.

At about 1.30pm on the previous day, John and Francis Longshaw, 23, were working for William Lardner of Manor Farm. John's job was to mind the horses on a dung cart. John and Francis started out of the farmyard with a load of dung on board the cart, but the wind was disturbing the thatch on the hayricks, so Longshaw was called back to secure it. John went on ahead with the cart.

The job took Longshaw about ten minutes, and then he went after John and the cart. He found the horses and cart at a stand-still on the far side of the bridge over the river Evenlode, but no sign of John. Longshaw returned to the farm with the cart, and enquired after John, but nobody had seen him. He informed Mr Lardner and John's father. John Pratley, a labourer, searched the river and found his son, dead, about 18 yards from the bridge.

John Pratley, 32, and his wife, gloveress Ellen, 32, had four other sons aged 7, 5, 4, and 1. The mysterious accident which took the life of John and Ellen's eldest son took place on a Friday when John should have been at school. But it would seem that, with so many mouths to feed, young John was required to miss school and make a contribution to the household budget by working for Mr Lardner.

Mr Lardner, whose own 13-year-old son was away at school in Charlbury at the time of John's death, had problems of his own. His wife Rhoda was mentally unstable, and eventually tried to slit her own throat with a razor in 1893, for which she was summoned to court. She was not convicted, but the bench advised that she should be attended day and night. She was lucky: she was blessed with two sons who lived with her until she died in 1916.

16 October

On this day in 1555, Hugh Latimer and Nicholas Ridley were burned at the stake in Broad Street for heresy.

They had been brought, along with Archbishop Cranmer, to the town prison in Oxford in the previous March, where they were to debate in public with Roman Catholic theologians. Ridley defended his beliefs with particular brilliance and Latimer dismissed his opponents as 'mass-mongers'.

The arch-conservative Stephen Gardiner, Bishop of Winchester and Lord Chancellor, presided over the trial for heresy at the end of September, when Latimer took the opportunity to deliver a blistering attack on the see of Rome as the enemy and persecutor of Christ's true flock. But there was never any doubt about the verdict. Ridley went to the pyre in a smart black gown, but the grey-haired Latimer, 70, who had a gift for what we now call the optics, wore a shabby old garment, which he took off to reveal a shroud. Ridley kissed the stake and both men knelt and prayed.

After a 15-minute sermon urging them to repent—the authorities would dearly loved not to have burned such senior clergymen—Latimer and Ridley were chained to the stake and a bag of gunpowder was hung round each man's neck. As the fire took hold, Latimer was stifled by the smoke and died without pain, but poor Ridley was not so lucky. The wood was piled up above his head, but he writhed in agony and repeatedly cried out: 'Lord, have mercy upon me, I cannot burn.' Cranmer, who was supposedly made to watch, would go to his own death the following year.

17 October

On this day in 1817, future Prime Minster Edward Smith-Stanley, 14th Earl of Derby, matriculated at Christ Church, only four months after the death of his mother.

As part of the smart Etonian 'set' within the college, Stanley was noted for his academic ability and boisterous self-assurance. In 1819 he led a group of drunken undergraduates who, late one night, pulled the figure of Mercury, erected in 1695, down from its plinth in the centre of Christ Church's Great Quadrangle. The college authorities drew a discreet veil over what was regarded as a gentlemanly escapade.

He was three-times Prime Minister of the United Kingdom and, to date, the longest-serving leader of the Conservative Party. He is one of only four British prime ministers to have three or more separate periods in office. However, his ministries each lasted less than two years and totalled three years and 280 days. Historian Frances Walsh has written that it was Derby 'who educated the party and acted as its strategist to pass the last great Whig measure, the 1867 Reform Act. It was his greatest achievement to create the modern Conservative Party in the framework of the Whig constitution, though it was Disraeli who laid claim to it'.

18 October

On this day in 1957, Woolworth at last moved into new premises in Cornmarket, Oxford.

F W Woolworth Ltd moved into its first Oxford shop in 1924; it was in the former Roebuck Inn on the east side of Cornmarket. It was so popular that the company had to find bigger premises. They bought the 17th-century coaching inn the Clarendon Hotel in 1930, planning to demolish it. Many years of battling with the Oxford authorities followed. The project was then put on hold during the Second World War, but the fight resumed in 1950.

Publicly the city authorities cited fears that such a large shop would encourage more traffic in a highly congested area. Privately they let slip that they felt that a larger Woolies would lower the tone and ill-suit the dreaming spires.

After 27 years a huge new store was finally approved, with the front made of

Shoppers check out the new Oxford Woolies in 1957

local Clipson stone, Bladon stone and grey slate. The new store, five times larger than its predecessor, featured a deluxe cafeteria, offices upstairs, a spectacular roof garden and a multi-storey car park. The building is now home to Boots the Chemist.

19 October

On this day in 727 (estimates vary), Oxford's patron saint Frideswide died. Rich and beautiful, she was the daughter of Saxon King Didan of Eynsham. She founded the Priory of St Frideswide, Oxford, and committed herself to celibacy. Her name means 'peace' (frithes) 'strong' (withe).

When the Mercian king Aelfgar pressed his suit to marry her rather too urgently and attempted to abduct her, she fled into the forests of Berkshire and hid in a swine-shed. Learning that her father was pining for her in Oxford, Frideswide snuck back into town. While she hid with the nuns at Binsey, they complained of having to fetch water from the distant river Thames, so Frideswide prayed to God and a well sprang up.

Aware that Aelfgar was pursuing her, Frideswide further prayed to God for protection and consequently God struck the king blind as he entered the gates of the city. Finally understanding the wrongness of what he had done, Aelfgar asked Frideswide for forgiveness. She took pity on him, bathing his eyes from the sacred spring at Binsey. Aelfgar's sight was restored. Frideswide went on to have a reputation as a healer and a beloved figure of great piety and prayerfulness.

The whole legend was written down 400 years later, so must be taken with a hefty pinch of salt. However, the well can still be found today at the Church of Saint Margaret in Binsey, a few miles up-river from Oxford. It is visited by pilgrims to this day, particularly by those with eye ailments.

20 October

On this day in 1836, John Ruskin matriculated at Christ Church. He would become the leading English art critic of the Victorian era, as well as an art patron, draughtsman, watercolourist, a prominent social thinker and philanthropist.

Ruskin first came to widespread attention with the first volume of *Modern Painters* (1843), an extended essay in defence of the work of J M W Turner in which he argued that the principal role of the artist is 'truth to nature'. From the 1850s, he championed the Pre-Raphaelites, who were influenced by his ideas. In 1869, Ruskin became the first Slade Professor of Fine Art at the University of Oxford, where he established the Ruskin School of Drawing.

Ruskin's sexuality has been the subject of a great deal of speculation and critical comment. In a letter to his physician John Simon in May 1886, Ruskin wrote: 'I like my girls from ten to 16—allowing of 17 or 18 as long as they're not in love with anybody but me.' However, there is no evidence that Ruskin engaged in any sexual activity with anyone at all—of whatever age.

21 October

On this day in 1882, *Jackson's Oxford Journal* reported a shocking accident at the Model Farm in Shirburn near Watlington.

Theresa Ann Brown, 20, was working in the oil-cake crushing mill. Oil-cake is the residue obtained after the greater part of the oil has been extracted from an oilseed. Oil-cakes are rich in protein and therefore valuable food for farm animals. Theresa 'incautiously' placed her hand in the hopper of the mill. The rotating wheels caught her hand and severely crushed the bones. Happily, at just that moment the steam had been turned off, so only the centrifugal force of the ten-foot fly-wheel remained. This, too, was arrested by the timely intervention of the attendant engineer. Showing great presence of mind, he cast off the driving band, and a fatal accident was averted. Clerk of works John Stockham, 36, rendered immediate assistance, and Theresa was reported to be going on well under the care of surgeon Mr Dixon. Not that well, though. Just over two weeks later, Theresa Anne died, and she was buried on 9 October.

22 October

On this day in 1789, two celebrated boxers, Tom Johnson and Isaac Perrins, fought on a 40ft turf stage at the Leys near Banbury. Perrins had issued a general challenge, offering to fight any man in England for a prize of 500 guineas, having beaten all challengers in the counties around Birmingham. The contest was billed as a battle between Birmingham and London as well as for the English Championship.

The two men were around the same age but physically very different. Perrins stood 6ft 2in (1.88m) tall and weighed 238lb (108kg), while Johnson was only 5ft 10in (1.78m) and weighed 196lb (89kg). The first five minutes saw neither man strike a blow and then, when Perrins tried to make contact, Johnson dodged and felled Perrins in return. Although Perrins recovered

Johnson (left) and Perrins (right) set to

to hold the upper hand in the first few rounds, Johnson began to dance around the ring, forcing Perrins to follow to make a fight of it. This 'shifting' confused Perrins because the custom at the time was for the fighters to stand still and hit each other, but the rules for this particular fight did not prevent it. Nor did they specify what should happen if a contestant fell to the ground, which is what Johnson did to avoid being hit; this action was thought by the spectators to be unsporting but was permitted by the two umpires. Before long first Perrins and then Johnson suffered cut eyes and further damage to their faces. By the fight's end Perrins' head was much knocked about.

The contest lasted 62 rounds, which took a total of 75 minutes to complete, until Perrins became totally exhausted. The contestants received 250 guineas each, with Johnson also receiving two-thirds of the entrance takings (after costs) and Perrins receiving the other third. The net takings were £800, with the number of spectators variously stated as being 3,000 or 5,000. Johnson called on Perrins and left him a guinea to buy himself a drink before leaving Banbury.

23 October

On this day in 1980, the last MG sports car rolled off the line at the Abingdon works. The MG Car Company had operated out of the old leather factory since 1929. A limited liability company was then incorporated on 21 July 1930. Manufacture of the MGB began in May 1962 and by the time production came to a end on 23 October 1980 half a million cars had rolled off the line, making it a world best seller. In 1966, a typical year, exports accounted for three-quarters of production with the Roadster outselling the GT by about two-to-one.

The six-cylinder MGC was introduced in 1967 followed by the MGB GT V8 in August 1973, both of which sold only in limited numbers. America was a big customer, too big to ignore, and when stringent US auto-legislation arrived in 1974/75 the MGB Roadster appeared for the first time with its controversial rubber bumpers.

Other changes included an increased ride height, hazard warning lights, servo brakes, and a single twelve-volt battery. Towards the end of October 1980 the final 1,000 Limited Edition cars brought production to an end at the

Sad, but proud: the last MG rolls off the production line in 1980

famous Abingdon works. MG production stopped in favour of the Triumph TR7 being built at Speke on Merseyside. The plant was auctioned off in March 1981.

24 October

On this day in 1728, diarist Thomas Hearne recorded the dismissal of troublesome Thomas Weeksy as a fellow of Oriel college.

'On Tuesday last Mr. Tho. Weeksy was deprived if his fellowship of Oriel coll., (and indeed expelled, his name being struck out of the book,) sentence being pronounced by the provost himself in the chappell, for contumacy and for having *uberius beneficium* [a benefice of greater value than the one he already held]. Both points were so plain and notorious that nothing can be alleged for him,' declared Hearne. 'This Mr. Weeksy (who stood himself to be provost) hath been so troublesome and vexatious that he did all that possibly he could to hinder the peace of the college. His living is about £19 in the king's books, whereas he cannot hold a fellowship of Oriel with a living above 10 marks [£6 13s 4d].

'He had been summoned three times before the society, particularly for detaining a register of the college and declining to surrender it, (tho' he and his crony Bowles had had it a great while, three quarters of a year or more,) notwithstanding the college had great occasion for it.'

Leading Oriel Whig Joseph Bowles came in for double doses of Hearne's ever-ready spleen because he had replaced the diarist himself as librarian at the Bodleian. Hearne describes Bowles as 'a pert, conceited coxcomb… who had the impudence to intrude into my place'.

A year later, Thomas Weeksy was restored to his fellowship, but this, according to Hearne, was only because the king's representative knew nothing about the workings of universities.

25 October

On this day in 1644, the siege of Banbury castle was lifted, the Royalist defenders having refused to capitulate.

In 1642 the English Civil War had broken out between the Royalist supporters of Charles I and the supporters of Parliament. Banbury Castle was initially held by William Fiennes for Parliament and the castle was hastily refortified. After the battle of Edgehill, Charles marched south and forced the surrender of the castle and its stock of 1,500 firearms. The fortifications were strengthened and in 1644 the castle was besieged again, this time by Parliamentary forces under the command of William Fiennes.

The royal governor, 18-year-old Sir William Compton, held out between July and October, when Compton's brother, James, relieved the siege. According to antiquary Anthony Beesley, during the entire 13-week siege William Compton never went to bed once. Compton continued governor of Banbury until the king left Oxford until, when the whole kingdom was submitting to Parliament, he surrendered upon honourable terms.

Oliver Cromwell called him 'the sober young man, and the godly cavalier'. He was one of the secret Sealed Knot association who managed all the eight attempts made for the restoration of Charles II from 1652 to 1659. After the war Banbury castle was slighted, or deliberately demolished, to prevent its further use; Parliament paid Fiennes £2,000 in compensation. Stones from the castle were later used to build houses in the town.

26 October

On this day in 1918, Albert Bowsher of Northmoor was fatally wounded on the Western Front. In June 1914, Albert had married Elizabeth Brooks, a laundress from nearby Aston. Albert gave his occupation at the time of his marriage as 'shepherd'.

Late in the war Albert's regiment was ordered to attack the village of Englefontaine on the Western Front. At 1.00am on 26 October the attack was launched. The enemy were strongly posted on the outskirts of the ruined village with machine-guns skilfully disposed to sweep the open ground. German machine-gunners opened fire as soon as the advancing platoons appeared out of the darkness.

In displays of astonishing individual bravery two machine-gun posts were captured; nevertheless there were many casualties. The attackers fought their way into the wrecked village and for a time a wild struggle raged around the ruins of the houses. Before dawn the German resistance was broken; and at first light on 26 October the last enemy troops in the village gave themselves up. Five men were killed and 34 wounded, including Albert. He died of his wounds a week after Armistice Day on 18th November 1918. He was 29.

27 October

On this day in 1938, a parliamentary by-election was triggered by the death in August of Robert Bourne, MP for Oxford since 1924.

On 29 September 1938, British Prime Minister Neville Chamberlain had signed the Munich Agreement, handing over the Sudetenland to German control. This issue polarised British politics at the time, with many Labour supporters, Liberals, and some Conservatives strongly opposed to this policy of appeasement. On 14 September, the Conservatives selected as their candidate Quintin Hogg, who was a fellow of All Souls and a former president of the Oxford Union Society. The Liberal and Labour candidates stood aside and both parties supported Sandy Lindsay, the Master of Balliol, as an Independent Progressive.

The campaign was intense and focused almost entirely on foreign affairs. Hogg supported Chamberlain's appeasement policy. Lindsay opposed appeasement;

his campaigners used the slogan 'A vote for Hogg is a vote for Hitler'. Lindsay was supported by many dissident Conservatives, such as Harold Macmillan, who were opposed to the Munich Agreement. A number of future politicians at the University at the time, including Denis Healey, Edward Heath and Roy Jenkins, all from Balliol, cut their teeth in the Michaelmas campaign. Hogg retained the seat for the Conservatives but his majority was halved by Lindsay.

28 October

On this day in 1882, *Jackson's Oxford Journal* published a compelling account of the floods around Witney.

'Wind, rain, snow, and thunder and lightning alternated during Tuesday morning until afternoon, when the fury of the tempest abated... The road to Southleigh was blocked by a prostrate tree, four upheaved trunks in succession disputed the passage of the road from Newbridge to Northmoor. Two more trees were precipitated across the line by the Witney railway station...

'At half-past five o'clock on Wednesday morning some of the residents of Bridge-street were awakened by the rush of water. On coming downstairs to ascertain the cause they found, in many instances, several inches of water already in their rooms. The work of removing all furniture, carpets &c., was at once commenced, which continued for some time. Whilst this was going on others were blockading their doors and gateways to prevent the fast-rising water entering their premises. When this was completed the back and front doors were thrown open and the water allowed to rush through the passages into the streets. Plenty of passengers were found by enterprising proprietors of vehicles willing to be conveyed through the water at the nominal charge of a penny each way. Others were seen in boats, on bicycles and tricycles, and even in tubs. About noon the water began to subside, and towards six in the evening there was very little water left in the streets, but it still remained in the low-placed houses when their inhabitants retired to rest for the night.'

29 October

On this day in 1642, Charles I arrived in Oxford, six days after the inconclusive battle at Edgehill, his troops flying colours captured from the Parliamentary

Civil War defences around Oxford: Castle Mound can be seen to the right

forces. The king was formally welcomed at Carfax by the mayor and aldermen, who presented the city's gift of £250, modest compared with the University's £10,000. Then Charles rode down Fish Street to Christ Church.

The king took up residence in the Deanery in Tom Quad, and Christ Church filled with courtiers, many of whom were also government servants or high-ranking officers. Lords Commissioners and a military governor were appointed to form a council of war. Though many important Royalists were resident in other parishes, some were in the best houses in St Aldate's, close by Christ Church.

In July 1643, Queen Henrietta Maria arrived from Holland and brought with her the considerable number of troops, heavy cannon, and arms which she had raised. Councillors agreed that 'the whole house shall repair to the Penniless Bench [at Carfax] in their best array and there stand ready at her Majesty's coming'. The streets were strewn with flowers, and after the ceremony the king conducted her to her own lodgings in Merton.

Oxford had become a garrison city. Buildings changed function and academic life ground to a halt. The Royalist ordnance office, which controlled the movement of military equipment in and out of the city, was based at New College, and small arms and powder were stored there. The Bodleian Library—one of the University's newest and most prestigious buildings—became a warehouse and repair depot. Heavy ordnance and repair sheds filled Magdalen Grove beyond the Eastgate, and mills on the outskirts of town were used to grind sword blades and manufacture gunpowder.

30 October

On this day in 1882, shop manager's wife Mrs Gibbs placed a bag containing £26 14s in gold and silver on the mantelpiece in her bedroom over the grocer's shop in Middle Row, Chipping Norton. She was up on the next floor for about ten minutes before she heard a noise in her own room. She went back down to her room and found a strange man standing there holding the bag of money, plus her gold watch and chain which had been near it.

Mrs Gibbs screamed loudly, and as she flopped down in a faint, the man escaped through the back bedroom. She did not recognise him, but she was sure he was wearing her husband's sealskin cap and a dark coat.

Her husband John Gibbs rushed upstairs and asked her what was the matter. She said that a man had taken the bag of money and her watch. After finding nothing on the top floor, Mr Gibbs searched the shop and the back of the house, and asked whether anyone had been seen leaving the premises. His enquiries proved fruitless. Searching more carefully upstairs, he found six dessert spoons and a pair of his wife's boots wrapped in his overcoat in the back bedroom. In the back sitting room downstairs he found his wife's watch and chain under a chair by an open window. On the same evening, in the company of Sgt Cope, Mr Gibbs found the bag of money secreted on top of the wardrobe in the back bedroom.

Edward Reeves, a groom who lived in a cottage at the back of the premises in question, was charged with the thefts, but as there was insufficient evidence to link him with the events in the shop, he was discharged to the accompaniment of much applause in court.

31 October

On this day 1956, vehement anti-Nazi Sir Franz Simon, physicist, died of coronary disease at the Radcliffe Infirmary.

Franz Eugen Simon was born into a wealthy Jewish merchant family in Berlin in 1893. By 1931 he was regarded internationally as the outstanding low-temperature physicist of his generation. After Hitler came to power he was at first exempt from persecution because he had been awarded the Iron Cross (first class) for his service on the Western Front in the First World War, but he wisely accepted an invitation to join the academic community in Oxford. He became Reader in Thermodynamics in 1936 and a student of Christ Church. From 1939 he was an important figure in the British 'Tube Alloys' Project and other aspects of atomic energy. In 1941 he was made a Fellow of the Royal Society, and the Chair of Thermodynamics at Oxford was created specially for him. He verified experimentally the third law of thermodynamics and under his guidance Oxford became the world's largest and most renowned centre for the study of low-temperature physics.

To the end of his life he could neither forget nor forgive the record of Nazi Germany and remained convinced that the spirit which made Nazism possible was still alive in Germany. He and his wife received countless refugees at their home at 10 Belbroughton Road.

1 November

On this day in 1568, foul-mouthed bishop of Oxford Hugh Curwen was buried at Burford church. He had been bishop of Oxford for only a year or so, having made himself unpopular in his most recent post.

For the previous 13 years he had been in Ireland; Queen Mary made him archbishop of Dublin in February 1555, in September he also became lord chancellor of Ireland, and he arrived in that country in October 1555. He preached his first sermon in Ireland in Advent 1555 at Christ Church, Dublin, where he also reinstated a marble statue of Christ taken down by Archbishop Browne. In 1559 the statue drew significant attention to itself when it was seen to bleed from the head during a Sunday service. Curwen, 'being displeased', bade a sexton investigate and a blood-soaked sponge was found concealed amid the crown of thorns. The fraudsters, were punished by being obliged to stand for three Sundays before the pulpit with their hands and legs tied.

Curwen's laziness exasperated his colleagues, with one complaining that he only 'preacheth now and then', and another that he ought to be 'provided for at home', ie, put out to grass. Archbishop Loftus of Armagh accused him of swearing 'terribly' in open court, adding: 'Is it not time and more than time that such a one be removed?' By now suffering from palsy (paralysis), Curwen was clearly unfit for the duties of his new diocese. He settled in Swinbrook where he died in October 1568.

> The Beatles at the Windrush Inn near Witney

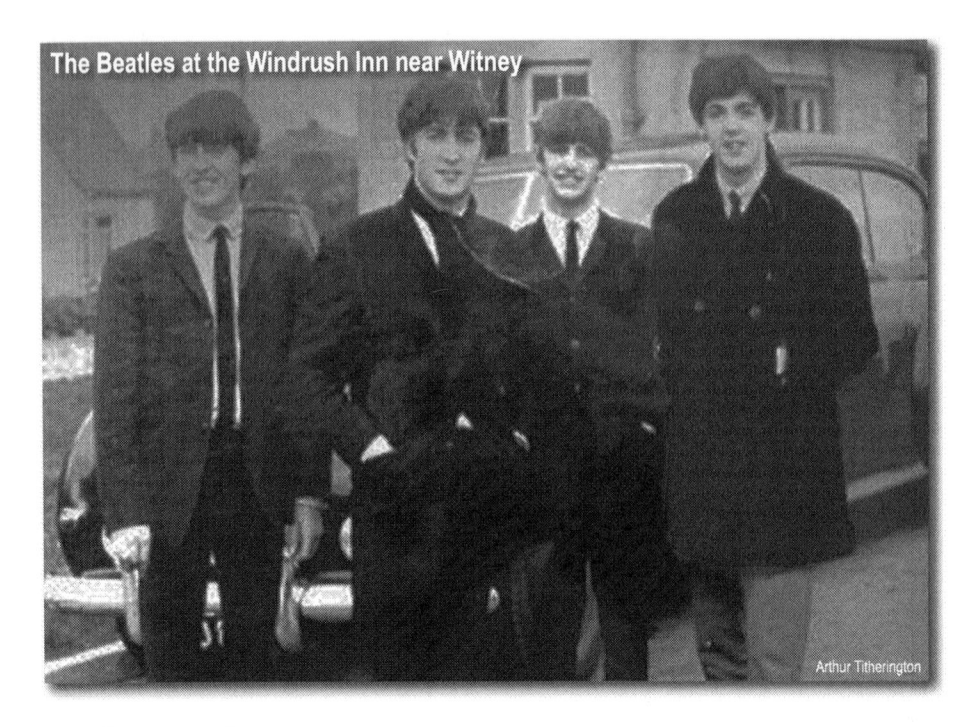

2 November

On this day in 1963, the Beatles stopped at the Windrush Inn on the Burford Road just outside Witney; the boys were on their way to Cheltenham. Their black Austin Princess stopped on the main forecourt outside the pub, and a member of their team went inside to ask if lunch could be served.

According to landlord Ted Thompson: 'The man said it was for the Beatles. They were feeling tired and could their presence be kept quiet?' Margaret Hill was waitressing in the dining room. 'I didn't know whether I was coming or going,' she said. Evidently Mr Thompson succeeded in his mission, because the boys managed to have a peaceful lunch and go on their way unnoticed.

Two days earlier, the band had experienced their first major airport reception at Heathrow on their return from Sweden. The group and their entourage flew back second class in a Scandinavian Airlines Caravelle aircraft. Upon their arrival in England there were thousands of fans at the airport, standing outside in spite of heavy rain. The Beatles initially thought the fans were waiting to see the Queen, but soon realised the extent of their popularity back home. Many of the fans were sporting Beatle haircuts, and the screams were so loud that they drowned out the noise of the jet engines.

3 November

On this day in 1835, gamekeeper Thomas Cooper, 68, left home in Woodeaton near Islip at around 3 o'clock in the afternoon, carrying his gun in order to procure game as requested by his employer, Richard Weyland MP. He was never seen alive again, except by his murderer.

At the inquest next day, Mrs Cooper revealed that she expected her husband home between 5 and 7pm. By 4 o'clock the following morning, Cooper had not returned, so Mrs Cooper sought the assistance of cordwainer George Phillips. Phillips sat with her until about 6.30am, and then went in search of Cooper.

He found the keeper's body under a hedge dividing East Wood from Middle Wood. Cooper, who was hard of hearing, had been shot at close range in the back of the head and then, after he fell, bludgeoned so fiercely with the butt of a gun that his face left an imprint in the mud. His gun was missing.

Several reports suggest that a gunshot was heard just after 5pm, and then an explosion at about 8pm—presumably Cooper's fully-loaded powder flask. Cooper's jacket was mostly burned away as a result of his powder flask igniting. Notorious poacher Thomas Clay was seen between 5 and 6pm walking casually towards his brother's cottage near Bushey Park, holding a gun.

Clay was apprehended the following day while working on the turnpike road. He maintained his innocence from first to last, and appeared confident he would be cleared. Footprints in the mud around the body were deemed to come from shoes belonging to Clay, although the shoemaker pointed out that he had made several pairs off the same last. On this circumstantial evidence, Clay was sentenced to death. In spite of the exhortations of the prison chaplain, Clay refused to make a last-minute confession, and was duly hanged in March 1836.

4 November

On this day in 1546, Christ Church was refounded as a college by Henry VIII under its present name.

Originally founded as Cardinal's College in 1524 by Cardinal Wolsey, then Henry VIII's chief advisor, the project embodied the Renaissance initiative to improve education and train young men for an active life in the church or state. The money for it was to come from closing monasteries, including the

Cardinal College, as founded by Cardinal Wolsey

St Frideswide's priory in Oxford, whose site was to provide the nucleus for the new college. St Frideswide's was an ideal starting point for Wolsey; it was on the edge of what was already a university town, with its own substantial priory church and buildings, but in 1520 there were only nine men living there. Wolsey hoped that by closing the monastery and turning it into a college he could prove his own credentials as a humanist intellectual, putting the wealth of the church to a more practical use.

The foundation stones were quickly laid and work began on the hall, but in 1529 Wolsey fell from power and his grand plans had to be revised. The college was taken over by Henry VIII and re-founded in 1546 as Aedes Christi, the House (or Church) of Christ. Henry had even more ambitious plans for the foundation. It was to be the cathedral church of a new diocese as well as a place of scholarship. Christ Church Cathedral School was also founded for the education of boy choristers.

5 November

On this day in 1997, historian Isaiah Berlin died at Headington House in Oxford.

A figure of towering intellect, Isaiah Berlin was one of the most important thinkers of the 20th century. His major concern was the assertion of individual freedom against the tyranny of absolute systems whether of philosophers or regimes. He was born in Riga in 1909 into a Russian-speaking Jewish family. In 1921 the family came to England. Berlin attended St Paul's School and in 1928 went up to Corpus Christi College, Oxford, where he took Firsts in Greats and PPE. He became a lecturer in philosophy and then Fellow of New College and also a Fellow of All Souls.

During the Second World War he was attached to the British Embassy in Washington and responsible for sending influential despatches back to Whitehall. In 1950 he returned to All Souls and in 1957 was elected to the Chichele Chair of Social and Political Theory. In 1966 he became the founding President of Wolfson College, the Oxford graduate college whose evolution owed much to his fund-raising skills and charisma. He remained there until his retirement in 1975.

He had been knighted in 1957 and became FBA in the same year. In 1971 he received the Order of Merit. In 1956, in his late 40s, he married Aline Halban, a daughter of the de Gunzbourg banking family, and came to live at Headington House where he remained until his death in 1997.

6 November

On this day in 1894, little Ethel Stockford, coming up for three, went into convulsions and died at her home in Little Rollright. It was not unexpected.

On the previous evening, Ethel had been sitting in front of the fire. A kettle of hot water was perched on the fire and, when the coals settled, it fell towards the child. Scalding water streamed down her left arm, leaving appalling burns. Ethel's parents labourer George Stockford and his wife Fanny frantically applied linseed oil to the wounds, and the following day medical assistance was summoned. But Ethel began to have convulsions, and died.

George Stockford's employer, farmer James Bliss, put a room in his house at the disposal of the police for the purpose of the inquest. Neighbour Mrs Mary Woodford, George Stockford, and W R Dix, assistant to Dr O'Kelly of Chipping Norton, gave evidence. Mr Dix explained that a serious scald to such a young child is very dangerous, and renders it liable to convulsions. A verdict of 'death from convulsions caused by being accidentally scalded' was returned. George and Fanny Stockford went on to have two more children.

7 November

On this day in 1883, poor Sidney Prewett unintentionally caused a sensation in Abingdon.

Prewett, 41, had taken charge of Abingdon lock at the beginning of the summer, having spent most of his working life in the Army and the Royal Navy. Soon after midday, Prewett spotted some wood floating on the current through the weir, and leaned over to try and retrieve it. Toppling over, he fell through the beams of the rushing weir and into the broiling weir pool. Nearby some Thames Conservancy workmen were building a new waterfall. They saw Prewett struggling in the water for a few moments, but they were powerless to help, the water level being very high and the current extremely strong. A party of men spent the afternoon dragging the river in search of a body, but without success. The fact that a man had been a sailor did not necessarily mean he could swim, and anyway the power and volume of rushing water passing through a weir is terrific.

It later emerged that Sidney had almost slipped into the river earlier that morning so, it was concluded, he must have been an inexperienced waterman. Nevertheless, he was considered locally a steady man, much respected by boating parties. Sympathy was expressed for his widow Rose and four small children.

Rose remarried in 1889 to biscuit factory labourer Edward Pyke, and the couple lived in Amity Road, Reading.

8 November

On this day in 1961, Norman Scott set off from Oxford to find Jeremy Thorpe MP.

Norman Josiffe was born in Sidcup, Kent, in February 1940—he did not assume the name Scott until 1967. In 1959 Josiffe moved to Kingham Stables near Chipping Norton where he learned dressage while working as a groom. The stables were owned by Norman Vater, the self-made son of a coalminer who, like Josiffe, had inflated his name and was known as Brecht Van de Vater. In the course of his rise, Vater had made numerous friends in higher social circles, among them Thorpe.

Norman Scott

In late 1960 or early 1961, Thorpe visited Vater at the Kingham Stables, and briefly met Josiffe. He was sufficiently taken with the young man to suggest that, should Josiffe ever need help, he should call on him at the House of Commons. Soon after this, Josiffe left the stables after a serious disagreement with Vater. He then suffered a mental breakdown, and for much of 1961 was under psychiatric care. A week after discharging himself from the Ashurst clinic in Oxford, Josiffe went to the House of Commons to see Thorpe.

He was penniless, homeless and, worse, had left Vater's employment without the National Insurance card which, at that time, was essential for obtaining regular work and access to social security and unemployment benefits. Thorpe promised he would help, and took Josiffe/Scott to his mother's home in Oxted in Surrey that evening. Thus began a relationship between the two men—illegal at the time—that would culminate in a badly-planned and bungled attempt to murder Scott in 1975. Thorpe was tried for conspiracy to murder, but acquitted amidst public unease.

9 November

On this day in 1892, the dissolute 8th Duke of Marlborough was found by his valet dead in his bed at Blenheim Palace, aged 48.

George Spencer-Churchill was gifted intellectually, and a member of the Liberal Party. At the general election of 1874 he bitterly opposed his younger brother Lord Randolph's candidacy as Conservative MP for Woodstock. Lord Randolph (father of Winston) won, and held on to the seat until 1885.

The Duke led a dissipated life which much depleted the family finances. In 1883 he was obliged to sell off many treasures from the Palace to meet the demands of his creditors. While married to his first wife, he fathered an illegitimate son, initially known as Guy Bertrand and later known as Guy Bertrand Spencer, by Edith Peers-Williams, wife of Heneage Finch, 7th Earl of Aylesford. Lord Aylesford launched a divorce suit which would have exposed the Churchills to unfavourable press attention so, in an attempt to pressure Lord Aylesford to drop the suit, Lady Aylesford and Lord Randolph Churchill threatened the Princess of Wales that they would subpoena the Prince of Wales as a witness in the divorce. The suit was dropped.

The Duke was also cited as one of four co-respondents in the sensational divorce trial of Lady Colin Campbell in 1886. Cold-shouldered by society, the Duke spent much time in America. In the winter of 1887 he met beautiful widow Lillian Hammersley, and married her in the following June.

10 November

On this day in 1789, at the Church of St Faith in Shellingford, a fisherman's granddaughter named Elizabeth Flower married Francis Warneford of Warneford Place, Sevenhampton near Highworth in Wiltshire.

Twenty-three years before, Elizabeth's mother Betty Ridge was six weeks pregnant when she married William Flower, Lord Ashbrook, in the little country Church of St Denys at Northmoor. Francis Warneford's mother, Catherine Calverley, objected strongly to her son marrying William and Betty's daughter Elizabeth Flower, but this was nothing new. The Warnefords were an extremely argumentative family who squabbled over everything.

Francis's brother Samuel Wilson Warneford augmented his own fortune by marrying Margaret Loveden of Buscot Park. After she died childless, Samuel resolved to put his money to good use, and founded the Warneford Lunatic Asylum in Oxford, now the Warneford Hospital. Margaret's brother Pryse Loveden Pryse of Buscot Park married Elizabeth Flower's sister Harriet. Harriet died following a mysterious fire at New Year 1813.

11 November

On this day in 1923, the Oxfordshire and Buckinghamshire Light Infantry war memorial at the foot of Rose Hill was dedicated.

It was originally proposed that the regimental memorial should be sited close to its barracks in Bullingdon Green, but it proved impossible to acquire a suitable site. Instead, it was built on land donated by Christ Church on Rose Hill. The location was specifically chosen so that the memorial could be seen against the sky. The memorial cost £878 10s and was unveiled by the regiment's colonel Major-General Sir John Hanbury-Williams.

Sir Edwin Lutyens was the leading English architect of his generation. Before the First World War his reputation rested on his country houses and his work at New Delhi, but during and after the war he became the pre-eminent architect for war memorials in England, France and the British Empire. One of the best-known is the Cenotaph in Whitehall in London.

12 November

On this day in 1971, Marston Ferry Road opened, replacing the ferry over the Cherwell. The name 'Marston' derives from the Anglo-Saxon equivalent of 'Marsh-town', and the road is named after the ferry that used to cross the River Cherwell at the village from at least 1279.

The first mention of a ferry at Marston is in 1279, when it was held as a freehold of the manor by two fishermen of Oxford. The position of this early ferry cannot be identified, and no ferry is shown on any map prior to the Ordnance Survey map of 1876. The ferry was at the nearest point of the Cherwell to Marston village, and a footpath led to Summertown. Latterly a punt could be pulled from one bank to the other using a tow rope, but carried pedestrians and bicycles only.

Until the 20th century there was no road-bridge between Magdalen Bridge and Islip, so that Marston was comparatively isolated: the distance by road to Carfax was more than 2½ miles. In 1942 Arthur Mee described Marston in *The King's England* as 'a quiet place among elms and green fields'. But in 1949 Reginald Turnor wrote in *Oxfordshire* that 'Summertown and an arterial road and Headington hedge it about too closely. It would be easy to be there "student and don", but hardly, I fear, "countryman".'

13 November

On this day in 1002, the St Brice's Day massacre took place in Oxford. It was royally-sanctioned murder of people of Danish heritage.

A royal charter issued by King Aethelred two years afterwards explains what happened: 'For it is fully agreed that to all dwelling in this country it will be well known that, since a decree was sent out by me with the counsel of my leading men and magnates, to the effect that all the Danes who had sprung up in this island, sprouting like cockle [weeds] amongst the wheat, were to be destroyed by a most just extermination, and thus this decree was to be put into effect even as far as death, those Danes who dwelt in the afore-mentioned town, striving to escape death, entered this sanctuary of Christ [the Church of St Frideswide], having broken by force the doors and bolts, and resolved to make refuge and defence for themselves therein against the people of the town and the suburbs; but when all the people in pursuit strove, forced by necessity, to drive them out, and could not, they set fire to the planks and burnt, as it seems, this church with its ornaments and its books. Afterwards, with God's aid, it was renewed by me.'

The skeletons of 34 to 38 young men, all aged 16 to 25, were found during an excavation at St John's College in 2008. Analysis carried out in 2012 by Oxford University researchers suggests that the remains are Viking. Charring on the bones is consistent with Aethelred's description of the church burning.

14 November

On this day in 1894, Oxfordshire continued to endure the worst floods for decades, with over an inch of rain added to an already inundated landscape. As *Jackson's Oxford Journal* pointed out, one inch of rain delivers a hundred tons of water per acre, and after a few days some places were three to four feet deep in the stuff.

A fortnight previously, the valleys of the Thames and Cherwell had experienced heavy downpours, then on Sunday 10 November a beautiful day terminated in a steady downpour which lasted through the night and almost all day on Monday. Port Meadow was virtually all submerged. Fine weather on Tuesday was succeeded on Wednesday by more violent storms than before,

Floods at Oxford, 1894. Abingdon Road.

Nothing got in the way of the beer delivery at the Fox and Hounds in Headington

and basements were flooded in Grandpont, Hinksey, Osney, Jericho, the Friars, and Paradise Square.

By Thursday evening the water was several inches deep in Albert Street and a man was seen paddling about in a tub at the corner of Clarendon and Wellington Streets. The Botley Road was two feet under water, and the railway was greatly disrupted, with nine inches of water on the line near the bridge at Cold Harbour.

Miles upon miles of meadow land was under water around Abingdon, and the postman was obliged to deliver letters in the town by means of a horse and trap, handing the post to residents through their bedroom windows. At Lower Mill cottages in Chipping Norton, gardens were flooded, and pigs had to be rescued from drowning in their styes. In the village street at Crowmarsh near Wallingford the water was described as being 'over a horse's knees'.

15 November

On this day in 1887, Chipping Norton saddler Joseph Walker was hanged for murdering his wife. Henrietta Collett was Walker's second wife; a heavy drinker, she disliked her step-children Fred, 19, Julia, 17, and Joseph, 14, and made sure everyone knew it. The unhappy atmosphere in the home in Market Street persuaded Fred to move out and Walker himself to take to the bottle. Noisy rows became a frequent occurrence along with mutual accusations of infidelity. Three weeks before the murder, Walker had received a knife wound to his eye during a row with his wife.

On 16 September Walker had sold two pigs to the landlord of the Chequers Inn. He spent part of the proceeds in the pub, and that evening Henrietta made her views on this clear. Tensions in the household were running particularly high at the time because of the suicide a fortnight before of 19-year-old Fred, who had hanged himself in Croydon. Walker berated Henrietta, blaming her for Fred's depressed state of mind.

Joseph junior retreated upstairs, but he soon heard renewed hostilities followed by a scream. Rushing downstairs, he found his father—a powerfully-built man—kneeling on a prostrate Mrs Walker in front of the fire. Her throat was deeply cut from ear to ear, and a razor-sharp cheese-knife had been thrown into the fender. Walker told his son to run for a doctor and a policeman, which he did. Far from expressing remorse, Walker more than once announced quietly: 'I have killed my wife, and I hope I have made a good job of it.'

On the day of his execution he thanked everyone who had looked after him in prison, and shook hands with the warder and with the executioner. A quarter of an hour before the appointed time, a bell began to toll. As Walker died a black flag was raised at the front of the prison, and the bell continued to toll for a further 15 minutes.

16 November

On this day in 1880, 14-year-old Daniel Howson died a few days after an accident while he was working on construction of the Didcot, Newbury, and Southampton Junction railway.

Work began on the construction of the railway in August 1879. According to the *Newbury Weekly News* of 4 August 1881: 'In the Upton cutting… a steam "navvy" is being used to tear away at the chalk with its three steel teeth: the chalk is then scooped into a bucket capable of holding about a ton: when full, the bucket is swung round to dump its load into a waiting wagon.

'The wagons are then pulled back through the cutting to be emptied further down the line where the Hagbourne embankment is being constructed….' It was one of these wagons that ran over poor Daniel on 11 November when his breaking stick slipped. Daniel's parents Daniel and Harriet were from Bedfordshire, but they moved around the country in pursuit of Mr Howson's work as a labourer. And it was the railway that brought the Howsons, and so many others, to Upton at this time. The families lived in railway huts.

Mrs Howson told the inquest at the George and Dragon on the day after her son's death that she 'blames no one in the matter, and thought it was a pure accident'. By 1891 the Howsons had sufficient savings to have set themselves up at The Goat public house in High Wycombe.

17 November

On this day in 1905, the northern lights could be seen from Bicester and as far south as Muswell Hill. The *Bicester Advertiser* reported: 'The sky on Wednesday evening had a most curious appearance caused by what is known as "Northern Lights". The attention of those who chanced to be out between the hours of eight and nine was attracted to the north-east, in which direction the sky had a beautiful crimson glow, and this appeared to move in various directions, caused by the clouds traversing in the light of the moon. We hear that from Muswell Hill a magnificent view of the phenomenon could be obtained.'

When the phenomenon appeared again in 2016, a more accurate explanation was offered by the *Guardian*: 'The aurora borealis was visible as far south as Oxfordshire on Sunday evening as the weather cleared, painting the night sky with shades of green, purple and blue. The ethereal spectacle is caused by charged solar particles interacting with the Earth's magnetic field and is usually only visible in the far north of Scotland.

A lucky combination of conditions in the lower atmosphere and in space meant the aurora was visible across swathes of the country, Met Office space weather adviser Amanda Townsend said. "Once in a while the solar winds are enhanced to levels stronger than normal, with particles at higher speeds, and on this occasion it has connected really well with the Earth's magnetic field." In addition to the cosmic weather being just right, conditions closer to the ground favoured those who ventured out into the cold to see the spectacle. Skies were clear over much of Scotland and England.'

18 November

On this day in 1883, two traps collided on the Hailey Road near Witney. One belonged to Witney notable, William Payne, 60, coal merchant, railway agent, and carrier of High Street, Witney. In the other trap was Frank Barnes, 28, plumber, glazier, and painter, who lived in Corn Street.

Barnes was on his way to Hailey. In Payne's trap was the Rev Alexander Fogwell, 41, Wesleyan minister of Mount House, driving back to Witney from Finstock accompanied by two other preachers. Barnes saw the danger and drew up to one side, shouting unsuccessfully to the driver of the Payne's trap 'but without attracting the attention of the occupants of the other trap until too late,' as *Jackson's Oxford Journal* put it, neatly transferring the blame away from the Witney bigwig Payne and his holy customers and onto the humble young house-painter Barnes.

Payne's trap hurtled on regardless, crashing into Barnes and pitching Rev Fogwell and his companions into the ditch. The horse broke away, taking the shafts of the vehicle with it. 'Not much injury' was done to either party, we are told, but Payne's vehicle and harness were badly damaged. No word reaches down to us about the fate of the horse.

19 November

On this day in 1669, at between 2 and 3am, according to *Jackson's Oxford Journal*: 'broke out a lamentable fier at Christ Church, in Dr. Richard's lodgings, viz., those next to the fields, which Dr. Henry Kyng built.

'All inside of them was clearly consumed and about 3 chambers on the south side of the bachelor's quadrangle, on the west side of the said lodging, consumed also. The lodgings also which Dr. Sebastian Smith lay in, joyning on the north side, were burnt and blowne up to prevent the fier from going towards the quadrangle. That part of Dr. Smith's lodgings took up the east side almost of the quadrangle. The fier began on the top of Dr. Gardiner's lodgings, in a cock loft [garret], by the negligence of a young scholar. It began on the 3rd storey (next under the cockle loft), in Mr. Chumley's chamber, a gent. commoner, who having made a larg fier over night, took hold of the joyst that ran under the chimney. He was forced to crawl upon the ridge of the house to save himself because the staircase was burning.' It is to Dr Gardiner, a canon at Christ Church, that Tom Quad owes its elegant central pond. His gift was intended to serve as a water source in a similar emergency in future. 'Chumley' was probably a son of Thomas Cholmondeley MP of Vale Royal in Cheshire.

20 November

On this day in 1888, an inquest took place at the White Hart Inn, Wolvercote, into the suicide of Mary Ann Paintin, aged 22.

Swinbrook carpenter's daughter Mary Ann, who was in service with the Wards at 'The Firs' in the Banbury Road, was pulled by some fishermen out of the canal on the previous Sunday afternoon—dead, but still warm to the touch. Mary had already hinted to her sister Elizabeth that she was expecting a child. She had even invited the young man in the question, John Wake of Abingdon, 23, to tea at her sister's house in Oxford. When he failed to reply to a letter she wrote in October, Mary Ann went, accompanied by a friend Flora Edgington, to visit him at his place of work—the place where she had originally met him.

The two had an awkward exchange. Wake asked: 'What have you come to see me about?' Mary Ann replied: 'You know what I have come about; you have got me into trouble.' 'No such thing,' retorted Wake. 'I have only walked beside you twice.' Mary Ann told him he would hear more on the matter.

A week later, realising that Wake was not going to stand by her, Mary Ann took poison before throwing herself into the canal. Under her pillow she had left a letter to her mother: 'My Dear Mother, I am writing to you the last letter that ever my hand will write to you. I shall be Dead and Cold before you receive it. I have always been a poor Despised Child and ill-treated wherever I have been. My life was a perfect misery. I have been Deceived twice and have been driven to do what I have done to Cause my Death… I have left all my clothes [and] my watch all to my only Darling Child Edie. Your daughter, Mary.'

Mary Ann's first illegitimate baby, Florence Edith, had been born in Headington Union workhouse in 1886. Florence appears to have enjoyed better luck in life than her mother. At 15, she worked as an assistant teacher at the National School. In 1929 she married decorator Albert Lynch at St Matthew's, Oxford. John Wake married Mary's friend Flora Edgington in 1890, and the couple set up home in Ock Street in Abingdon.

21 November

On this day in 1596, the so-called Oxfordshire Rising commenced on Enslow Hill north of Oxford. Falling agricultural wages coincided with rising food prices and the imposition of much-despised enclosures deprived ordinary people of commonland to graze their animals. A small group of impoverished men developed a plan to seize weapons and armour and march on London, hoping to attract 200 or 300 men from various towns along the way, and then to link up with the highly-politicised (and numerous) London apprentices.

They met at 9am on the appointed day, but only four men turned up: Hampton Poyle carpenter Bartholomew Steer, Thomas Horne, a servant from Hampton Gay, Robert Burton, a Beckley mason, and Edward Bompass, a fuller who had promised to bring support from the neighbouring village of Kirtlington. Their proposed violent methods may have put others off. The plotters were quickly arrested after a servant, Roger Symonds, whom Steer had tried to recruit, informed his landlord of the plan.

Sir Edward Coke advised that the ringleaders were liable for charges of treason, 'making war against the Queen', under a 1571 Act, although it appears that not all the statute's legal requirements had in fact been met. Five principal ringleaders—Steer, James and Richard Bradshaw, Bompass, and Burton—were taken to London tied to the backs of horses and closely guarded to prevent their conversing with one another. There they were lodged in separate prisons and interrogated. Around 20 other men were also imprisoned or interrogated, though not charged with treason as the ringleaders eventually were.

As the authorities were eager to discover if any gentry were involved in the conspiracy, the use of torture was authorised, and Coke pursued the charges with extreme aggression, despite the misgivings of several judges regarding his interpretation of the statutes. Steer and James Bradshaw probably died in prison. Burton and Richard Bradshaw were executed on Enslow Hill, within sight of the enclosures they had wished to remove.

22 November

On this day in 1900, little Thomas Hughes, 3, went missing at Duck End Farm, Great Rollright. After lunch his mother had let him out to play; he

Duck End House at Great Rollright

liked to fill his wheelbarrow with sticks. Domestic servant Edith Grafton, 13, saw him trundling happily past the window with his barrow. After about five minutes, Mrs Hughes called to Edith from upstairs to go and check on the boy.

When Edith went outside, she saw Tommy's little wheelbarrow outside the boiling-house. The boiling-house was so-named because inside was a tank used for mashing meal, milk, and food scraps for the pigs. The frame of the tank was level with the floor, and on this particular day the lid had been left open and there was a layer of milk about 18 inches deep at the top. Tommy lay, face-up in the liquid, his straw hat floating beside him.

Edith called out for help to groom Alfred Coles, 27, who rushed into the boiling-house and pulled the boy out. But Tommy was already dead. Around the time Tommy first came outside to play, Alfred had popped in to the boiling-house for a rake and left the door open.

The coroner's inquest was held in the dining-room at Duck End Farm, and medical practitioner Henry Whitley from Chipping Norton declared that Tommy must have peered over the edge to look into the tank and toppled in. The boy never uttered a sound.

23 November

On this day in 1990, author Roald Dahl died at the John Radcliffe hospital, aged 74. Dahl was born in Llandaff, near Cardiff, in September 1916. In April

1942, aged 25, Dahl was posted to Washington DC to join the British Embassy as assistant air attaché. In the US he became a spy working in a division of MI6 alongside Ian Fleming, the creator of James Bond. (Dahl later adapted Fleming's novel *You Only Live Twice* for the 1967 Bond film.)

In December 1960, while the family was living in New York City, Dahl's four-month-old-son Theo was hit by a taxi and suffered traumatic brain injury. As a result Theo developed a medial condition called hydrocephalus—a build-up of fluid on the brain. Together with neurosurgeon Kenneth Till and toymaker Stanley Wade, who specialised in making small hydraulic pumps that supplied fuel to model aeroplane engines, Dahl designed a cerebral shunt used to drain excess fluid from the brain. The device has since been used in thousands of operations, although Theo himself recovered from his accident and did not require the valve.

In November 1962 Dahl's eldest daughter, Olivia, died from measles encephalitis, aged just seven. And in February 1965 his wife, actress Patricia Neal, suffered a series of strokes while filming in Los Angeles. The strokes left Patricia in a coma for three weeks; after regaining consciousness she was semi-paralysed and unable to speak. However, with Roald's help, she learned to walk and talk again. At the time of her stroke Patricia was three months pregnant with their fifth child (and fourth daughter), Lucy, who was born on 4 August.

24 November

On this day in 1899, the Kaiser visited Blenheim Palace, accompanied by the Prince of Wales. The royal train arrived at Woodstock station at 1.15pm prompt. Awaiting the important personages on the platform were the Duke and Duchess of Marlborough and various other dignitaries, plus a guard of honour furnished by the Woodstock Troop of the Queen's Own Oxfordshire Hussars. The entire party drove in an open-topped carriage drawn by four horses with postilions past cheering crowds in a town gaily decorated with flags, and then entered the park through the famous arch.

In the afternoon the Kaiser was shown some of the treasures inside the palace, and drove round the grounds. He planted a conifer in the park to commemorate his visit. At half-past four a crowd assembled at the station to give the royal party a hearty send-off. The Duchess of Marlborough at the time was the

American railroad heiress Consuelo Vanderbilt. Aware that her husband loved another woman, Consuelo shocked society by leaving her husband in 1906.

25 November

On this day in 1993, the first minibus of immigration detainees arrived at Campsfield House detention centre in Kidlington. Formerly a young offenders' institute, Campsfield was converted into an immigration detention centre in 1993 amid a storm of protest from local residents.

Within six months of opening Campsfield experienced a major problem when six asylum seekers escaped following a rooftop protest. In June 2005 a group of six Zimbabwean asylum seekers went on hunger strike for three days. A few days later, detainee Ramazan Komluca, committed suicide. The 19-year-old from Turkey had been detained for about six months, and had made three unsuccessful bail applications.

The centre continued to be plagued by arson, riot, hunger strikes and breakouts. One escapee was apprehended by a resident living nearby who said it was the third time he had found a detainee in his garden. In November 2018 the Government finally announced that the 216-bed facility would shut after 25 years. The last detainees left in the following month.

26 November

On this day in 2018, a gold seal ring found in Bampton was sold for £10,000 at Hanson's Auctions in Derbyshire. Paul Wood, 64, a driving instructor from Dorset, discovered the ring with a metal detector in August 2016 while exploring land sold for housing development. It is engraved with an elaborate coat of arms and crest which is believed to represent the Skinner family. According to research carried out by Mr Wood, the Skinners

The Bampton ring

were prominent in the Bampton region from the 13th century onwards. There are many entries for the Skinner family in the parish registers for the 1600s and 1700s.

James Brenchley of Hanson's said: 'Due to [the ring] being rather small, it may have belonged to a lady. The coat of arms features an elegant chevron decorated with small dots between three birds' heads. Above the shield is a well-detailed helm, from which emerges elaborate mantling on either side. Just above the helm, the crest consists of another bird's head rising from a battlement, its mouth open and neck decorated with thin lines to indicated ruffled feathers.'

27 November

On this day in 1678, at one o'clock in the morning, a fire broke out at Burroughs' ironmonger's in the parish of All Hallows, Oxford. It spread to the lower back room of Souche the milliner's next door. Souche and his wife slept in the room above where the fire reached their house; choking on the smoke woke them up. While Mr Souche ran downstairs to quench the flames, Mrs Souche passed out and was burnt to death where she lay. By this time, Burroughs' house was thoroughly alight, but the dragoons managed to put out the conflagration. They were awarded £5 by the University for their vigilance.

Rumours sprang up that the whole business was the responsibility of Papists. This was the year of the totally fictitious but widely-believed Popish Plot in which it was alleged that Jesuits were planning the assassination of King Charles II in order to bring his Roman Catholic brother, the Duke of York (afterward King James II), to the throne.

28 November

On this day in 1695, antiquary Anthony Wood died in Oxford. Wood was born in 1632 in Postmasters' Hall which was leased by the family from Merton College. He attended schools in Oxford and Thame and entered Merton where he was considered a mediocre student, not destined for an academic career. His interest turned instead to antiquarian research.

Wood set about amassing a huge quantity of information which involved

Anthony Wood, Oxford antiquary

gleaning university, college and parish archives, trawling through bookshops, and gathering information in the shires and in London libraries and record offices. He lived and worked throughout his life in the attic rooms at the top of Postmasters' Hall.

He was a cantankerous and vituperative character who fell out with everyone sooner or later. In 1693 he was sued in the vice-chancellor's court for libelling Edward Hyde, Earl of Clarendon; his book was publicly burnt and he was expelled from the University. He bequeathed his thousands of books and manuscripts to the old Ashmolean and they are now held in the Bodleian. He never married, and led a life of self-denial, entirely devoted to antiquarian research. Bell-ringing and music were his chief relaxations. He was always suspected of being a Roman Catholic, and invariably treated Jacobites and Papists better than Dissenters in his writings, but he died as a member of the Church of England. He was laid to rest in the parish church of St John, now Merton chapel, where his fine monument can be seen.

29 November

On this day in 1880, brothers George and John Jerome, aged 16 and 13 respectively, were charged before Henley's mayor and town magistrates with stealing two-ounce packs of tobacco from Mr J Rowe's shop in Hart Street.

The boys went into the shop for two halfpenny pipes, and each helped himself to a packet of tobacco off the glass counter while the assistant's back was turned. When apprehended in the street outside, they denied all knowledge of the crime, even though John was found to have a two-ounce packet of tobacco in his pocket. Once under lock and key, George admitted taking the other packet.

George had figured in the police court before, so he asked to have the charge dealt with at once. He was sent to Oxford gaol for two months' hard labour. John was detained for another day in order that he might be given 12 lashes of the rod.

The skeletons of young adults from a mid-19th-century graveyard in Whitechapel, East London, show evidence of pipe notches in the front teeth. Since grooves worn into the incisors take a few years to develop, these individuals must have taken up smoking as children. Whilst smoking may have been a necessary narcotic for many hungry and cold Victorian street children, the Jerome brothers appear to have been motivated more by a timeless boyish devilment. More shocking to modern perceptions is that Mr Rowe should blithely sell smoking apparatus to young boys. It was not until the Children's Act of 1908 that the sale of tobacco to under-16s was forbidden.

30 November

On this day in 1874, Winston Churchill was born at the family's ancestral home, Blenheim Palace. Direct descendants of the Dukes of Marlborough, his family was among the highest levels of the British aristocracy, and thus Winston was born into the country's governing elite.

His father, Lord Randolph Churchill, had been elected Conservative MP for Woodstock in 1873. His mother, Jennie Churchill (née Jerome), was from an American family whose substantial wealth derived from finance. The couple lived beyond their income and were frequently in debt; according to the biographer Sebastian Haffner, the family was 'rich by normal standards but poor by those of the rich'. Throughout much of the 1880s Randolph and Jennie were effectively estranged, and during this time she had many suitors. There has been speculation that Randolph was not Winston's biological father. Churchill had virtually no relationship with his father; referring to his mother, Churchill later stated: 'I loved her dearly—but at a distance.'

His relationship with his brother Jack was warm. The brothers were cared for primarily by their nanny. Churchill nicknamed her 'Woomany', and later wrote: 'She had been my dearest and most intimate friend during the whole of the twenty years I had lived'. But, of course, his future wife, the striking Clementine, had not yet come into his life (see 11 August 1908).

1 December

On this day in 1714, the funeral took place in the University Church of St Mary, Oxford, of Dr John Radcliffe. Radcliffe had a great reputation as a physician in the late 17th century, and was one of Oxford University's leading benefactors. His memory is perpetuated in an observatory, two libraries, a college quadrangle, a square, a road, travelling fellowships for medical students and two hospitals.

The son of an attorney, Radcliffe was born in Wakefield, Yorkshire, in 1650. He matriculated at University College, Oxford when he was 13 and was elected to a fellowship at Lincoln College in 1669 aged only 18. He became a lecturer in Logic in 1671 and in Philosophy in 1672. When he was living at Lincoln College, Dr Bathurst, President of Trinity College, called upon him and was surprised to see so few books in his room. Radcliffe is said to have pointed to a skeleton and a couple of vials containing herbs, declaring: 'This is Radcliffe's library!'

He was obliged to resign from his job at Lincoln in 1677 when, under the statutes of the college he was called upon to take holy orders. He moved to London, where he started work earning 20 guineas a day. In 1690 Radcliffe was elected MP for Bramber, and for Buckinghamshire in 1713. Despite being a Jacobite (ie, a supporter of the Stuarts), he became physician to William III and Mary, and attended the king frequently until 1699 when, examining James' skinny frame and swollen ankles, he offended the monarch by remarking: 'I would not have your Majesty's two legs for your three kingdoms.'

2 December

On this day in 1885, 11-year-old Lizzie Miles drowned when Osney Bridge collapsed at 8.30am. Several other people were rescued, but little Lizzie was swept away by the strong current and her remains were not recovered for three years.

Jackson's Oxford Journal reported that a crack appeared in the roadway on the 120-year-old bridge just after 8am and almost immediately part of the stonework on the north side fell into the river. The fourth pier from the Oxford side split in the middle and gave way, and this caused the parapet, the footpath

Osney Bridge on 2 December 1885

and about two or three feet of the roadway and the arch to collapse and fall into the swift-running waters. Four people were thought to have been thrown in the river, one or more of whom were rescued by bootmaker Ebenezer Greenaway, 46, of Mill Street, Osney, who 'gallantly jumped into the water'.

A little girl walking with Lizzie—probably Ada Mole, 12, of Bridge Street—had also gone into the water but, though she tried to hold on to Lizzie's hand, she had to let go because of the current. Ada was pulled into a boat, but Lizzie sank just before she reached it. A reward of 20 shillings was offered to anyone finding Lizzie's body.

Almost three years later on 18 November 1888, Lizzie's remains were eventually spotted in the river near Osney lock by an angler named Brooking. Her step-brother Henry Williams told the inquest jury that Lizzie had been sent to the railway station for a morning paper when she drowned.

3 December

On this day in 649, or some say in 650, Birinus, first Bishop of Dorchester, died. He was known as the 'Apostle to the West Saxons' for his conversion of the Anglo-Saxon kingdom of Wessex to Christianity.

A Frankish Benedictine monk (ie, hailing from the area between the Lower and Middle Rhine), Birinus had been commissioned by Pope Honorius I to convert the West Saxons from paganism to Christianity. In 635, Birinus persuaded the West Saxon king Cynegils to allow him to preach. At the time, Cynegils was trying to create an alliance with Oswald of Northumbria, with whom he intended to fight the Mercians. At the final talks between kings, the sticking point was that Oswald, being a Christian, would not ally himself with a pagan. Cynegils then converted and was baptised. He gave Birinus Dorchester-on-Thames for his episcopal see.

Birinus is said to have been very active in establishing churches in Wessex. Tradition has it that Birinus built the first church at Ipsden, as a small chapel on Berins Hill, about two miles east of the present church. Eventually Winchester displaced Dorchester as the seat of the see, with the bishopric being transferred there in 660. Birinus's relics were eventually translated to Winchester after his death. Dorchester again became the seat of a bishop in around 875, when the Mercian Bishop of Leicester transferred his seat there.

The diocese merged with that of Lindsey in 971; the bishop's seat was moved to Lincoln under the Normans in 1072.

4 December

On this day in 1880, Thomas William Pratt was welcomed for lunch at the Bell Inn at Great Bourton near Banbury, home of his friend William Mercer, publican. After lunch, when Mercer, 40, went out on foot to Little Bourton, Thomas cleared off with his host's horse for a lark.

Thomas managed to do this without being seen from the front of the pub. He gave Joseph Young, 17, a shilling to get Mercer's horse out of the stables. Thomas then led the chestnut horse up through the orchard and Young was instructed to take out a couple of sections of the fence, so that Thomas and the horse might get out on to the main road. Horse and rider then disappeared for the day.

Thomas was a 16-year-old carpenter who lived in Cropredy. His father was a miller, the latest of several generations of millers in the village. In the evening Thomas called at several pubs in Banbury, trying to offload the stolen horse. He called at the Catherine Wheel in Bridge Street and offered the horse for sale for £40, telling the landlord that he was the son of Stephen Hands, an innkeeper in Shenington. Having had no luck, he called at the Town Hall

Tavern at 11pm and asked for a bed, offering the horse for £30 and putting it in the stables. Next morning Thomas rode the horse back home to Cropredy and put it in one of the fields of miller and farmer Richard Hadland of Bourton House. It was found there by PC White the following day.

At the Quarter Sessions in the New Year, Mercer claimed that he would not have prosecuted had the police not become involved. Defending young Thomas, Mr Sim said that the prank was a joke that had got out of hand. Thomas was acquitted with a caution not to carry impudence too far in the future.

5 December

On this day in 1927, in the early hours of the morning, two armed and masked thieves, Frederick Browne and William Kennedy, held up Eynsham station on the Oxford, Witney and Fairford Railway. Browne had formerly lived in Eynsham and was on the run from the police after having shot dead a policeman, PC Gutteridge, in Essex in September 1927. Kennedy was also wanted, as Browne's accomplice.

Browne drove along the line from near South Leigh to Eynsham. A porter, Frederick Castle, arriving by motorcycle, discovered the thieves and challenged them. They held Castle at gunpoint and tied him to a chair in the stationmaster's office. Castle had no key to the safe so Browne and Kennedy tried unsuccessfully to detach it from the floor. They moved Castle from the stationmaster's office to the building housing the ground frame, then escaped with several parcels and the stationmaster's typewriter.

Both were arrested the following January and, after trial at the Old Bailey, they were hanged in May 1928 for the murder of PC Gutteridge. Eynsham station closed to passenger traffic in June 1962 and to goods in April 1965.

6 December

On this day in 1827, at about 11.30pm, two young women looked in at the windows of a Brasenose College student's room. They were Ann Price from Hereford, 24, known in Oxford as Ann Crotchley, and her companion Harriet Mitchell, 18. Within an hour, Ann would be found dying in Blue Boar Lane.

The two girls had known one another only for a couple of days before they spent that Thursday night racketing about the town. The occupant of the college rooms was evidently entertaining at the time because seven or eight young men came to the window. Ann Crotchley asked for a glass of wine and one of the undergraduate guests, Houstonne John Radcliffe (no connection with the John Radcliffe of the Camera, Observatory and hospitals), replied that he had no wine but that he would give her brandy if she would drink it. When she agreed he handed out a tea-pot filled with brandy. Both Ann and Harriet drank and it was estimated that Ann may have had as much as a pint. She then asked for wine again but none was forthcoming.

In due course, Radcliffe bade his host good night and departed from the party. Harriet and Ann split up after leaving Brasenose. Soon afterwards, a watchman found Ann lying insensible in Blue Boar Lane. She was taken to her lodgings where she was attended by a doctor, but she died on Saturday morning from internal injuries inflicted by a sharp stick.

Both city and University offered £100 as rewards for information leading to conviction, but nobody was ever tried for the crime. Radcliffe was sent down for the rest of the academic year and never returned. Brasenose received notice of his death aged 23, less than two years after his departure.

7 December

On this day in 1943, Sir Oswald and Lady Mosley arrived under house arrest at the Shaven Crown Inn in Shipton-under-Wychwood.

Committed Fascists, the Mosleys had been interned since 1940, spending most of the war in a house in the grounds of Holloway prison. They were driven in a modest car round to the back of the hotel in order to

Diana and Oswald Mosley

avoid press attention. On Friday 10 December, Supt Johnston of Oxfordshire Constabulary arrived to serve the couple with the terms of their detention. They were to restrict themselves to their private apartments at the hotel. The family nanny and their two youngest children were with them. Their movements outside the hotel were restricted to a radius of seven miles, and within the county of Oxfordshire. Effectively, this reduced the radius to 3 miles on the Gloucestershire side. There were no other guests in the hotel.

Shaven Crown proprietor Kathleen Jude expressed concern at the persistence of press photographers besieging her business. Indeed, as the police left that day, eight reporters were waiting outside. On the following day, information was received that protestors would be arriving at midday to demonstrate against the presence of the Mosleys in Oxfordshire, but in fact nobody turned up. Foreseeing food shortages after the war ended, Mosley had expressed a wish to acquire a farm locally. By January the couple had found Crux Easton House near Newbury.

8 December

On this day in 1893, 30-year-old housekeeper Kate Dungey was murdered at lonely Lambridge Wood farmhouse near Henley-on-Thames.

The house was leased to a businessman who resided there only during the summer and on occasional visits throughout the rest of the year. Kate spent most of her time alone at the house, but local carpenter John Frome's sons James and Henry, 12 and 10, slept there most nights.

On that Friday evening, James and Henry had their tea at home in Lower Assenden as usual, and arrived at the farmhouse at about 8.30pm to sleep. They knocked on the door several times, but there was no reply. Assuming that Kate was out, they went to shelter from the pouring rain in the well-house. A while later, they went back to see if she had returned. Peering through the glass door, they could see a light burning in the kitchen; the clock stood at 9.50pm. Distressed, the boys ran home to their parents in tears.

John Froome and James went back to the house, calling upon the bailiff, George Dawson, on the way. Once again the three men knocked on the door and tapped on Miss Dungey's bedroom window, but still there was no response. Finding that a top portion of the bay window was unlocked, they managed to slip inside and, with the light of a small lantern, they began to search the house. They found cups and saucers set out for two people. In the passage, they spotted bloodstains on the wall, the floor and on the front door handle.

Suddenly they heard moaning coming from the woods. About 25 yards into the trees, they saw Kate Dungey's body lying on the ground. She had been savagely attacked. George Dawson immediately took a horse and trap into Henley to fetch the police. Near Kate's head, Supt Keal found a thick stick used on the farm for smashing potatoes. Inside the house, he discovered a poker with blood and hair on, and a brooch and hairpin belonging to Kate by the front door, but nothing had been taken.

George Dawson's brother-in-law Walter Rathall, 22, was tried for the murder, but acquitted. Nobody was ever convicted of the crime.

9 December

On this day in 1899, readers of *Jackson's Oxford Journal* were treated to all the salacious details of the divorce between Mary Pill, 37, and her husband John, 52.

The couple kept a coffee house at 4 Cornmarket Street in Oxford, and had four children. Mary enumerated many examples of her husband's violence and cruelty towards her, and called multiple witnesses to these distressing incidents. Usually under the influence of drink, John had struck her, sloshed soup over her, lobbed a basin at her, tossed bread at her, and cut her forehead by pitching a spoon at her face. She also suspected the nature of the relations between her husband and a young woman named Ada Walton, 25, a dressmaker living in Castle Street.

John Pill denied these accusations, and in turn cast aspersions upon Mary's behaviour with other men. For example, one day he says he came home to find Mary reclining on a sofa with a man named Halliwell who was feeding her with a spoon. Mary said Halliwell was actually showing her niece how to administer medicine for her cold. Eventually, the couple separated in May 1898, and John went to live in Castle Street, where he ran another café.

Spotting John and Ada walking past her shop late one evening, Mary began to follow them. John Pill also let rooms in the house at 4 Castle Street, and various spies were commissioned to ascertain the sleeping arrangements there.

Mary established to her satisfaction that John and Ada were co-habiting. Pill saw that events in court were turning against him, and announced that he preferred not to take up any more of the court's time. His Lordship pronounced a decree nisi. Two children were born to Ada and—presumably—John Pill in the next couple of years: Hilda Walton in 1902 and Harold in 1903. However, later in 1903 Ada married cabdriver Henry Rippington, and by 1911 the Rippingtons had three children of their own, plus Ada's two, all squeezed into their home in Cranham Street in Jericho.

10 December

On this day in 1644, noted mathematician and Royalist Thomas Lydiat wrote to the governor of Banbury, William Compton, complaining that his house in Alkerton near Banbury had been pillaged four times by Parliament's forces from Compton House, to the value of at least £70. For three months he hadn't even had a shirt to wear and had to borrow one.

Furthermore, he had twice been seized and taken from his house. The first time he was taken to Warwick on a 'poor jade' [a clapped out nag], roughly treated by the soldiers at Warwick, and so sorely hurt that he was, at the time of writing of the said letter, 'not throughly whole', and doubted he ever would be again. On a second occasion he was taken to Banbury. The cause of this shabby conduct by Parliamentarian soldiers was, Lydiat claimed, that he had denied them money and had defended his books and papers and then, while a prisoner in Warwick Castle, he had 'spoken up for the king.'

Lydiat eventually died peacefully at his own home in Alkerton. He is now believed to have beaten Johannes Kepler, to the idea of an oval orbit in astronomy.

11 December

On this day in 1867, Supt Hedger attended the home in Besselsleigh of the Rev Charles Dundas Everett and took the housekeeper into custody.

Sarah Carter, 31, was accused of concealing the birth of an illegitimate child, the baby's mother being Sarah's niece and fellow servant, Elizabeth, 19. The escaped father of the child was George Gooding, 18, formerly a groom for the

Lenthalls; George did a runner weeks after Elizabeth announced that she was pregnant in June. The birth occurred while Rev Everett was away from home, and Sarah and Elizabeth claimed they had gone home to Elizabeth's mother in Liddington in Wiltshire for the event. Indeed, when Rev Everett had asked Elizabeth whether she was 'in the family way', she had said yes, and the rector had dismissed her with a letter explaining his reasons to her mother.

But the letter was never delivered to Mrs Carter, and Elizabeth in fact gave birth to a stillborn boy in Rev Everett's house. She said that the body was wrapped in carpet and taken away. Supt Hedger found fragments of tiny bones and charred carpet in the fire which heated the copper. Both Elizabeth and Sarah were sent for trial, but acquitted when it was pointed out that they had not concealed the birth at all; Elizabeth had confessed her pregnancy to several people.

Elizabeth returned to her parents' home in Wiltshire and worked as an agricultural labourer. Bizarrely, it soon emerged that Sarah Carter had also been expecting a child at the same time as her niece. This baby, too, was evidently born dead, and buried in the rectory garden. A separate case of concealment against Sarah was dismissed and she continued as housekeeper for Rev Everett. Heroic George Gooding worked as a sawyer and lived in Marsh Baldon with his wife, dairywoman Annie, and their son Arthur.

12 December

On this day in 1790, the roof of Banbury church fell in, the resulting crash being heard two miles away. The Gothic church was due for demolition on the following day, a development much disapproved of by Banbury historian

The old and new churches in Banbury

Alfred Beesley. In the face of claims of extreme dilapidation (which the spontaneous collapse of the roof might be seen to support), Beesley recounted several professional opinions that only small repairs were required. But the next day the tower fell in as well.

To be fair to Beesley, it did take gunpowder to destroy the doughty old walls. 'And at length, by means such as these,' Beesley lamented, 'and to the lasting disgrace of the Town, the venerable Church was at length made a heap of ruins'. The more interesting monuments were to be transferred to the new church at the expense of persons connected with them, but as all relevant family members had by then died off, not one of them was re-erected.

Beesley concluded: 'Banbury Cross was destroyed during the fever of Puritanism, because it was considered to be a relic of Popery. Banbury Castle was taken down from a fear that such a stronghold might be again used to the injury of the inhabitants of the town. It remained to complete the destruction of all the noble buildings of antiquity in Banbury by this last and far greatest act of vandalism.'

13 December

On this day in 1883, Robert Jefferies of Stert Street, yeast merchant, found himself up before the magistrates on a charge of assaulting his wife Rachel.

Mrs Jefferies, 33, was at home at about 9.15pm on the previous evening when her husband came home very drunk. Mr Jefferies, 29, knocked the furniture about and punched his wife in the head. She retreated to the kitchen with her mother, and a while later the women emerged into the sitting room again. Jefferies seized Rachel, threw her down and struck her several times with his fist, once in the eye, causing severe bruising. By this time Rachel's friend Jane Plowman had arrived, and the police were called.

Supt Robotham found Jefferies very noisy and intoxicated. He tried to calm things down by persuading him to go to bed and sleep it off. But at 11pm that night he heard cries of 'Murder!' and 'Police!' coming from the house. He went in to find Jefferies once again pinning his wife to the floor. Pulling Jefferies off, he saw marks of violence and blood on Rachel's face. The room was in great confusion, with the supper things smashed.

The magistrates ordered that Jefferies should find two sureties of £5 each to keep the peace for six months, or undergo one month's imprisonment. After he had been in the lock-up for a few hours, Jane's husband carrier Thomas Plowman and grocer John Kirkpatrick served as sureties for the £10 and Jefferies was released.

14 December

On this day in 1650, servant girl Anne Greene, 22, was hanged at Oxford Castle. A few hours later she was up and about again.

As a scullery maid at the Duns Tew home of local bigwig Sir Thomas Reade, 22-year-old Anne was seduced by Reade's grandson, Jeffry, 16. Eighteen weeks later, while turning malt, Greene felt ill and miscarried in the privy. She buried her stillborn son near the servants' cesspit, but she was soon found out and put on trial for infanticide. (Under a statute of 1624, any woman who concealed the death of a child could be presumed guilty of infanticide.) Reade himself prosecuted the trial.

Greene claimed to be unaware that she had been pregnant, and midwives testified that the fetus was very premature. However, Greene was found guilty and sentenced to be hanged in December.

The unsuccessful execution of Anne Greene

She bequeathed her clothes to her mother and her last words condemned the 'lewdness' of the Reade family. At the time hanging usually resulted in slow strangulation after being 'turned off a ladder' rather than instant death from a broken neck of later trap-door hangings. Friends and relatives would help speed death by pulling on the victim's legs. Greene's friends and family did so, but the under-sheriff stopped them, fearing that the rope might break.

Eventually Anne was thought to have expired and her body was given for dissection to William Petty, a surgeon and anatomical researcher. When her coffin was opened, Petty's assistant observed that she was still breathing, so to end her sufferings he stomped on her chest and stomach with full force. Petty himself soon arrived with three other physicians, and they chose to revive her.

Greene recovered and was speaking again within 12 hours. She was given her coffin as a souvenir. Sir Thomas Reade died a few days later, which was seen by some as a divine indication of her innocence and retribution for his complicity in her trial. Greene is said later to have married, had three children, and to have died in childbirth at the age of 37.

15 December

On this day in 1880, a small boy was seen crying in the street in Deddington, struggling along with a chimney brush, his clothes black with filth.

Little Edward Yeobury, 9, told Inspector Wyatt that he did not like chimney work, and rival sweep Thomas Evans, 36, claimed that Yeobury's master, Charles Dixon, 54, of Castle Street in Deddington, was in breach of the law in employing a child under 10.

Children were widely used as human chimney sweeps in England for about 200 years; they were required to crawl through chimneys which were only about 18 inches wide. The ideal age for a chimney sweep to begin working was said to be 6 years old, but sometimes they were used beginning at age 4. The child would shimmy up the flue using his back, elbows, and knees. He would use a brush overhead to knock soot loose, and the soot would fall down over him. Once the child reached the top, he would slide down and collect the soot pile for his master, who would sell it. Children often became stunted in their growth and disfigured because of the unnatural position they were required to adopt before their bones had fully developed. Their knees and ankle joints were most often affected. Their lungs would become diseased, and their eyelids were often sore and inflamed. Then in February 1875, a 12-year-old chimney sweep named George Brewster became stuck in Fulbourn hospital chimneys. An entire wall was pulled down in an attempt to rescue the boy, but he died shortly after the rescue. Brewster's master was found guilty of manslaughter. A bill was pushed through parliament in September 1875 which put an end to the practice of using children as human chimney sweeps in England.

In Deddington in 1880, Charles Dixon claimed that the boy was merely conducting his man, George Garden, 34, to properties requiring his services while he himself was indisposed. The magistrates fined Dixon one pound plus ten shillings costs. Edward Yeobury was actually Dixon's own grandson.

16 December

On this day in 1664, antiquary Anthony Wood reported seeing a 'blasing star' as he made his way along Botley Causeway from Cumnor at between 5 and 6pm in the evening. On the same night that the comet was observed by fellows at the University, it was also witnessed by the king and queen at Whitehall, as well as being visible as far away as the south-west of England.

Indeed, Samuel Pepys gave an account of it in his diary on 15 December: 'To the Coffee-house, where great talke of the Comet seen in several places; and among our men at sea, and by My Lord Sandwich.' On Christmas Eve Pepys continued: '... saw the Comet which is now, whether worn away or no I know not, but appears not with a tail, but only is larger and duller than any other star, and is come to rise betimes, and to make a great arch, and is gone quite to a new place in the heavens than it was before: but I hope, in a clearer night, something more will be seen.'

The comet had been first spotted in Spain on 17 November 1664. It remained visible through to the end of January 1665.

17 December

On this day in 1939, Rev Canon John Stedwell Stansfeld died aged 85 a few days after a two-hour walk in the rain at night to visit the dying wife of his churchwarden.

Until well into middle age Stansfeld earned his living as a civil servant but gained a degree in medicine from Exeter College by studying part-time. While studying, he lived at 67 Banbury Road with his mother and sister. He was described as an 'Officer of Inland Revenue 2 Class'. Stansfeld was rector of St Ebbe's between 1912 and 1926, at a time when the parish was poor and overcrowded. He set up a medical dispensary in the rectory garden and campaigned to get public baths built in Paradise Square. His nickname was 'the Doctor' and his passion was giving pre-medical treatment to the poor. He worked to improve living conditions and set up clubs for boys and young men where they could socialise. In 1919 he used his personal resources, by no means ample, to purchase 20 acres of land at Shotover. Here he set up summer camps and developed a country retreat for the urban poor of St Ebbe's. Stansfeld started off with a tree-house called the Crow's Nest. Later he installed rough huts or bungalows where whole families from St Ebbe's could go for a country holiday, but which would allow the breadwinner to walk each day down to Oxford to his work. In 1926, at the age of 72, the tireless Stansfeld travelled to Africa to set up a mission school in Kenya. On his return to England in 1929 he was appointed rector of All Saints, Spelsbury. His funeral at Spelsbury was attended by more than 100 mourners from St Ebbe's, and three bishops were at a crowded thanksgiving service in Bermondsey parish church in January 1940.

18 December

On this day in 1880, there was an unpleasant scene at Christ Church in Banbury. In the course of his sermon, curate the Rev J G Barnsdale expressed his sympathy for certain clergymen currently imprisoned for their liturgical practices; they were known as 'Ritualists'. From the 1850s to the 1890s, several liturgical practices espoused by many ritualists led to some occasional and intense local controversies—and to prosecutions. Ritualists wished to restore the use of elaborate vestments, incense, thurible and incense ('bells and smells'), and other practices that smacked to many of Catholicism. Barnsdale felt confident that conscientious attitude of these ministers would create such feeling in the country that the people would rise up and demand that the services should be rendered according to their wishes. Evidently Barnsdale's confidence was misplaced because, to express his disapproval of these sentiments, parish warden Mr Hood immediately rose from his seat and marched out of the church, accompanied by two other members of the congregation.

After the service the curate was rounded on by the vicar and the churchwardens, and at the evening sermon the vicar tried to soothe ruffled feathers. He appealed to his hearers to exert themselves as peacemakers at this festival season, and to bear and forbear with one another. Goodwill did not, however, extend to all men; the curate was asked to submit his resignation.

19 December

On this day in 1387, the Battle of Radcot Bridge was fought between troops loyal to Richard II, led by court favourite Robert de Vere, and an army captained by Henry Bolingbroke, the future Henry IV.

Bolingbroke and his colleagues objected to Richard's tyrannical and capricious rule and his use of favourites like de Vere. De Vere's army arrived at the twin Thames bridges, only to find the first sabotaged and the second guarded by Bolingbroke's troops. The Duke of Gloucester's men were still approaching from the north. Undeterred, de Vere gave the command to storm

Robert de Vere's escape; he may actually have been obliged to swim

the crossing. At this point, a larger force of Bolingbroke's men arrived from the north, effectively surrounding the Cheshiremen. The Royalists turned and deserted at the first shock of Bolingbroke's pikes. They could only surrender or else make desperate rushes over or through the river in an attempt to escape.

According to 16th-century chronicler Raphael Holinshed: 'Eight hundred men fled into the marsh, and were drowned; the rest were surrounded, stript, and sent home.' Such figures should be taken with a pinch of salt, but it does seem that Robert de Vere managed to escape only by swimming across the Thames and then fleeing to France. Richard II now had no choice but to comply with the rebels, who had now succeeded completely in breaking up the circle of favourites around the king.

Henry Bolingbroke would become king in 1399 and rule as Henry IV—the first king of England since the Norman Conquest whose mother tongue was English, not French.

20 December

On this day in 1610, Wadham College was founded by Nicholas and Dorothy Wadham. But it was Dorothy who, as a widow, piloted the job through.

Nicholas Wadham, a member of an ancient Somerset family, died in 1609 leaving his fortune to endow a college at Oxford. The hard work of translating his intentions into reality fell to his formidable widow, Dorothy—aged 75 at her husband's death. She fought all the claims of Nicholas's relations, lobbied at court, negotiated the purchase of the site of the former college of Trinitarian Friars, and drew up the college statutes. She appointed the architect William Arnold, the first warden, fellows and scholars, and even the college cook, with such efficiency that the college was ready for opening within four years of Nicholas's death. She added considerably to the endowment from her own resources, and kept tight control of its affairs until her death in 1618, although she never actually visited Oxford from her home in Devon.

21 December

On this day in 1682, Mrs Eunice Lazenby, landlady of the Mitre Inn, died of fright at 3 o'clock in the morning. Three members of All Souls had spent a long evening celebrating the re-opening of the Mermaid Tavern after a three-month closure. At midnight they fancied something to eat, so they called at the Mitre Inn and a boy let them in.

The young men asked for food, but the boy explained that everybody was in bed. Where did Mrs Lazenby sleep, they asked? Innocently, the boy indicated the window of a ground floor room and, of course, the revellers were soon hammering on the glass, demanding meat. She told them it was too late, and she had no intention of getting out of bed, whereupon the rowdy visitors began to abuse her terribly. They called her a 'Popish bitch', an 'old Popish whore', and suggested that she deserved to have her throat cut. A terrified Eunice Lazenby fell into fits and died three hours later.

The masters of All Souls' were examined by the vice-chancellor. The young men in question were Thomas Baker, 29, of Grafton near Worcester, John Aldworth, 29, of Hurst in Wiltshire, and Ralph Olliffe, 22, from Bristol. Poor Mrs Lazenby was kept above ground for an unusually long period for the time; presumably because the Christmas festivities intervened, she was not buried until 27 December.

22 December

On this day in 1900, readers of *Jackson's Oxford Journal* became acquainted with the motto of a tramp named Walker: 'No boots, no work.'

Walker had been admitted to Faringdon workhouse on the previous Friday night, wearing boots which were 'in the most dilapidated condition it is possible for even boots to assume'. He was put to work as was usual but, sneered the newspaper, he refused to comply unless provided with better footwear than 'the pieces of leather he was privileged to call his property'. Bearing in mind that the work traditionally required of men was stone-breaking, one can perhaps see Walker's point of view.

Faringdon Poor Law Union was formed on 2 February 1835, one of the first unions to be declared following the Poor Law Amendment Act 1834. A regime of hard labour and strict discipline prevailed. Its operation was overseen by an elected Board of Guardians, 34 in number, representing 30 constituent parishes. Assistant Poor Law Commissioner Edward Gulson reported: 'Order and regularity were kept up to a high degree in this workhouse; the classification of the inmates, and the separation of the sexes, have been rigidly enforced; and the able-bodied paupers were employed in digging stone out of a pit, which was situated on a piece of land attached to the workhouse.'

A new union workhouse was built in 1846. The main building was an unusual U-shaped layout, three storeys in height. The area within the U was divided into four walled exercise yards for the different classes of workhouse inmate. A single-storey entrance block fronted onto Union Street at the north of the site, with a chapel located at the west side. A workhouse school was located at the far south of the site. After 1930, the former workhouse building was converted into flats which continued in use until the late 1960s. No trace of the workhouse now remains.

As a result of his insurrection, Walker was gaoled for 14 days—probably exactly what he wanted over the Christmas period.

23 December

On this day in 1881, an inquest was held at Hornton into sudden death of Joseph Simpkins. Simpkins, a 41-year-old agricultural labourer, had other family in the village, but he lodged with fellow single labourer Henry Durham, 50. Both men worked for William Bacchus, 34, a gentleman farmer of 500 acres at Hornton Grounds Farm. While Bacchus had a wife, Ethel, three children, and four servants, Durham's cottage was virtually naked of furniture.

Simpkins was known on occasion to drink too much, which might explain any difficulty living alongside family members. According to Durham, at the time of his death, Simpkins had no money or food, although the medical examiner Jeremiah McGreal reported that Simpkins' body was 'fairly well nourished' and had plenty of muscle coverage, suggesting that he did not die of starvation. However, Simpkins frequently complained of chest pains for which he applied a mustard plaster. Dry mustard, flour and warm water were mixed to a paste and spread on to a cloth. The cloth was folded to protect the skin, then wrapped around the chest and left for around 20 minutes. Sometimes Simpkins also resorted to a teaspoonful of pepper in a little warm water or tea.

It seems unlikely that any of this would have worked because, in the opinion of Mr McGreal, Simpkins was suffering from a diseased heart. His housemate Henry Durham died a few years later, aged 57.

The remnants of Beaumont Palace in 1785

24 December

On this day in 1166, King Henry II's favourite son John was born at Beaumont Palace in Oxford.

King Henry and Duchess Eleanor of Aquitaine had five sons: William IX, Count of Poitiers, who died before John's birth; Henry the Young King; Richard I, Count of Poitiers ('the Lionheart'); Geoffrey II, Duke of Brittany; and John. Nicknamed John 'Lackland' because he was not expected to inherit significant lands, John became the king's favourite child following his surviving brothers' failed revolt of 1173–74.

When Henry II died in 1189, having been predeceased by Henry the Young King and Geoffrey, Richard became king and Geoffrey's son, Arthur, the heir presumptive. But after Richard's death in 1199, John felt that the way forward involved dealing with Arthur. The annals of Margam Abbey in Wales offer the following colourful narrative: 'After King John had captured Arthur and kept him alive in prison for some time, at length, in the castle of Rouen, after dinner on the Thursday before Easter, when he was drunk and possessed by the devil ['*ebrius et daemonio plenus*'], he slew him with his own hand, and tying a heavy stone to the body cast it into the Seine.'

Beaumont Palace became a monastery, but at the Reformation most of the structure was dismantled and the stone reused in Christ Church and St John's College. The last remnants were destroyed in the laying out of Beaumont Street in 1829.

25 December

On this day in 2016, pop star George Michael died in bed at his home in Goring-on-Thames, aged 53. He was found by his Australian partner, Fadi Fawaz, who appeared to have been sleeping in his car.

Cause of death was confirmed on 7 March by the senior coroner for Oxfordshire; George died of heart disease. Previously, Fawaz's social media accounts stated that the star's death was suicide, claiming: 'The only thing George wanted is to DIE. He tried to kill himself many times…' and 'finally he managed'. Fawaz claimed it was Michael's fifth suicide attempt, despite the coroner concluding that he died of natural causes. But Fawaz later claimed he had been hacked. George had previously spoken about contemplating suicide as he did not want to watch all of his loved ones die before him.

George Michael's death ruined Christmas 2016 for many middle-aged women

26 December

On this day in 1899, the Headington morris men knocked at the door of Sandfield Cottage in Headington. It was an important moment in the English folk dance and music revival.

In the spring of that year the building firm of Knowles & Son had done some work on the house, and concertina player William Kimber had been the foreman of the gang. Bad weather in the run-up to Christmas had led to a shortage of work, so now the men were trying to earn a bit of extra money. Music teacher and composer Cecil Sharp, his wife Constance, and their three young children were spending Christmas at the house with Constance's mother. The meeting between Sharp and Kimber led to the revival of morris-dancing in England.

Sharp saw the dancers performing *Laudanum Bunches* with Kimber playing the concertina, and he asked Kimber to come back the next day to play the tunes while he wrote them down. At this time, morris dancing was almost extinct, and the interest generated by Sharp's notations kept the tradition alive. In 1911 Sharp founded the English Folk Dance Society, which promoted the traditional dances through workshops held nationwide, and which later merged with the Folk Song Society in 1932 to form the English Folk Dance and Song Society. Sandfield Cottage has now gone; it was where Horwood Close is now.

27 December

On this day in 1893, Martha Combe died, and bequeathed most of her collection of Pre-Raphaelite art to the Ashmolean Museum.

Martha's husband was Thomas Combe, superintendent of the Clarendon Press at Oxford. In 1849, he met John Everett Millais in Oxford, who painted portraits of Combe's family. Thomas and Martha became keen patrons of the arts, and particularly of the Pre-Raphaelites.

The Pre-Raphaelite Brotherhood was formed in 1848 by a group of young painters, sculptors and writers who intended to restore to English art the freshness and close study of nature that they found in early Italian painting before Raphael. The original group included Millais, Rossetti, Holman Hunt, and the sculptor Thomas Woolner. The later Pre-Raphaelites became particularly closely associated with Oxford and Oxfordshire: stained glass at Christ Church and Harris Manchester Colleges, the sumptuous Victorian chapel at Exeter College, and William Butterfield's assertive Keble College with its intimate chapel, which houses William Holman Hunt's *The Light of the World*. The library at the Oxford Union contains early and important murals by William Morris, Dante Gabriel Rossetti and Edward Burne-Jones. Kelmscott Manor was the country home of the writer, designer and socialist William Morris from 1871 until his death in 1896.

28 December

On this day in 1665, George FitzRoy, 1st Duke of Northumberland, was born at Merton College, Oxford. He was the third and youngest illegitimate son of King Charles II of England; his mother Barbara Villiers, Countess of Castlemaine, was still married at this time to Roger Palmer, Earl of Castlemaine, so the boy was known at first as George Palmer.

In March 1686, Northumberland married a great beauty, Catherine Wheatley, the daughter of a poulterer, Robert Wheatley of Bracknell in Berkshire. Catherine was the widow of Thomas Lucy of Charlecote Park, a captain in the Royal Horse Guards. Soon after the marriage, Northumberland regretted his rashness, and allegedly engaged the help of his brother, Henry FitzRoy, 1st Duke of Grafton, to bundle poor Catherine abroad to live out her life in an English convent in Ghent, Belgium.

Of all of King Charles II's children, Northumberland was said to be the most accomplished—extremely handsome and athletically-built.

29 December

On this day in 1894, readers of *Jackson's Oxford Journal* could thank their lucky stars while they read the sad details of the suicide of grocer's assistant Francis Cornish, 31.

Francis was the son of Thomas Cornish, 60, of Mount Farm, Churchill. Mr Cornish had endeavoured to persuade his son to stay at home and help him on the farm, but Francis insisted he must seek his fortune in London. For the month prior to his death, Francis had been lodging with Frank Hart in Regina

Churchill village

Road in Holloway. During this time Francis had been out of work, and 'was not steady in his habits', ie, he drank too much.

On Friday 21 December Francis visited Hornsey Road baths. Bath attendant George Crook said that Francis seemed to be taking an unusually long time over his ablutions, so he knocked on the door to check that all was well. Receiving no reply, Crook forced open the door. Cornish lay dead in the still-warm bath, having cut his own throat. Police Sgt Coveney found in Francis's possession two pawn tickets and two letters of rejection of his applications for employment. The coroner declared that Francis had apparently become despondent and ended his life, and that he would have been much better off staying in Churchill to help his father.

30 December

On this day in 1999, George Harrison and his wife Olivia were attacked by an intruder at their home, Friar Park in Henley.

At about 3.20am Olivia Harrison woke her husband to say she had heard smashing glass. While Mrs Harrison phoned the police, Harrison went down to the kitchen and found a window broken. Lying nearby was a fragment from a stone statue in the garden. He smelled cigarette smoke and shouted to his wife that someone was in the house.

Friar Park, Henley

He went back upstairs on to a gallery that overlooks the ground floor. Glancing down, he saw an intruder in the main hall. Harrison said: 'He stopped in the centre of the room and looked towards me. He started shouting and screaming.'

The intruder advanced up the stairs. Harrison lunged at him. 'We fell to the floor. I was fending off blows with my hands. He was on top of me and stabbing down at my upper body.' Mrs Harrison came out and began hitting the man with a brass poker. The intruder chased her and grabbed her by the throat. Harrison said: 'I vividly remember a deliberate thrust to my chest. I could hear my lung exhaling and had blood in my mouth. I believed I had been fatally stabbed.'

Mrs Harrison grabbed a heavy table-lamp and began swinging it at the attacker, who gripped the cord of the lamp and pulled it towards him. She threw the lamp at him and ran downstairs to find that the police had arrived.

Michael Abram, a 34-year-old man suffering from paranoid schizophrenia, served just under two years in a secure psychiatric unit for the attack.

31 December

On this day in 1999, during the fireworks that accompanied the celebration of the millennium, thieves broke into the Ashmolean Museum and stole

***View of Auvers-sur-Oise**, by Paul Cézanne—do say if you spot it anywhere*

Cézanne's landscape painting *View of Auvers-sur-Oise*. Valued at £3 million, the painting has been described as an important work illustrating the transition from early to mature Cézanne painting.

The work depicts a cluster of small white cottages set in a tree-filled valley and dates from around 1880. Police said the thieves appeared to have broken in through the main gallery's glass roof as thousands of revellers were celebrating on the city's streets. They seemed to have gained access from the adjoining library, which was undergoing building work, before clambering over rooftops to reach the museum itself. The painting was the only item taken, suggesting that it was stolen to order.

The theft came four days after the former head of Scotland Yard's art and antiques squad predicted a surge in art crime because police had to cut back on their specialist squads.

Sources

abingdon.gov.uk; ancestry.com; aviation-safety.net; banburyguardian.co.uk; battlefieldstrust.com; bbc.co.uk; beatlesbible.com; berkshirehistory.com; bl.uk (Jackson's Oxford Journal, Leeds Mercury, Morning Chronicle); blhs.org.uk; bnc.ox.ac.uk; britisharchaeology.ashmus.ox.ac.uk; british-history.ac.uk; britishlistedbuildings.co.uk; catalogue.millsarchive.org; chch.ox.ac.uk; churchtimes.co.uk; conclarendon.blogspot.com; culture24.org.uk; dailymail.co.uk; danq.me; davidkidhewitt.wordpress.com; deddingtonhistory.uk; dirkdeklein.net ; eleusinianm.co.uk; gw.geneanet.org; headington.org.uk; heraldseries.co.uk; historic-uk.com; historyextra.com; historytoday.com; hyperallergic.com; ijmet.org; jadn.co.uk; landmarktrust.org.uk; localhistoryisawesome.co.uk; magnacarta.cmp.uea.ac.uk; maritimetas.org; open.ac.uk; oxforddnb.com; oxfordjewishheritage.co.uk; oxfordmail.co.uk; oxfordshireblueplaques.org.uk; oxfordshirebuildingstrust.co.uk; oxfordshirehealtharchives.nhs.uk; oxfordtimes.co.uk; oxoniensa.org; pixture.co.uk; projects.history.qmul.ac.uk; quod.lib.umich.edu; rafabingdon10otu.co.uk; reginascott.com; sandfordonthames.co.uk; southoxford.org; st-edmundcampion-mh.co.uk; telegraph.co.uk; thamehistory.net; thames.me.uk; truecrimelibrary.com; truthequalsfiction.blogspot.com; usbornefamilytree.com; winstonchurchill.org; witneyblanketstory.org.uk; workhouses.org.uk

Bibliography

Acland, Henry Wentworth, *Memoir on the cholera at Oxford, in the year 1854* (London, Oxford, 1856)

Beesley, Alfred, *The history of Banbury, including copious historical and antiquary notices* (Banbury, 1841)

Bliss, Philip, ed, *The remains of Thomas Hearne of Edmund Hall* (John Russell Smith, 1869)

Blomfield, James Charles, *The History of the Present Deanery of Bicester, Oxon* (Bicester, 1884)

Bloxham, Christine, *Oxfordshire Folklore* (Tempus, 2005)

Clarendon, Edward Hyde, Earl of, *The history of the rebellion and civil wars in England* (Oxford, 1826)

Clark, Andrew, ed, *The life and times of Anthony Wood, antiquary of Oxford, 1632–1695* (Oxford, 1891)

Dacombe, Rod, *Rethinking Civic Participation in Democratic Theory and Practice: The Theories, Concepts and Practices of Democracy* (Palgrave Macmillan; 1st edition, 2017)

Dunkin, John, *The history and antiquities of Bicester, a market town in Oxfordshire* (London, 1816)

Hamper, William, ed, *The life, diary, and correspondence of Sir William Dugdale, knight* (London, 1827)

Johnstone, H Diack, 'Handel at Oxford in 1733', *Early Music*, Vol 31, No 2, pp 248–260 (May 2003)

Kennett, White, *Parochial antiquities attempted in the history of Ambrosden, Burcester, and other adjacent parts in the counties of Oxford and Bucks* (Oxford, 1818)

Mallet, R and J W, *The Earthquake Catalogue of the British Association* (London, 1858)

Tanner, Michael, *The Oxford Murder* (AuthorHouseUK, 2015)

Verney, Frances Parthenope, Lady, *Memoirs of the Verney family* (London, 1892)

Also by Julie Ann Godson

THE WATER GYPSY
How a Thames fishergirl became a viscountess
At dusk on a snowy evening in 1766 a tired young couple made out the welcoming lights burning in the windows of creaky old Shellingford Manor in the Vale of the White Horse, the house that was to be their home. He was Viscount Ashbrook, she was Betty Ridge, daughter of a humble Thames fisherman. Earlier that day they had been married in a little village church, and now Betty—a real-life Cinderella—was embarking on a new life in the alien world of the aristocracy.

SCANDAL IN HIGH SOCIETY OXFORDSHIRE
Twenty tales of toffs in trouble
SECRET LOVE AFFAIRS, murder, blackmail, poisoning and extortion: most of us enjoy a good scandal. And it's even more fun when it involves our so-called 'betters'. This book tells twenty tales of Oxfordshire toffs in trouble, from the Tudor period right up to the modern age. Few readers will fail to be impressed by the sheer variety of ways in which the upper classes of the county have contrived over the centuries to behave badly—and often to get away with it.

1066: OXFORDSHIRE AND THE NORMAN CONQUEST
Why it all started and finished in our county
IT WAS AN EVENT which changed the country forever. And from the birth of a prince to the formal surrender after the Battle of Hastings, Oxfordshire frequently provided the background for the board-room take-over that was the Norman Conquest of England.

OUR BOYS 1914–1918
Who were the fallen of one Oxfordshire valley?
From the workhouse boy who became an early submariner to the officer who proved to be not quite a gentleman, all of life is here. This is not a book about war and death, it is an exploration of the lives of 48 men and boys from a peaceful rural valley before war crashed in on them.

NORTHMOOR THROUGH THE YEARS
A fascinating collection of photographs, maps, documents and newspaper cuttings charting the history of a village by the river Thames in Oxfordshire and the changing lives of its residents.

www.julieanngodson.com
Facebook @julieanngodson
amazon.co.uk

Printed in Great Britain
by Amazon